24 Hours

to the Law Enforcement Exams

John Gosney

ARCO
THOMSON LEARNING

Australia • Canada • Mexico • Singapore • Spain • United Kingdom • United States

ARCO

THOMSON LEARNING ™

An ARCO Book

ARCO is a registered trademark of Thomson Learning, Inc., and is used herein under license by Peterson's.

About Peterson's

Founded in 1966, Peterson's, a division of Thomson Learning, is the nation's largest and most respected provider of lifelong learning online resources, software, reference guides, and books. The Education Supersite[SM] at petersons.com—the Web's most heavily traveled education resource—has searchable databases and interactive tools for contacting U.S.-accredited institutions and programs. CollegeQuest[®] (CollegeQuest.com) offers a complete solution for every step of the college decision-making process. GradAdvantage[™] (GradAdvantage.org), developed with Educational Testing Service, is the only electronic admissions service capable of sending official graduate test score reports with a candidate's online application. Peterson's serves more than 55 million education consumers annually.

Thomson Learning is among the world's leading providers of lifelong learning, serving the needs of individuals, learning institutions, and corporations with products and services for both traditional classrooms and for online learning. For more information about the products and services offered by Thomson Learning, please visit www.thomsonlearning.com. Headquartered in Stamford, Connecticut, with offices worldwide, Thomson Learning is part of The Thomson Corporation (www.thomson.com), a leading e-information and solutions company in the business, professional, and education marketplaces. The Corporation's common shares are listed on the Toronto and London stock exchanges.

For more information, contact Peterson's, 2000 Lenox Drive, Lawrenceville, NJ 08648; 800-338-3282; or find us on the World Wide Web at: www.petersons.com/about

ISBN: 0-7689-0613-X

Printed in Canada

10 9 8 7 6 5 4 3 2 1   03 02 01

About This Book

24 Hours to the Law Enforcement Exams has been designed not only to give you outstanding tips, hints, and strategies in passing the written law enforcement exams but also to give you practical no-nonsense advice on what you need to know about the other requirements for becoming a law enforcement officer (such as the physical exams, background checks, academic requirements, and so on). This book also provides information on what the various law enforcement positions consist of, including such issues as salary, general requirements, working conditions, and employment outlook.

Law enforcement, in all its various permutations, can be an incredibly rewarding career. *24 Hours to the Law Enforcement Exams* has been designed to help you achieve your law enforcement goals.

Who Should Use This Book?

The answer to this question is simple: Anyone who must take the various law enforcement exams and who must perform well on them. The field of law enforcement is incredibly competitive—it is an excellent idea that you perform as well as you can on the examinations (both written and physical) to help set yourself above the competition. Although it's impossible to anticipate every type of question that may be asked of you, *24 Hours to the Law Enforcement Exams* gives you the best proven, generalized strategies (and lots of practice questions!) to help you achieve the highest scores.

Contents

Introduction

Welcome to *24 Hours to the Law Enforcement Exams*. Here, you'll get a fast but effective overview of law enforcement careers and the tests you have to pass to enter those fields. In just twenty-four well-organized and easy-to-follow one-hour lessons, you get the information you need to succeed on exams for such law enforcement positions as Police Officer, State Trooper, Federal Agent, Correction Officer, Border Patrol Agent, and more. This book assumes that you have a strong interest in achieving the highest possible score on the law enforcement exams; this book will help you on your way by letting you know what to expect on the exams and by giving you lots of practice questions and answers to help you prepare for the exams. The book also gives you lots of information that can help you decide whether or not you're ready to accept the challenges and responsibilities that come with being a law enforcement official.

How This Book Is Organized

24 Hours to the Law Enforcement Exams is arranged in three parts; each chapter represents an hour in your 24-hour study plan:

• **Part I   An Inside Look at Law Enforcement**

Aside from learning strategies to do well on the tests, it is also necessary to have a solid understanding of what the various law enforcement positions are, the general requirements for them, their working conditions, their benefits and promotion structures, and how they differ from one another. Hours 1 through 4 introduce you to several fields of law enforcement and give you a solid background in what each of these fields is and what individuals who serve in them do.

• **Part II   Learn What It Takes to Get In**

Whether you are interested in becoming a Police Officer, a Correction Officer, or a Special Agent for the Border Patrol or are seeking a position with the Secret Service, you'll find general qualification requirements in the hours covered by Part II. In Hours 5 through 13, you learn more details about the written exams, strategies for doing well on them, and other requirements.

• **Part III   Practice the Exam Questions**

Part III is the heart of the book. During these hours, you practice for your exam by looking at several sample questions. Hours 14 through 24 provide detailed answer keys and answer explanations in addition to the sample questions so that you can quickly understand your incorrect answers.

In addition to the 24 hours of detailed instruction, you will also find two appendixes. Appendix A provides a comparison of the various law enforcement positions, and Appendix B discusses how to prepare for training programs.

As you read through this book, you will notice several "special elements" in the form of margin notes. These special elements are designed to provide you with supplementary material that enhances the text proper as well as to draw your attention to topics or issues of special importance.

Tip
Look for these Tip boxes to provide you with "insider" information and other useful advice that can help you stay ahead of the competition.

Note
When you see this element, look for supplementary information to what is presented in the text. Additional topics of interest that are related to the text can often be found in these Note boxes.

Caution
Cautions warn you of troublesome possibilities and are generally designed to keep you from making a major error on the exams. In addition, several Caution boxes throughout the book warn you of potentially dangerous situations that may arise in your role as a law enforcement officer.

Make Connections
These cross-references point out related material in other sections of the book.

Finally, many hours include a "Q&A" section, where you'll find the answers to questions you're most likely to have regarding the material you covered in that hour. Look to the "Q&A" sections for a more conceptual discussion of some of the issues discussed in that specific hour. You can use these sections as a way of sharpening your skills as you prepare for the exam. Then check "The Hour in Review" section to make sure you note the key concepts learned in the hour. Good luck!

Part I

An Inside Look
at Law Enforcement

HOUR 1

Learn the Range of Law Enforcement Jobs Available to You

What You'll Learn in This Hour

In this hour, you'll learn about the wide range of law enforcement positions and the unique and challenging opportunities presented by each. After reading through this chapter, you should not only have a solid understanding of the various positions in the field of law enforcement, you should also be able to differentiate between each field.

Here's a list of your goals for this hour:

- Learn the definition of *law enforcement*
- Learn about municipal police enforcement
- Learn about county police enforcement
- Learn about state law enforcement

• Learn about federal law enforcement

• Learn about the role of Correction Officers

Understanding the Definition of Law Enforcement

Law enforcement agencies today reflect the social, urban, and industrial complexities of society. In discussing this career area, it is more accurate to use the term "law enforcement" than "police" because responsibility for enforcement now rests with a variety of government agencies. In the United States, some 40,000 separate law enforcement agencies represent municipal, county, state, and federal government. All these agencies enforce the law by investigating, apprehending, and assisting in the prosecution of persons violating the law.

Note
Law enforcement in America is decentralized and specialized, owing primarily to the basic distrust Americans have of the concept of a national police force. More often than not, this decentralized system works to the advantage of both law enforcement officials and the citizens they serve because those who choose to violate the law can be recognized—and apprehended—virtually anywhere.

In many instances, the large number of enforcement agencies in the United States means duplication of law enforcement activities. In fact, most law enforcement professionals work in conjunction with multiple enforcement agencies at the local, state, and federal levels. A careful examination of career opportunities and responsibilities within this decentralized system by level of government (i.e., municipal, county, state, and federal) is the focus of Part I of this book.

Tip
Crime prevention is one aspect of law enforcement that can really benefit from cross-jurisdiction. Effective crime prevention requires that law enforcement agencies be able to motivate, coordinate, and work effectively with individuals and organizations within the community. Strong communication and "people" skills are a must for those preparing to enter most areas of law enforcement today.

The Role of Municipal Police

At the local level, the two most important examples of law enforcement are *municipal* and *county* police agencies. Despite the development of criminal activities that crisscross local, state, and national boundaries, the first line of defense against most crime in America occurs at the local level. Consider these facts:

- More than 90 percent of all felonies occur in the jurisdictions of local police agencies.
- The vast majority of criminal laws are local ordinances prohibiting offenses ranging from vandalism to murder.
- The size of local police agencies in the United States is as varied as the number of laws they seek to enforce. Some smaller communities function with two or three officers, while large municipalities such as New York City have forces exceeding 25,000 officers.

Highly trained police officers are found in both large and small cities. Of the more than 17,000 cities in the United States, fifty-five have populations exceeding a quarter of a million, and these cities employ about one third of all police personnel. Many police problems in America are concentrated in the cities, and the cities present the greatest challenges to law enforcement.

All police agencies, large or small, have similar problems and responsibilities. All engage in common activities that prevent crime and disorder, preserve the peace, and protect individual life and property.

> **Make Connections**
> All law enforcement officers must pass specific (and often rigorous) testing and physical training requirements. The qualifications, testing, and training requirements for positions in each area of law enforcement are discussed in Part II of this book.

Municipal police departments, in both personnel and management practices, are generally organized along semimilitary lines:

- Police officers are ranked according to a military system such as sergeant, lieutenant, captain, or colonel.
- Police officers wear uniforms that reflect their rank.
- Police officers are governed by the specific, written rules and regulations of their agency.

Municipal police activities can be divided into two functions: line and staff. *Line functions* involve activities that result directly in meeting police service goals; *staff activities* help administrators organize and manage the police agency.

Understanding Patrol and Other Line-Function Duties

The line functions common to most municipal police departments include patrol, investigation, vice, traffic, juvenile, and crime prevention.

At the center of police law enforcement is *patrol*. Patrol involves movement of uniformed police personnel (on foot, in vehicles, or on horseback, bicycle, motorcycle, or other conveyance) through designated areas. In most departments, at least half of all police personnel are assigned to patrol. Officers on patrol have a variety of duties, including the following:

- Interviewing and interrogating suspects and arresting lawbreakers.
- Controlling crowds at public gatherings and enforcing laws regulating public conduct.
- Intervening in personal, family, and public disputes.
- Issuing warnings and citations.
- Providing miscellaneous services to members of the public.
- Participating in community crime-prevention programs, both by educating people about the steps they can take to prevent crime in their neighborhoods and by serving as "contact points" between the police department and the public at large.

Although Patrol Officers spend more time carrying out routine police services than in catching criminals, their importance can't be overstated. Because their primary duties are performed on the street, Patrol Officers are the most visible representatives of local government. The following sections provide more details on some of these important duties.

Note
The high visibility of the Patrol Officer is perhaps the most subtle aspect of police work, and one of the most important. The Patrol Officer provides a powerful reminder that the law is always in effect and always ready to be enforced.

1

Investigation Activities

Investigation activities come into play when Patrol Officers are unable to prevent a crime or arrest a suspect in the act of committing a crime. Investigative specialists (better known as *detectives*) help to solve crimes by skillfully questioning victims, witnesses, and suspects; gathering evidence at crime sites; and tracing stolen property or vehicles connected with a crime. Detectives investigate many types of crime, including murder, robbery, rape, aggravated assault, burglary, auto theft, forgery, embezzlement, and weapons violations. They spend considerable time reviewing physical evidence, clues, interviews, and criminal methods. In addition, they coordinate information provided through the investigations of Patrol Officers, laboratory personnel, records clerks, and concerned citizens.

Vice Operations

Vice operations in the local police agency combat illegal activities that corrupt and destroy the physical, mental, and moral health of the public. Vice operations direct their activities principally against illegal gambling, narcotics violations, traffic in liquor, prostitution, pandering, pornography, and obscene conduct. Organized crime is involved in many vice crimes, and vice crimes are directly linked to other types of street crime.

Juvenile Law Enforcement

Juvenile law enforcement guidelines and the methods used to enforce them can vary among different agencies and often depend on the needs of individual communities. In some cases, Police Officers are given special training and are assigned to juvenile cases on a full-time basis.

A juvenile becomes a *delinquent* by committing an act that, if he or she were an adult, would be a crime. The police have responsibilities in juvenile matters greater than merely enforcing laws by taking youthful offenders into custody. In the case of juveniles, police efforts are aimed at identifying neglected and dependent children, detecting and preventing predelinquent behavior, finding and investigating delinquency breeding grounds within the community, and properly disposing of juvenile cases.

Crime Prevention

Police serve all segments of the community, but they cannot preserve law and order and control crime unless the public cooperates and participates in the law enforcement process. Hostility between citizens and the police can create explosive situations and even promote crime in the community. In many (if not most) municipalities, police agencies have introduced such crime-prevention techniques as neighborhood security and watch programs. Police Officers assist in coordinating these programs and are responsible for maintaining constant, effective communication with these citizen groups. Other crime-prevention responsibilities include addressing citizen and school groups, working with community leaders and civic organizations, and establishing strong relationships with individual members of the community.

Understanding Staff Functions

Staff functions are activities performed by Police Officers to help administrators organize and manage the police agency. Here are some examples of staff functions:

- Personnel recruitment, selection, and training
- Planning and finance
- Employee services, public relations, and use of civilian personnel

Staff is the costliest and most important of all the resources committed to the law enforcement process. A police agency is only as able and effective as its personnel. To be effective, police departments must plan and organize numerous around-the-clock operations such as patrolling, providing constant communication between officers in the field and the agency headquarters, and preparing for emergency responses. The unpredictable nature of police work, however, and the problems that arise from emergency situations sometimes make planning difficult.

Note
A widespread practice is the use of civilian personnel in certain jobs within police agencies. These personnel are assigned to duties (for example, clerical work, sanitation work, prisoner booking, and so on) that do not include the exercise of police authority or the application of the skills and knowledge of professional law enforcement personnel. As such, entry into these positions rarely demands the same level of law enforcement testing and training required for law enforcement officers.

In addition to these primary staff functions, important *auxiliary staff services* help line and administrative personnel to meet police objectives. These services include the following:

- **Crime laboratory.** Because solutions to many crimes are found through the application of the physical and biological sciences, the crime laboratory is of great value to law enforcement officers. Crime laboratory personnel are responsible for fingerprint operations, ballistics, polygraph tests, blood and alcohol tests, and examination of questioned documents. Also, given the constant improvements in

1

this type of work, crime lab personnel may be called upon to perform advanced analysis of evidence (for example, DNA testing).

- **Property and detention.** Regardless of size, locale, or functions, police agencies are responsible for evidence, personal property, and articles of value confiscated when carrying out police business. Each police department must ensure the safe-keeping of all property and evidence and make provisions for their storage, retrieval, and disposition to authorized police personnel. Detention activities involve the temporary confinement of persons arrested and awaiting investigation or trial; detention activities include booking, searching, fingerprinting, photographing, and feeding prisoners.

- **Transportation.** Police mobility is crucial to crime prevention. Typical means of police transportation include automobiles (patrol and unmarked), motorcycles, trucks, buses, motor scooters, aircraft, watercraft, and horses. Local geographic features play a crucial role in determining the type and function of police transporta-tion in each area.

- **Communications.** Communications is the lifeline of any police agency. Most police department communication systems have three parts: the telephone system, com-mand and control operations, and radio communications.

- **Police information systems.** This staff service can also significantly affect efforts to reduce crime. The major functions of police information systems are the report-ing, collecting, and recording of crime data and the storage and retrieval of informa-tion.

- **Intelligence.** Intelligence operations gather information (through research, commu-nity-watch contacts, and other informants) to keep police officials attuned to happenings in their area of jurisdiction. Effective intelligence-gathering activities provide insight into community conditions, potential problem areas, and criminal activities.

The Role of County Law Enforcement

A *county* is the largest territorial division of local government within a state. The chief law enforcement office for most counties is that of the *Sheriff*. The County Sheriff is generally an elected official. To provide law enforcement services, Sheriffs employ a force of uniformed *Deputies*. The size of the force is most often determined by the size of the county; as a rule, Deputy Sheriffs operate freely in unincorporated areas (that is, those areas not within city or town limits).

> **Note**
> Deputy Sheriffs may perform extensive police services—including patrol, juvenile, vice, and investigative activities—in much the same way as their counterparts in municipal law enforcement agencies do.

In addition to countywide police and sheriff departments, other county law enforcement personnel, such as designated Constables, Marshals, and Police Officers, enforce the law in villages, towns, townships, and boroughs. Also operating at the county level are special-purpose police units whose jurisdictions include tunnels, parks, bridges, freeways, and harbors.

The Role of State Law Enforcement

Two of the best-known state-level enforcement units are the *state police* and the *highway patrol*. There is a definite distinction between these agencies in terms of responsibility and authority. State police engage in a full range of law enforcement activities, including criminal investigation. Highway patrol units are concerned almost entirely with traffic control and enforcement and have limited general police authority.

> **Make Connections**
> This hour provides a good overview of the roles and responsibilities of a state law enforcement officer. See Hour 3, "Learn About Positions in State Law Enforcement," for more detailed information about the specific duties, working conditions, training, and promotion opportunities in this field.

A law enforcement career at the state level is not limited to the state police or highway patrol. In most states, various agencies have jurisdiction over other specialized functions that differ from the usual policing activities. Some examples of these are listed here:

- Crime laboratories
- Investigation bureaus or departments that conduct civil and criminal investigations for various state agencies, departments, and commissions (and, in some cases, local police agencies requesting assistance)
- The protection and conservation of natural resources
- Enforcement of public health and safety codes

The Role of Federal Law Enforcement

The federal government offers various opportunities to persons considering a career in law enforcement. Although the goals of federal agencies differ and their authorities cover broad geographic areas, the scope of most agencies is specific and limited. Some, such as the Drug Enforcement Agency, have enforcement duties that deal with criminal or regulatory matters. Others, such as the Secret Service, deal with affairs of national security. Many federal law enforcement positions require extensive travel, and most entail relocation at some time during the officer's career.

Make Connections

Hour 4, "Learn About Positions in Federal Law Enforcement," provides a more detailed look at the working conditions, responsibilities, training, and promotion opportunities at the federal law enforcement level.

Federal law enforcement positions offer glamour overlaid with hard work, long hours, and (in many cases) personal danger. The following sections briefly describe some of the major federal law enforcement agencies.

Bureau of Alcohol, Tobacco, and Firearms (BATF)

The objective of the BATF is to enforce voluntary compliance with laws relating to alcohol, tobacco, firearms, and explosives and to minimize willful violations. To do so, the bureau has two enforcement units: criminal and regulatory. The criminal unit seeks to eliminate the illegal possession and use of firearms and explosives, reduce traffic in illicit alcohol, and assist state and local law enforcement agencies in reducing crime and violence. The regulatory law enforcement unit helps ensure full collection of revenues due from legal alcohol and tobacco industries; it also aids in preventing commercial bribery, consumer deception, and improper trade practices.

Federal Bureau of Investigation (FBI)

The FBI is responsible for investigating violations of all federal laws except those specifically within the jurisdiction of other federal agencies. The FBI deals with violations such as sabotage, treason, and espionage as well as with internal security matters. Although the jurisdiction of the FBI is limited, the bureau has responsibility for enforcing numerous federal laws, including these:

- Kidnapping, extortion, and bank robbery
- Offenses involving interstate transportation
- Civil rights violations
- Assaulting or killing a U.S. president or federal officer
- Violating the security of personnel employed by the federal government and property owned by the government

> **Note**
> The FBI also maintains these resources: a centralized system of fingerprint identification; the National Crime Information Center (NCIC) to supply information on known or suspected criminals; crime laboratory services (also available to local enforcement agencies); and training programs to increase law enforcement effectiveness at all levels of government.

General Services Administration (GSA)

The GSA, one of the largest federal agencies, provides our government with the most economic and efficient methods of managing its programs and resources. These efforts include the following:

- Management of property and records
- Construction and operation of buildings
- Purchase and distribution of supplies
- Management of communications, traffic, and transportation
- Direction of the governmental automatic data processing program

> **Note**
> Also within the GSA is the very large Public Buildings Service (PBS), which is responsible for the protection of life and property in most federally owned or leased buildings throughout the country. To carry out its protective mission, PBS employs a uniformed security force staffed with Federal Protection Officers.

U.S. Secret Service

The U.S. Secret Service, created in 1865, is one of our nation's oldest law enforcement agencies. It was originally formed as a bureau of the Department of the Treasury and was given responsibility for eliminating the counterfeiting of our currency, and the forgery and cashing of government checks, bonds, and securities.

The Secret Service is perhaps best known for its protection of the president. After the attempted assassination of President Truman, Congress granted the U.S. Secret Service its permanent protection authority. Here are some areas of jurisdiction within the Secret Service:

- **Technical Security Division (TSD).** This operation supports headquarters, field offices, and the protective details through new concepts in lock, alarm, and video systems. The TSD also handles chemical, biological, and nuclear concerns involved with protecting the president and other dignitaries.

- **Forensic Services Division (FSD).** This operation includes specialists in finger-printing, visual information, graphic arts, and audio visual. One area the FSD is currently investigating, for example, is the use of computerized voice recognition and computerized handwriting recognition.

- **The Uniformed Division.** This group is the most familiar of the areas within the Secret Service. These personnel are responsible for security at the White House and other government buildings, including the Treasury Building. (Although the uniformed division is clearly the most visible, isn't the plainclothes, poker-faced group protecting the president the most familiar?)

Other Areas of Federal Law Enforcement

The preceding sections described only a few of the major federal agencies. Here are a few others:

- Drug Enforcement Administration
- Immigration and Naturalization Service
- Internal Revenue Service
- U.S. Customs Service
- U.S. Department of Agriculture
- U.S. Department of Defense
- U.S. Department of Health and Human Services
- U.S. Department of the Interior
- U.S. Department of Labor

- U.S. Marshals Service
- U.S. Postal Service
- U.S. Department of Transportation

The Role of Correction Officers

Employment of Correction Officers is expected to increase much faster than the average for all occupations through the year 2001. This trend is predicted because additional officers are needed to supervise and counsel an increasing inmate population and to relieve tensions in already crowded correctional institutions. Expansion and new construction of correctional facilities are also expected to create many new jobs for Correction Officers.

Employment of Correction Officers is not usually affected by changes in either economic conditions or the overall level of government spending because security must be maintained in correctional institutions at all times. Even when corrections budgets are cut, Correction Officers are rarely laid off.

Tip
With additional education, experience, or training, qualified officers may advance to Correction Sergeant or other supervisory, administrative, or counseling positions.

Here is a brief list of some responsibilities and duties of Correction Officers:

- Participating as members of corrections teams of caseworkers, psychiatrists, psychologists, teachers, and others working to help individual inmates.
- Carrying out a wide variety of tasks dealing with institutional security, such as making periodic rounds and checking for faulty bars, gates, locks, and so on.
- Administering first aid in emergencies.
- Using a firearm in emergency situations (such as during inmate riots and attempted escapes).

Correction Officers work in maximum, medium, and minimum security facilities. Because institutional security is a 24-hour responsibility, Correction Officers may be required to work nights, holidays, weekends, and overtime during emergencies.

Make Connections
For more information about qualifying for a position as a Correction Officer, see Hour 5, "Qualifying for Local Law Enforcement Positions."

1

Q&A

Q: With the law enforcement system in the United States being so fragmented, how can it possibly work to bring criminals to justice?

A: Although the fragmentation is based largely on Americans' inherent distrust of large, organized law agencies, the fragmentation actually works to everyone's advantage. Criminals—and their activities, which span several areas of interest (and geographical boundaries)—can be recognized and combated by the various law enforcement agencies, ranging from the local to the federal level.

Q: I'm interested in law enforcement, but I am concerned about the amount of time I'll need to put into a preparing for the exams. Is preparing for the exams really that time consuming?

A: The amount of time you'll need to spend preparing for the exams depends on your own background and knowledge and the exam of the individual law enforcement agency for which you're preparing. In this book, you get a good overview of the requirements for different law enforcement agencies, and you also can practice some of the types of questions from the exams. You really can complete this book in 24 hours, and you really can be pretty well prepared for most of the major law enforcement exams at the end of that time.

Q: It seems that people who know or are related to law enforcement officials have such an advantage over those of us who are coming into the field as "rookies." Is this true?

A: As with any job, those people who possess "inside knowledge" can use it to their advantage, and law enforcement is no exception. However, by carefully studying this book, by reading the job postings from the agency in which you're interested, and by having the discipline to prepare yourself for the exams and field-specific training, you can succeed. Don't let your fear of "not knowing anyone" prevent you from pursuing a career in law enforcement if that is where your true interests lie.

The Hour in Review

This hour introduced you to the exciting range of possibilities within the field of law enforcement. The remaining hours of your study will be devoted to learning more about the various positions. In Part II of this book, you'll learn strategies (and be provided with lots of sample questions) for passing the exams. Remember these points from this hour:

- Law enforcement covers an incredibly diverse range of positions, ranging from city policeman to a Special Agent in the FBI.

- All areas of law enforcement work together to serve the public. Although the law enforcement system in the United States may seem quite fragmented, individual agencies often work together to combat crime and bring fugitives to justice.

- Federal law enforcement positions are far more varied than that of an FBI Special Agent. You can secure work in the Secret Service; the Bureau of Alcohol, Tobacco, and Firearms; as well as many other divisions and agencies.

- The best law enforcement personnel are those who are adept with both their mind and their physical skills. Use this book as your guide to explore and understand what is tested on the exams, as well as to prepare yourself physically for the rigors of law enforcement work.

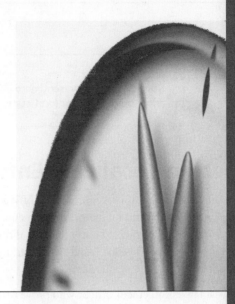

HOUR 2

Learn about Positions in Local Law Enforcement

What You'll Learn in This Hour

In this hour, you'll learn about the various positions available within local law enforcement agencies. You'll review a variety of local and county law enforcement positions, as well as the different extensions of these positions (for example, bomb squad and narcotics detective). You'll also examine the typical working conditions of these positions and touch briefly on training and promotion opportunities.

Here's a list of your goals for this hour:

- Learn about careers in local law enforcement
- Learn about the duties of a Police Patrol Officer
- Learn about the duties of a Police Detective
- Learn about working in county law enforcement

Connections

Hours 5, 6, and 7 present more information about the training specifications and requirements for local, state, and federal law enforcement positions.

Careers in Local Law Enforcement

By far, the majority of law enforcement officers working in the United States today are employed by local and municipal departments. Law enforcement personnel at the local level can count on working close to home throughout their careers. These officers are seldom called upon to travel, and when reassigned within the department, do not have to uproot and relocate their families.

A local law enforcement officer who proves effective in early assignments can look forward to promotion to positions of greater responsibility or specialized assignments, depending on the area in which the officer works and the size of the department.

The cornerstone of the local law enforcement unit is the Police Officer. Although you can work your way into some local law enforcement departments through civilian auxiliary staff positions, it's more common to enter the system as a Police Officer. After basic training, most Police Officers are assigned to patrol duty.

Duties of a Police Patrol Officer

Patrol Officers have two basic responsibilities: to prevent crime and to provide day-to-day police service to the community. Unlike specialists, Patrol Officers must perform well in a number of different roles. They have to make on-the-spot decisions about whether to advise or arrest, how to interpret the law, and the differences between lawful dissent and disturbing the peace. Patrol Officers must first protect citizens' constitutional guarantees. and second, enforce the law. In meeting these overriding responsibilities, the duties of a Police Officer are wide-ranging:

- Police Officers patrol assigned sectors in motor vehicles or on foot, working alone or with a partner, paying close attention to area conditions and inhabitants.

- During patrol, Police Officers observe suspicious behavior or conditions or activities in their sector and report incidents by radio to a superior officer before taking any action.

- Traffic control is an important part of patrol duty. Police Officers may direct traffic, monitor parked and moving vehicles for traffic violations, and issue warnings or citations for violations.

- Police Officers investigate incidents and question the individuals involved to determine violations of the law. They respond to radio calls sent by police dispatchers or superior officers ordering them to the scene of incidents such as burglaries, bank robberies, homicides, rapes, and other crimes in progress.

- When necessary, Patrol Officers arrest suspects at crime scenes (or after pursuits) and can use physical force and firearms to subdue suspects. When making arrests, officers advise suspects of their constitutional rights and transport them in police vehicles to police booking and detention facilities.

- Police Officers may be called on to testify in court to provide evidence for prosecuting attorneys.

- At the end of their daily patrol, officers prepare a written activity report that logs all encounters, arrests, and other patrol incidents and submit that report to a superior officer.

> **Note**
> Patrol duty involves many "community service" functions. Patrol Officers often check entrances and exits of commercial facilities for security during hours of darkness, inspect residential buildings for safety, and suggest methods for improving security. In addition, they respond to requests from citizens, settle disputes, and respond to emergency situations—often by administering first aid.

Specialized Assignments for the Police Officer

As you've seen, Patrol Officers are generalists, but the complexities of modern police work have created the need—and opportunity—for many areas of specialization. Smaller communities tend to need fewer specialists, but large departments in highly populated areas can provide a variety of specialized assignments. Some of these assignments are described here.

- **Community Relations Officers.** These officers help develop and maintain contact between the police department and community groups, organizations, and schools in the area. In this role, your objective is to promote understanding of the police role in the community, develop closer working relationships, and keep open the lines of communication between citizens and the police department.

- **Bomb Squad Officers.** These officers are highly trained police personnel who respond to incidents of bomb threats and report to locations where bombs have been detonated. As a Bomb Squad Officer, you may use sophisticated equipment and specially trained dogs to locate and disarm explosive or incendiary devices.

- **Canine Officers.** These officers team with specially trained dogs to provide assistance to other police units within the department. Canine Officers train their dogs (with the help of professional instructors) and are responsible for the dogs' general care.

- **Crime Prevention Officers.** These officers conduct security surveys of multiple dwellings and commercial establishments and suggest methods for improving security (for example, the use of burglar alarms, window gates, and better locking devices). If you are interested in becoming a Crime Prevention Officer, you must be comfortable working with and speaking to the public. In this role, you'll be called upon to speak before civic groups on the topic of crime prevention.

- **Emergency Service Officers.** These officers are highly trained police personnel who are brought into situations that other Police Officers are not equipped to handle. As an ES Officer, you'll deal with problems ranging from people threatening suicide to persons trapped in automobile wreckage.

- **Harbor Patrol.** This group of officers is a specialized unit in which Police Officers are responsible for patrolling municipal harbors to detect and apprehend criminals and to aid people in distress.

- **Hostage Negotiation.** Working in teams, members of these units are specially trained, having the difficult task of rescuing hostages from their captors without bloodshed or violence.

- **Mounted Police Officers.** These officers are specially trained to patrol their assigned areas on horseback or motorcycle.

- **Police Instructors.** These training officers instruct Police Officer recruits in basic phases of police work and in the duties and responsibilities of the Police Officer.

- **Traffic Officers.** These officers are members of specialized police units whose aim is to produce voluntary obedience to traffic regulations and to provide maximum mobility of traffic with a minimum of interruption.

Note
In addition to these specialized roles, Police Officers may belong to special-ized units (a *unit* is usually defined as a smaller subgroup within a police department, rather than a specialization). Some examples include intelli-gence, juvenile, sex-crime, and street-crime units.

Working Conditions of the Police Officer

Police Officers work in locations ranging from boroughs, townships, and counties to urban areas of varying size. Working conditions vary considerably according to location, size, organization, and jurisdiction of the police agency. If you work in small towns and rural communities, you'll most certainly face problems different from those met by your counterparts in the inner city. The pace, types of criminal activity encountered, and availability of necessary manpower and services definitely aren't the same in rural and urban police departments.

As a rule, most officers work outdoors in all types of weather to conduct patrols or carry out other assignments. Some officers on special duty may perform their duties indoors at police facilities. Depending on the size of the department, Police Officers may work alone or have a partner. Because police agencies operate 24 hours a day, officers are usually required to work five-day rotating shifts, including holidays and weekends.

2

Caution
Regardless of where they work, all Police Officers share certain problems: They constantly deal with human suffering, yet must always maintain self-control and act in a calm, efficient manner. They must face danger, difficulty, and frustration on a daily basis. They work long, irregular hours and, in some communities, lack public support. All Police Officers live with the very real threat of serious injury or death. You must give these facts careful consideration when you're thinking about a police career.

As a Police Officer, you can expect to have a number of fringe benefits that include some or all of the following:

- Paid vacations
- Sick leave
- Holidays
- Overtime pay
- Life, medical, and dental insurance
- Tuition assistance or refund programs for college studies
- Retirement pension

> **Note**
> In some departments, officers may retire after 20 years of service if they are from 50 to 55 years of age. In departments with different standards, Police Officers may retire after 20 years of service regardless of age.

Training and Promotion Opportunities for the Police Officer

Following the completion of your training, you'll be assigned to work under the supervision of a veteran officer. The experienced officer will evaluate your work performance from time to time during the probationary period, which may last from one year to 18 months. After successfully completing this probationary period, you'll become a permanent licensed or certified law enforcement officer; you are then sworn in and awarded a badge.

Promotional prospects for Police Officers are generally good and are usually governed by merit or by civil service system regulations. As a rule, Police Officers become eligible for promotion after a specified number of years (three to five in most police agencies). Promotions are made according to the officer's position on a promotion list and determined by scores on a written, competitive examination, as well as by ratings of on-the-job performance.

Duties of a Police Detective

Police Detectives, key members of the police law enforcement team, conduct investigations to prevent crime, protect life and property, and solve criminal cases that can range from misdemeanors to homicide. As a rule, uniformed Police Officers are the first to investigate crimes; they apprehend suspects, question witnesses, and preserve evidence. If those officers don't make arrests or the crime remains unsolved, detectives take over the criminal investigation.

Working in plain clothes, detectives assigned to a case report to the scene, where possible, and determine the nature of the incident, the exact location and time of the occurrence, and the probable reason for the crime. They obtain reports from other Police Officers and search the area to obtain clues and evidence.

Detectives use all the resources of the police agency to find solutions to crimes. They work with ballistics experts, police chemists, laboratory technicians, computers, and other resources. Once they've compiled all the available information, detectives analyze the results to determine the direction the investigation will take. As evidence begins to develop, court-approved wire tapping or electronic surveillance methods may be used to gather data pertinent to the investigation. Detectives conduct surveillance of suspects, on foot or in vehicles, to uncover illegal activities.

> **Note**
> An important responsibility of Police Detectives involves the preparation of criminal cases scheduled for trial. This entails preparing a written summary of the facts gathered during the investigation, including evidence obtained and official statements made by witnesses, victims, Police Officers, and defendants. If you become a detective, you'll spend many hours in court testifying as an arresting officer and appearing as a witnesses for the prosecution.

Specialized Assignments for the Police Detective

The following are some of the specialized assignments available to Police Detectives:

- **Bombing/arson cases.** For these cases, detectives investigate incidents of suspected arson or the use or presence of explosive devices.

- **Fraud and embezzlement.** Detectives can specialize in crimes involving embezzlement, fraud, forgery, and counterfeiting.

- **Homicide.** These officers investigate criminal homicide cases in which one person is killed by another or other cases in which death appears imminent as the result of aggravated assault.

- **Narcotics.** These detectives conduct specialized investigations to identify and apprehend persons suspected of illegal use or sale of narcotics and dangerous drugs. Narcotics Detectives also work on a cooperative basis with other police agencies involved in this type of investigation and with federal agencies such as the Drug Enforcement Administration (DEA).

- **Motor vehicle and truck hijacking.** This is another type of investigative specialty. Detectives question salvage and junkyard operators, motor vehicle and motor parts dealers, and owners of retail stores to uncover possible leads.

- **Vice squad.** These detectives investigate establishments and persons suspected of violating morality and antivice laws pertaining to liquor, gambling, and prostitution.

> **Note**
> As with other areas of police specialization, the range of and opportunities for specialization as a detective vary according to the size of the respective department and the needs of the community it serves.

Working Conditions of the Police Detective

Local, county, and state police agencies employ detectives, and the working conditions depend on the size, location, organization, and jurisdiction of the agency. During investigations, detectives spend considerable time in office work, reviewing files, gathering data, evaluating and preparing reports, and meeting with other Police Officers.

Detectives drive unmarked vehicles. They may work alone or with partners. As a detective, you can expect your work schedule to be rotating shifts of five days a week, eight hours a day, including weekends and holidays. Detectives are on call at all times and may be recalled to duty during periods of emergency.

> **Caution**
> Although detective work is a challenging career, there are times when it is tedious, routine, and frustrating. Don't forget—if you become a detective, you'll often be exposed to the risks of bodily injury and death during the course of criminal investigations.

In most police agencies, detectives receive fringe benefits including some or all of the following:

- Paid vacation
- Sick leave
- Overtime pay
- Life, medical, and disability insurance
- Tuition assistance or refund programs for college studies
- Retirement pension

> **Note**
> In most agencies, detectives can retire after 20 years of service if they are in the 50-to-55-year age bracket. Other departments may have different standards, and detectives may retire after 20 years of service regardless of age.

Training and Promotion Opportunities for the Police Detective

After successfully completing training, new detectives remain on probation. You will work with experienced investigative personnel who provide practical guidance and assistance under actual field conditions. Newly hired detectives get permanent assignments after they've demonstrated the ability to perform this job on an independent basis. Advancement prospects for detectives are governed by work performance as well as the personnel practices and size of the agency. Promotional opportunities are usually good and are made according to a merit system or civil service regulations. Detectives are, as a rule, eligible for promotion after satisfactory service for a specified period of time (usually two to four years). As a detective, you can develop your skills through training, experience, and further education. Then you can compete for the position of Sergeant, the first step in the promotion ladder.

Working in County Law Enforcement

The jurisdiction of county law enforcement officers varies greatly from state to state but generally includes all areas not in the domain of municipal or town law enforcement departments (except for areas patrolled by state police). The county law enforcement officer can work close to home with a minimum of extended travel. The amount of daily travel is dictated by the size of the county and the officer's specific assignment.

> **Tip**
> If you become a county law enforcement officer, you probably won't need to worry about having to relocate or uproot your family.

Most counties throughout the United States have the office of Sheriff, which has varying degrees of responsibility for county policing, jails, and court activities. Most Sheriffs' agencies provide full police services. Depending on the size of the county and the extent of its legal obligations, county Sheriff departments employ forces of uniformed Deputy Sheriffs (often referred to simply as Deputies) to meet these responsibilities.

Duties of a Deputy Sheriff

Deputy Sheriffs patrol assigned districts within their jurisdiction. Here are some of the duties of the Deputy Sheriff:

- Observing people, conditions, and events for evidence of suspicious or criminal activities, either as a routine part of daily patrols or in response to radio calls from superior officers.

- Detaining and questioning suspects or apprehending and arresting suspects at crime scenes or after pursuit. When making arrests, Deputies advise suspects of their constitutional rights and escort them to department headquarters for booking and confinement. Deputies sometimes work with backup units and use physical force or firearms when necessary.

- Conducting routine traffic patrol on county roads and issuing warnings and citations as necessary.

- Transporting suspects to and from jail, courtrooms, district attorneys' offices, or medical facilities. Deputies also may serve as extradition officers by transporting wanted persons across state lines to stand trial.

- Becoming involved in criminal investigations in which Deputies may work as plainclothes officers to investigate a wide range of cases involving vice, narcotics, juvenile offenses, burglaries, car thefts, homicides, and missing persons.

- Enforcing laws (including environmental, fish, and game laws) in county and state parks and game preserves.

- Preparing daily written reports of all work activities, maintaining accurate police records, and testifying during court proceedings.

> **Note**
> In addition to patrol, criminal investigation, and traffic duties, some Deputy Sheriffs have unique responsibilities related to the county court system. They serve civil papers and orders of the court, such as subpoenas, garnishments, and property executions. They serve warrants, evict people from property, and confiscate real or personal property as designated by court order.

Working Conditions of a Deputy Sheriff

Deputy Sheriffs work primarily outdoors, in all types of weather conditions, while on patrol duty in county areas. Depending on the size of the department, Deputies work alone or with a partner. Although they're not directly supervised, they do maintain radio contact with their communications center and with superior officers to report in and to receive new or revised orders. Generally, sheriffs' departments operate 24 hours a day; Deputies are usually required to work five-day rotating shifts, including holidays and weekends. As with other law enforcement officers, Deputy Sheriffs are on call at all times and, during periods of emergency, may work extended tours of duty.

> **Caution**
> As a Sheriff's Deputy, you may be involved in the apprehension of suspects who are armed and dangerous, and you may participate in high-speed chases. When you consider a job in county law enforcement, you must be aware that the job carries the potential for serious physical injuries—or even death.

2

In most county sheriffs' departments, Deputies receive fringe benefits that include paid vacations, sick leave, and holidays; overtime pay; life, medical, and disability insurance; uniform allowances, and retirement pensions.

Training and Promotion Opportunities for a Deputy Sheriff

The training program for Deputy Sheriffs is followed by a 6- to 18-month probationary period. Probationary Deputies work with experienced Deputies to develop their skills. Because Deputies must often work alone, they aren't hired as permanent members of the force until they have demonstrated their ability to work independently. If you are hired as a Sheriff's Deputy, your advancement prospects depend on the size of the agency you work for and its personnel policies. As your experience, training, and education increase, you can compete for promotions to Sergeant, Detective, Lieutenant, Captain, or Chief Deputy—depending on which of these positions are available in your department.

Q&A

Q: As a law enforcement official, I'll spend most of my time in the field, right?

A: This depends on the type of law enforcement position you take, as well as the location of your employment and other factors. Although you can, of course, expect to spend a good deal of time "out in the streets," an equally important (and time-consuming) part of your job can be spent writing reports, testifying in court, educating the public, or participating in other duties that are not strictly patrol-related.

Q: I really love the idea of becoming a local law enforcement official, but I don't want to spend all my time writing traffic citations. Is that all there is to it?

A: Although enforcement of motor vehicle laws and regulations is an important and critical duty of the local law enforcement official, there are many other duties that require the time and commitment of the local law enforcement official (such as those duties mentioned in the first question above). In addition, you can focus on numerous "specialized" areas, including Bomb Squad, the Canine Unit, Harbor Patrol, and so on (of course, these "specialized" areas may be limited because of your geographical location and the size of the department).

Q: Is the position of Police Detective considered a promotion above the job of Police Officer?

A: No, the two positions are considered to be lateral. In other words, they're at the same level on the local law enforcement "hierarchy." However, many detectives start out as Police Officers and then move into the job of Police Detective.

Q: What are the promotional opportunities within a typical local law enforcement agency?

A: Generally, opportunities for promotion are quite good. As with any job, tenure and ability are favorable qualities when it comes to promotion. However, because of the (sometimes) high turnover at police agencies and the various "lateral" promotion opportunities that exist (for example, moving from Police Officer to Police Detective), promotional opportunities can be quite diverse.

Q: I'm concerned about the benefits available to a law enforcement official....

A: Although benefits can vary, most include health insurance, retirement pension plans, educational reimbursement, and holiday and vacation pay.

The Hour in Review

- The majority of law enforcement positions in the United States are in local agencies. Local law enforcement includes municipal and county law enforcement agencies.

- Most local law enforcement officers aren't asked to relocate. Generally speaking, you can be reasonably sure that you won't have to move if you take a job in local law enforcement.

- Most local law enforcement agencies offer some form of training program and require new officers to complete a probationary period.

- Most Police Officers are "generalists" with a wide range of duties and responsibilities, including close interaction with the public through education and other police-community partnerships. Opportunities for specialization vary depending on the size and nature of the local agency.

- Police Detectives function in tandem with most local law enforcement agencies. Although detectives share many of the same benefits and working conditions of other local law enforcement officers, they may spend more of their time in conducting criminal investigation and providing court testimony.

- Most county law enforcement agencies have a Sheriff and Sheriff's Deputies. These officers provide the same police services as do municipal Police Officers, although specific responsibilities and working conditions may be quite different from those in urban agencies.

HOUR 3

Learn about Positions in State Law Enforcement

What You'll Learn in This Hour

In this hour, you'll learn about the law enforcement position of State Trooper. You'll also learn about the working conditions, promotion opportunities, and general characteristics of this challenging position.

Here's a list of your goals for this hour:

- Learn about the duties and responsibilities of the State Police Officer (also called a *Trooper*)

- Understand the typical working conditions of a state law enforcement officer

- Know what training and promotion opportunities are available to you as a State Police Officer

- Judge for yourself: Do you have the qualities the state looks for in a Trooper?

> **Make Connections**
> Hours 5, 6, and 7 focus more specifically on the training specifications and training requirements for local, state, and federal law enforcement positions.

Duties and Responsibilities of a State Police Officer

State law enforcement is the connecting point between local and federal law enforcement agencies. State Police Officers provide services to the public by patrolling state and interstate highways, turnpikes, and freeways and by enforcing motor vehicle and criminal laws. Powers of the state police vary widely among the states; some forces have full, statewide police powers, while others are restricted to highway patrol and traffic regulation. No matter what state you serve as a State Police Officer or Trooper, you'll perform a vital service in ensuring the safety of all citizens.

In many ways, State Police Officers are "generalists"; as do local law enforcement officers, State Police Officers perform a wide range of general law enforcement duties. The following is a partial listing of work activities for State Police Officers:

- In most cases, state police units are organized into posts, or *troops,* within specified geographic areas. Each troop, or post, is housed in a headquarters building that contains a communication center, barracks, lockup, crime laboratory, pistol range, and motor pool. The work day begins at the headquarters location where state police officers report daily for roll call, inspection, and duty assignment.

> **Note**
> The vast majority of State Police Officers use specially equipped patrol cars in performing their assignments. In addition, some state police forces drive motorcycles or fly helicopters.

- When on patrol, State Police Officers carefully observe conditions, strictly enforce motor vehicle codes and criminal laws, watch for traffic violations, and issue warnings or citations to offenders.
- State Police Officers assist motorists on the highway. Troopers furnish road information and directions to drivers and may even give details about restaurants, lodging, or tourist attractions in the area.

- State Police Officers respond to accident scenes, assisting with the injured, calling for additional emergency personnel, and directing traffic when serious crashes block normal traffic flow. They also may investigate the causes of such accidents and prepare detailed written reports concerning the accident victims and the circumstances leading up to the accident.

- State Police Officers are responsible for providing help to victims of fires, floods, and other disasters.

- State Police Officers also may have to take on the functions of municipal and county police, particularly in areas that don't have local police forces. In those situations, the state police can investigate burglaries, take part in roadblocks, help apprehend escaped criminals, and respond to civil disturbances.

> **Note**
> Unlike federal law enforcement officers (whom you learn more about in Hour 4), state law enforcement officers usually aren't specialists in narrow fields of investigation, prevention, control, or protection. State law enforcement officers have to be able to do it all—responding with whatever skill or task is necessary to enforce the law in their state.

3

Working Conditions of a State Police Officer

The conditions under which State Police Officers work vary according to assignment. For the most part, they work outdoors in all types of weather while patrolling highways and roads in their sectors. Officers work alone or with a partner and, because of the nature of their duties, do not receive direct supervision. They do, however, maintain constant contact with their communication centers to report to superior officers and to receive new or revised orders.

Because the state police operate around the clock, officers are subject to rotating shifts, usually consisting of a 5-day, 40-hour work week, including weekends and holidays. In addition, they are on call at all times and may work for extended periods during emergencies.

> **Caution**
> Although the job of State Trooper offers the possibility of an exceptionally rewarding career, you must carefully consider the dangers involved. State Police Officers risk serious injury or death from high-speed pursuits, the general dangers of working so close to speeding vehicles, and the tremendous risks of apprehending criminals who may be armed and dangerous. Even if you've thought these things over, you should think them over again.

Fringe benefits that State Police Officers receive usually include the following:

- Paid vacation
- Sick leave
- Holiday pay
- Overtime pay
- Life, medical, and disability insurance
- Uniform allowances
- Tuition-refund programs or tuition assistance
- Retirement pension

> **Caution**
> If you pursue a career as a State Police Officer or Trooper, you must be prepared to relocate. State law enforcement officers can be transferred to any part of the state in which they serve. As manpower needs change throughout the state, you could be temporarily—or permanently—reassigned to another barracks.

Training and Promotion Opportunities in State Law Enforcement

As is the case with nearly all law enforcement positions, prospective State Police Officers must successfully complete training and a probationary period before they're considered permanent members of the force. Probation can last from six months to a year, depending on the state. During the probationary period, the new officer gets valuable experience at the side of a veteran officer.

Advancement opportunities in state police agencies are based on merit; promotional examinations are scheduled periodically. All qualified people can compete for promotional opportunities. The first level of advancement is to Sergeant. After you become a Sergeant, you can use your education and experience to advance to the positions of First Sergeant, Lieutenant, Captain, Major, Inspector, Deputy Superintendent, and Superintendent.

> **Make Connections**
> For information on qualifying for positions in state law enforcement, see Hour 6, "Qualifying for State Law Enforcement Positions."

State Police Training School

When a number of vacancies occur or appear to be imminent, a group of prospective State Police Officers is selected from the civil service list. These recruits enter training school on a probationary basis. If you're one of these trainees, you'll be expected to complete an intensive training program of approximately 12 to 16 weeks. In training, you'll receive instruction in a variety of subjects, such as criminal law; state motor vehicle codes; laws of evidence, arrest, and search and seizure; methods of patrol, surveillance, and communications; accident prevention and traffic control; crime prevention and criminal investigation methods; and police ethics as well as several other topics.

Candidates who successfully pass this training are assigned to duty on a probationary basis for a period ranging from six months to one year or longer, depending on state police policy. While on probation, you'll work with experienced Troopers until you're skilled enough to function independently. When you've successfully completed probation, you'll receive permanent employment status as a State Police Officer or Trooper.

> **Note**
> Some police agencies have cadet programs for high school graduates under the age of 21 who are interested in a law enforcement career. Cadets work as civilian employees, performing non-enforcement duties, but they also receive instruction in the various facets of police work. Some cadets attend colleges that offer programs in law enforcement and criminal justice as preparation for a police career. In addition, some jurisdictions offer their cadets special testing sessions. The exam is the same as the open competitive exam, but those who pass it are placed on the promotional list. Eligibles are always hired from the promotional list before the open-competitive list is tapped.

Self-Evaluation: Do You Have the Qualities the State Expects in a State Police Officer?

State police work differs from city police work only in the proportion of time spent at various duties. State Police Officers deal with traffic control and with helping motorists in distress. But the high-speed traffic that the state police deal with presents problems quite different from the heavy-congestion traffic common to most local law enforcement sectors. The traffic accidents to which state police are called typically include more vehicles and more damage to persons and property.

State law enforcement differs from local law enforcement in many ways. State police are more likely to deal with highjacking, drug traffic, and smuggling—and are less likely to deal with domestic violence and burglary. Although the location you serve as a State Police Officer may determine the emphasis of your law enforcement work, the traits desired in—and expected of—a State Police Officer are the same regardless of the duties or the location.

If you're interested in a career as a State Police Officer, read through the following partial list of expectations and honestly assess how you measure up to each of them.

- **A State Police Officer must be intelligent.** As a recruit, you must be intelligent enough to make it through the Police Academy or whatever training program the particular department offers. You'll need good reading and listening skills, and you must be able to remember what you're taught. Both as a recruit and as a State Police Officer, you must be able to synthesize material—that is, you must be able to learn rules and then apply them to hypothetical or actual situations.

- **A State Police Officer must be healthy and physically strong and agile.** Police work is physically taxing. State Police Officers must be able to spend many hours on their feet or on the road; to move quickly; to see and hear accurately; and to lift, move, or carry as the situation requires. Obviously, an officer who is ill or who cannot perform all physical activities adequately is not acceptable. Police departments have strict medical standards so that they hire only recruits in excellent health.

Make Connections

For more information on physical qualifications, see the section, "Physical Qualifications for a Position in Law Enforcement," in Hour 5, "Qualifying for Local Law Enforcement Positions."

- **A State Police Officer must be emotionally stable.** A Police Officer carries a gun. Obviously, anyone who is armed must be even tempered, well adjusted, and impartial. When it comes to dealing with firearms, there is no room for error. It is vital that the officer not become excited or react from prejudice or any other emotional state that would cause him or her to act irrationally or "too soon." The state police force has no room for brutal, insulting, or prejudicial behavior in its officers. That's why applicants undergo one or more psychological tests and interviews to determine that they have the stability required for responsible behavior befitting a police role.

- **The State Police Officer must be honest.** The person charged with upholding the law must have a clean record as a law-abiding citizen. Youthful infractions of the law must be few, of a minor nature, and explainable. A dishonest character or history of bad behavior is unacceptable in any law enforcement officer.

- **The State Police Officer must be self-confident and tactful.** State Police Officers must have the self-confidence to make quick decisions and stick with them. Unwavering decisions and firm actions are vital in maintaining control. Tactful, gentle, and firm—these are the hallmarks of the effective, successful Police Officer. You're judged on these qualities during your interviews, and these aspects of your personality are the final refinements on which the decision will be made to hire—or not hire—you as a State Police Officer.

Q&A

Q: Are my opportunities for a state law enforcement career basically the same, throughout the United States?

A: Every state (except Hawaii) has a state police force, but the size of that force can vary widely. For example, California maintains a force of over 5,000, but North Dakota's state force typically has only about 100 officers.

Q: I know you said that State Police Officers are generalists, but what types of special training might be available to them?

A: Some State Police Officers are given special training and serve as radio dispatchers, instructors at police academies, or as police aircraft pilots. They can also work with canine and mounted units or be assigned to protect governors and legislators.

Q: Do State Troopers have to do the same amounts of paperwork you described for local law enforcement?

A: Yes. If you work in law enforcement, you can't avoid the paperwork. At the end of every tour of duty, State Police Officers must prepare a written report of the day's activities. They must also maintain accurate police records and be prepared to draw on those records when testifying in court proceedings.

The Hour in Review

State Police Officers are a distinguished group of individuals—a group that carries a long tradition of aiding the public in many different situations. If you think you're interested in this field, remember these things:

- State Police Officers are responsible for maintaining the law on the state's highway, freeway, and turnpike systems. Some states give their Troopers statewide law enforcement responsibilities, while other states limit the activity of their Troopers to highway patrol and traffic regulation.

- Although State Troopers may have special training, they must operate as law enforcement "generalists" by providing broad law enforcement support to areas that aren't served by local law enforcement systems.

- Most State Troopers must complete some form of Police Academy training and a probationary period.

- State police work brings with it unique sets of risks. Heavy, fast-moving traffic, high-speed chases, and pursuit of armed fugitives in flight are just some of the special challenges for this field.

- Because of the nature of state police work, much of your duty time will be spent alone and unsupervised.

- Self-confidence, trustworthiness, and patience are key attributes of any State Police Officer.

HOUR 4

Learn about Positions in Federal Law Enforcement

What You'll Learn in This Hour

In this hour, you'll take a brief look at the incredible variety of positions available to you in the federal law enforcement realm. From Postal Inspector to Secret Service Agent, federal law enforcement positions afford great variety but are as demanding as (perhaps even more demanding than) any other law enforcement position. If you want to learn more about the opportunities available to you, read on!

Here's a list of your goals for this hour:

- Learn about the duties of a Bureau of Alcohol, Tobacco, and Firearms Special Agent

- Learn about the duties of a Drug Enforcement Administration Special Agent

- Learn about the duties of an FBI Special Agent

- Learn about the duties of a Border Patrol Agent
- Learn about the duties of an Immigration Inspector
- Learn about the duties of an Immigration and Naturalization Service Criminal Investigator
- Learn about the duties of an Internal Security Inspector for the Internal Revenue Service
- Learn about the duties of an Internal Revenue Service Special Agent
- Learn about the duties of a Customs Inspector
- Learn about the duties of a Secret Service Special Agent

Duties of a Bureau of Alcohol, Tobacco, and Firearms Inspector

An important part of the Bureau of Alcohol, Tobacco, and Firearms (BATF) law enforcement effort is its inspection force. BATF Inspectors must be constantly alert to the possibility of fraud, negligence, or illegal activities. When they uncover evidence of criminal activities, inspectors turn it over to BATF Special Agents responsible for criminal investigations. If you become a BATF Inspector, you'll carry out your duties in a variety of work settings. Inspections may take you to such locations as breweries; wineries; distilleries; plants that manufacture distilled spirits for industrial, scientific, and medical use; and laboratories conducting scientific research projects. Your work also may take you to wholesale liquor establishments, cigar and cigarette manufacturing plants, firearms and explosives retailers, and manufacturers and importers.

When, as a BATF Inspector, you are given your work assignments, you visit business establishments alone or as part of an inspection team. You contact and interview company representatives and gather basic data about procedures and operations. You acquire financial statements as well as business and public records to verify information and to make certain that required taxes have been paid. In addition, you determine that the business has the various special licenses, permits, and other authorizations required by federal law. You are also responsible for judging whether facilities and equipment meet legal standards and if manufacturing processes and operations are being conducted in accordance with the law. If you detect violations, you advise company representatives and arrange for correction of these conditions. In cases of criminal violations such as fraud, tax evasion, or falsified inventories, you prepare detailed summaries of evidence to assist agents in preparing cases for criminal prosecution. You will prepare written reports of your work activities, may serve legal papers in violation of federal laws, and sometimes testify as a government witness during court proceedings.

Working Conditions

BATF Inspectors may be assigned to workstations anywhere in the United States and are required to travel when performing field inspections. Working hours are usually regular and average 40 hours per week. The fringe benefits you receive as a BATF Inspector include paid vacations, sick leave, overtime pay, low-cost medical and life insurance, and retirement annuities.

Promotion Opportunities

BATF Inspectors are chosen from the top of the list of eligible candidates meeting the entry standards of the Bureau of Alcohol, Tobacco, and Firearms. Prospects for advancement in this work are generally favorable. Promotions are not automatic but rather are based on satisfactory performance and the recommendations of supervisory staff. As you show ability to assume more complex assignments, you are recommended for promotion in line with such responsibilities. If you so desire, you may choose an alternative advancement route by becoming a BATF Special Agent. Many of the experience requirements for Special Agents may be fulfilled by years of satisfactory service as a BATF Inspector. Federal agencies give preferential treatment to job applicants from within the agency.

Duties of a Bureau of Alcohol, Tobacco, and Firearms Special Agent

The work of a BATF Special Agent is far from routine; if you accept a position in this field, you'll face ever-changing situations while carrying out your duties. The major responsibilities of a BATF Special Agent are twofold. First, BATF Special Agents enforce federal laws concerned with the sale, transfer, manufacture, import, and possession of firearms and explosives. In addition, agents inspect the records and inventories of licensed firearms or explosives distributors to check compliance with federal laws and to uncover possible evidence of unlawful activities. To be an effective BATF Special Agent, you need an extensive knowledge of firearms and explosives. You will likely be asked to probe a variety of cases involved with illegal transport of firearms and explosives across state lines. Your efforts will be particularly directed at organized criminal elements and at terrorist groups operating in this country as you seek to eliminate illegal arms possessions and investigate bombing incidents.

The second major responsibility you will have as a BATF Special Agent involves the difficult task of enforcing federal liquor and tobacco regulations. You will investigate and uncover illicit distillery operations and will be empowered to seize and destroy contraband and illegal production facilities. You'll work to reduce contraband cigarette smuggling and

4

bootlegging of untaxed tobacco products, and you'll investigate reputable distillers, breweries, and manufacturers to make certain that they're following regulations.

Regardless of the type of case assigned to you, as a BATF Special Agent, working alone or in teams, you'll gather all available data and plan the conduct of the investigation. You'll make use of the technical resources of your own bureau as well as those of other law enforcement agencies in obtaining additional information relevant to the case. You will interview, observe, and interrogate suspects, informants, and witnesses connected with the investigation. You may also conduct surveillance activities and work undercover. Where indicated, you may seize, search, and arrest suspects and gather contraband and other evidence as authorized by appropriate legal warrants. BATF Special Agents are trained in self-defense tactics as well as in the use of various types of firearms; they employ these skills as needed during the course of an investigation. You may assist the U.S. Attorney in preparing and presenting cases in court, and you also may make court appearances to testify for the prosecution during criminal proceedings.

Working Conditions

As a Special Agent, you may be assigned to work locations anywhere in the United States and travel frequently during the course of your investigation. You are also subject to transfers and work assignments based on the needs of the bureau. The working hours of Special Agents are often irregular and in excess of 40 hours a week. Besides working under stressful and dangerous conditions, the work is often physically strenuous and is performed in all kinds of environmental conditions. These factors should be weighed carefully when considering this career. The fringe benefits available to you as a BATF Special Agent include the following:

- The opportunity to join group health and life insurance plans, with the government sharing the costs. Immediate family members of Special Agents are included in health and benefit plans.
- Sick leave earned at the rate of 13 days a year, which may be accumulated without limit.
- Annual leave earned at the rate of 13, 20, or 26 days a year, based on the length of government employment.
- Eligibility for retirement at age 50, with 20 years of service in the criminal investigative field.

Promotion Opportunities

When hired as a BATF Special Agent, you usually enter duty at the GS-5 level. Promotions are contingent on satisfactory work performance at each level and require the recommendations of supervisory personnel. As you demonstrate your capabilities, you are given progressively more responsible assignments and promotions commensurate with those responsibilities.

The journeyman level for a Special Agent is GS-11. Selections for promotion to positions above the GS-11 level are made as vacancies occur, in accordance with the bureau's merit promotion procedures.

> **Note**
> For BATF Special Agents, the minimum waiting period in each grade is one year. Periodically, you may receive within-grade "step increases" even if you remain at the same grade level. For the most part, prospects for upward mobility are favorable within the BATF. If you demonstrate the ability to assume more difficult and responsible assignments, you're likely to be recommended for promotion by supervisory personnel.

Duties of a Drug Enforcement Administration Special Agent

The illegal manufacturing and distribution of drugs is a worldwide problem that can be resolved only through the international efforts of all countries. The primary mission of the U.S. Department of Justice Drug Enforcement Administration (DEA) is to enforce the drug laws and regulations of the United States of America. The DEA is charged with bringing to justice individuals and organizations involved in the illegal growing, manufacture, or distribution of drugs in the United States. The DEA also recommends and supports nonenforcement programs aimed at reducing the availability of illegal drugs on the domestic and international market.

As a DEA Special Agent, your primary mission will be to enforce laws dealing with narcotics and dangerous drugs by investigating the alleged or suspected criminal activities of major drug traffickers on both the national and international scene. You'll concentrate your efforts on locating and eliminating illegal sources of supply and distribution that quite often involve secret manufacturers of drugs and sources of drugs diverted from legitimate channels.

As a DEA Special Agent, you'll work alone or in teams to review and analyze all the available case data the agency has on file and to make preliminary plans about the ways in which the investigations will be conducted. You'll be responsible for obtaining additional facts and evidence by interviewing, observing, and interrogating witnesses, suspects, and informants with knowledge of the case. You'll examine financial and inventory records or other sources of information to uncover new evidence indicating criminal activities. In some cases, as a Special Agent, you'll undertake the very risky job of assuming other identities and working undercover. You'll conduct surveillance activities, and you'll often be responsible for coordinating investigations among various agencies to make sure that information is disseminated as necessary and to prevent the duplication of efforts. You'll evaluate the investigation results and consult with supervisory personnel to determine what legal actions should follow.

> **Caution**
> A position as a DEA Special Agent is a stressful, demanding activity requiring long hours and close association with some of society's most undesirable elements.

DEA Special Agents are well trained in the use of firearms and self-defense methods and employ these skills as needed during arrests. As an agent, you'll prepare detailed, written reports of each case in which you take part, and you'll cooperate with government attorneys in trial preparations and testify for the prosecution during trials and grand jury proceedings.

> **Note**
> Special Agents have full police power to enforce all federal laws anywhere in the United States. They can arrest suspects and seize evidence and contraband as authorized by appropriate legal warrants. These actions are carried out by teams of Special Agents or by groups of agents who are part of a strike force unit.

The Drug Enforcement Administration is also responsible for regulating the legal trade in narcotics and dangerous drugs. As a Special Agent, you must have the versatility to conduct accountability investigations of drug wholesalers, suppliers, and manufacturers. In overseas operations, DEA activities are aimed at developing international awareness of the criticality of the illegal drug problem and at obtaining support for drug trafficking suppression measures. As an agent, you'll also give lectures, make speeches, and serve as a panel member for civic, social, community, and other types of organizations expressing concern and interest in the drug-abuse problem.

Working Conditions

DEA Special Agents are the backbone of the agency and represent half of its total workforce. If you begin a career as a DEA Special Agent, you can look forward to many opportunities for diversified experience and assignments at many domestic and international posts of duty. In fact, you must be willing to accept assignment to duty stations *anywhere* in the United States after appointment and at any time thereafter—and don't overlook the possibility of foreign assignments. The work involves frequent travel as well as irregular hours and overtime. This job involves hazardous duty, working under stress, and the possibility of physical injury during dangerous assignments.

The fringe benefits you receive include paid vacation and holidays, sick leave, overtime pay, low-cost medical and life insurance, financial protection in the event of job-related injury or death, and a liberal retirement pension. As a Special Agent with 20 years of service in criminal investigation activities, you can retire at age 50.

Training and Promotion Opportunities

The training program you must undergo to become a DEA Special Agent is so rigorous that many applicants don't make it to the first cut. Continued employment with the agency is contingent on successful completion of the training program. As a candidate, you'll have to sign a statement indicating that you understand that contingency. Once you're hired as a DEA Special Agent, your prospects for upward mobility are generally good. You're eligible for promotion after one year of satisfactory work performance at the entry level. Promotions are based on job performance, demonstrated ability to perform the duties of the higher-level job, and the recommendations of supervisory personnel.

Most Special Agents are appointed at GS-7, and the position has promotion potential to GS-12. Promotions beyond GS-12 are made through DEA's Merit Promotion Plan.

Duties of an FBI Special Agent

The FBI is a fact-gathering agency; its Special Agents function as investigators only. This agency does not prosecute cases but turns over facts and evidence to a U.S. Attorney who makes the decision regarding legal action.

As an FBI Special Agent, you are responsible for enforcing a wide variety of federal laws within your jurisdiction, dealing with such matters as kidnapping, bank robbery, thefts of government property, organized crime activities, espionage, sabotage, civil rights violations, and white-collar crimes such as bank embezzlements or bankruptcy fraud. You can be assigned to any of these various cases; however, where possible—if you have a specialized background such as accounting or science, for example—you are given cases in which your skills can best be used.

An agent's most important function is gathering evidence in cases where specific federal laws have been violated and then presenting findings to the office of a U.S. Attorney.

Agents plan, coordinate, and conduct investigations, using the considerable resources of the bureau. Working alone or in teams, agents conduct surveillance, work undercover, and can seize and arrest individuals as authorized by legal warrants. FBI Special Agents must be skillful in the use of several types of firearms as well as hand-to-hand defensive tactics. They're also required to prepare detailed, written reports on all aspects of cases in which they're involved. They assist the staff of U.S. Attorneys' offices in preparing cases for trial and appear as witnesses during trials and grand jury hearings.

Working Conditions

As an FBI Special Agent, you are assigned to one of the 59 divisional offices located in cities throughout the United States and Puerto Rico, or you work in FBI headquarters in Washington, D.C., or in FBI resident agencies scattered across the nation. Work in excess of 40 hours a week is common, and you may be called on to travel during the performance of duties. You must be available for assignments at any time and are subject to call 24 hours a day. In addition, transfer to different work locations is usually required at some point during your career.

> **Caution**
> Hazardous duty, working under stress, and the prospect of physical injury resulting from participation in dangerous assignments are essential aspects of the work of an FBI Special Agent.

The fringe benefits Special Agents receive include paid vacations, sick leave, life insurance, full medical insurance, overtime pay, and retirement annuities. All FBI Special Agents with 20 years or more of service are required to retire at age 55.

Training and Promotion Opportunities

As a newly appointed FBI Special Agent, you serve a one-year probationary period before achieving permanent status. Once your appointment is permanent, you have a great deal of job security. FBI Special Agents don't receive automatic promotions, but supervisory and administrative positions are filled by agents from within the organization, and promotions are based on demonstrated leadership qualities and work expertise.

Duties of a Border Patrol Agent

The Immigration and Naturalization Service (INS), an agency of the U.S. Department of Justice, administers and enforces laws that govern the admission, exclusion, deportation, and naturalization of aliens. Through a variety of law enforcement activities, the INS protects the national security of the United States and its legal residents. An essential part of the INS law enforcement effort is carried out by a group of highly trained officers known as the Border Patrol.

The Border Patrol is a highly mobile, uniformed enforcement organization whose primary responsibilities are to detect and prevent the illegal entry or smuggling of aliens into the United States. The Border Patrol must also detect, take into custody, and arrange for the deportation of those living illegally in this country. Border Patrol Agents work along the more than 8,000 miles of land and coastal areas that make up the international boundaries of the continental United States. In many cases, these borders are barely visible lines located in rugged and uninhabited mountains, canyons, and deserts. Agents patrol designated areas to uncover attempted or actual illegal entries into this country using electronic communication systems, electronic sensing devices, pursuit vehicles, jeeps, fixed-wing aircraft, helicopters, and patrol boats. Agents perform line-watch duties at points that provide good visibility and use binocular devices to scan areas for illegal entrants.

> **Note**
> Border Patrol Agents use some ingenious methods to catch illegal immigrants. In sandy areas, agents use an age-old technique called "sign cutting" to detect illegal entry. They smooth these areas over, then return to examine them for footprints and tracks, which can indicate the number of people who have crossed the "sand trap" and the direction in which they've traveled. Agents also use jeep-plane teams to enforce immigration laws in remote areas. These teams coordinate aerial surveillance or search activities with ground operations over wide expanses (such as agricultural areas) to pinpoint the location of possible lawbreakers.

4

Border Patrol Agents also investigate other possible means of illegal entry into this country and use foreign language skills where appropriate. They stop vehicles at traffic checkpoints on roads and highways leading from the border and determine the citizenship of occupants. Agents also make inquiries into the immigration status of farm and ranch employees. As a Border Patrol Agent, you may be required to inspect and search trains, buses, trucks, aircraft, ships, and passenger and cargo terminals to locate illegal aliens.

During these searches, you may uncover evidence of smuggling activities, and if you discover illegal aliens, you will be authorized to arrest them without a warrant, using firearms and physical force if necessary. As a Border Patrol Agent, you will make detailed written reports of cases in which you are involved and may be called on to give testimony during court proceedings.

Working Conditions

As a newly hired Border Patrol Agent, you are assigned initially to duty stations in the southern border states of California, Arizona, New Mexico, and Texas. Many of these locations are situated in small, isolated communities. Some of these areas may have poor schools and medical facilities.

> **Caution**
> Border Patrol Agents may find it difficult to transfer to a remote workstation from an area where they prefer to live. If your heart is set on living in a specific location, consider this drawback before you decide to pursue this area of law enforcement.

Border Patrol Agents are required to work overtime and may work long hours. Sixty-hour weeks and 10- to 16-hour days are not uncommon. As an agent, however, you may earn from 10 percent to 25 percent additional pay for the performance of extra duty time. Agents work irregular rotating shifts every two to four weeks, and these shifts are subject to change, often on short notice. Agents work under stressful and dangerous conditions and are subject to the hazards of physical injury during the performance of duties.

Fringe benefits you will receive include paid vacation (13 days in the first three years, 20 days per year after three years of service up to 15 years, 26 days per year after 15 years of service), holidays, and sick leave of 13 days per year, which can be accumulated if not used. Agents are also eligible for low-cost medical and life insurance, and receive an annual $480 uniform allowance.

> **Note**
> New Border Patrol Agents must make the initial outlay of about $1,275 (tax deductible) for uniforms for the first year, $300 of which is due before entering the training academy.

When, as a Border Patrol Agent, you have at least 20 years of service, you are eligible for special retirement with a good pension at age 50. This special provision also applies to other law enforcement officers and certain supervisory personnel who have been promoted from law enforcement positions. Retirement is mandatory at age 55, allowing you to pursue a new career or hobby while collecting retirement pay.

Promotion Opportunities

Initial appointment is at grade GS-5. Career progression generally follows at one-year intervals to GS-7 and to journeyman at GS-9. Promotions and salary increases occur even during the three-year conditional appointment period. The prospects for advancement are excellent. As a Border Patrol Agent, you may compete for other assignments within the Border Patrol or for supervisory-level positions, or you may apply for other positions within the Immigration and Naturalization Service.

Duties of an Immigration Inspector

An integral position in the Immigration and Naturalization Service (INS) uniformed officer corps is that of the Immigration Inspector. Approximately 300 million people enter the United States annually. The Immigration Inspector is usually the first United States official a person meets when entering this country.

If you accept a position as an Immigration Inspector, your key responsibility will be to prevent the entry of people who are ineligible to enter the United States and to properly admit those who are eligible to enter. Immigration Inspectors work primarily at land ports, airports, seaports, and other places where people enter the United States. As a trainee Immigration Inspector, you will perform certain phases of inspection work under fairly close supervision and will assist higher-grade officers in other inspection processes.

4

Working Conditions

Immigration Inspectors must wear an official uniform while on duty, must enforce laws and regulations that may conflict with personal beliefs, and must work in high-pressure situations where complaints and criticism from the public are frequent. Inspectors work long, irregular hours under constantly varying conditions. Overtime is frequently required, and Immigration Inspectors may earn substantial overtime pay for the performance of extra duties.

Promotion Opportunities

Initial appointments are at grade GS-5. Career progressions to grade GS-7 and to journeyman at grade GS-9 generally follow at one-year intervals. Promotions to higher graded positions are made through the competitive procedures of the Federal Merit Promotion System.

Duties of an Immigration and Naturalization Service Criminal Investigator

The Immigration and Naturalization Service (INS) is responsible for determining whether aliens may enter or remain in the United States, evaluating the applications of aliens seeking U.S. citizenship, reviewing applications for visas, guarding against illegal entry into this country, and representing the U.S. Government at official immigration hearings. To meet these responsibilities, the Immigration and Naturalization Service employs a force of highly trained officers known as Criminal Investigators. This force of nonuniformed officers has the mission of investigating and gathering facts in all cases falling within the jurisdiction of the INS. Most cases involve administrative proceedings and criminal prosecutions.

Your primary responsibility as a Criminal Investigator in the INS will be to investigate alleged or suspected violations of federal immigration and naturalization laws. When you receive your assignment, working alone or in teams, you will identify the charges or issues involved and evaluate all the available information concerning each case. Based on this evaluation, you'll plan the preliminary direction, scope, and timing of the investigation. You'll interview, observe, and interrogate suspects and witnesses who are parties in a case, and you'll make use of informants.

As a Criminal Investigator, you examine various types of legal records and immigration documents to see whether they are genuine or to uncover evidence of fraud, conspiracy, or other immigration law violations. You may be required to conduct surveillance or assume other identities and work undercover. This is an often risky and demanding activity that involves long and irregular hours as well as close association with criminal elements. Information gathered during the course of an investigation is analyzed and distributed within the INS to aid in planning and to avoid duplicate effort. In cases where evidence is uncovered about illegal actions in the jurisdiction of other agencies, you'll relay this information and may coordinate your activities with the agency in question. When, as an INS Criminal Investigator, you decide that sufficient evidence has been gathered to justify action, you'll be authorized to seize, arrest, and take suspects into custody and to seize evidence using court-obtained warrants where required.

Immigration Inspectors are skilled in the methods of self-defense as well as in the use of firearms; inspectors use these skills as required. Inspectors prepare reports of their investigations, may assist INS attorneys in the preparation of cases, and may be called on to testify in court.

Working Conditions

The INS uses Criminal Investigators throughout the United States. The larger field offices are usually in metropolitan areas. The work may involve irregular hours, travel, and overtime as part of normal duties. Certain parts of this job involve hazardous duty, working under stress, and the possibility of physical harm. Benefits include paid vacation, sick leave, and holidays; overtime pay; low-cost medical and life insurance; financial protection in the event of death or injury; and a retirement annuity. When you have 20 years of experience in federal law enforcement as a Criminal Investigator, you are eligible for retirement at age 50. Retirement is mandatory at age 55.

Promotion Opportunities

Initial appointments are at grade GS-5. Career progressions to grades CS-7, GS-9, and journeyman at GS-11 generally follow at one-year intervals. Thereafter, promotions are made through the competitive procedures of the Federal Merit Promotion System. As a Criminal Investigator who demonstrates the skills required to perform complex assignments, you may compete for supervisory or other high-level positions.

Duties of an Internal Security Inspector, Internal Revenue Service

4

The Inspection Service is an essential part of the Internal Revenue Service (IRS). The Inspection Service is responsible for keeping the IRS honest at all levels. The Inspection Service's two basic operations are Internal Audit and Internal Security. Members of Internal Audit review all levels of operations of the Internal Revenue Service to be sure that the agency is being managed and run effectively. Internal Security makes up the law enforcement wing of the Inspection Service.

If you take a job as an Internal Security Inspector, you'll be part of the IRS's own investigative unit whose duties are varied and often complex. Internal Security Inspectors conduct detailed character and background investigations of prospective IRS employees, including applicants or appointees to technical or nontechnical jobs and those involved with the handling of funds; public accountants and former IRS employees who apply to represent taxpayers at IRS hearings; and those involved in charges of unethical conduct by lawyers, accountants, or others involved in IRS proceedings. Inspectors also investigate complaints or information that indicate possible wrongdoing by IRS employees, and they respond quickly to any attempts to bribe IRS employees or to interfere with the administration of IRS statutes. Inspectors are often assigned as armed escorts, responsible for protecting IRS employees and government witnesses in legal proceedings. Other duties include investigating cases where federal tax information was illegally disclosed and cases of accidents involving IRS employees or property that result in civil law suits. Sometimes the Secretary of the Treasury, the Commissioner of the IRS, or some other high-level official may direct Internal Security Inspectors to conduct special investigations. This agency works cooperatively with law enforcement personnel of other agencies and at times may assist in providing security for the president of the United States and other American or foreign dignitaries.

By its very nature, the job of the Internal Security Inspector is often more difficult than many others in the investigative field. When you work in this role, most of your criminal investigations involve secret or concealed crimes, so you first have to learn that the crime has been—or is going to be—committed. Then you must discover where and how it occurred and who is involved. When you've accomplished all that, you have to secure all the necessary evidence, arrange for the apprehension of those responsible, and prepare the material that will lead to successful prosecution. The average Criminal Investigator rarely has so complex a problem. In burglary or homicide, for example, someone usually reports the crime, and thus there is evidence that the crime did occur. The sole remaining problems are to find out who did it and prove it; much of the critical evidence remains at the scene of the crime.

Note

Internal Security Inspectors are faced with extremely heavy workloads as the following excerpt from the Commissioner's Annual Report of 1982 attests. In reading the record of indictments and convictions, keep in mind that the majority of investigations lead to innocent persons:

The Internal Security division's investigations to protect the integrity of the IRS resulted in the arrest or indictment of 95 taxpayers and tax practitioners and 272 current or former IRS employees. There were convictions or guilty pleas in the cases of 121 individuals arrested or indicted in 1982 or earlier. Of these convictions, 18 were for bribery and 21 for assault; the rest involved conspiracy to defraud the government, embezzlement, impersonation of a federal officer, narcotics, and other offenses.

The Internal Security division completed 5,495 background investigations of employees during the year and conducted police record checks on all persons considered for temporary appointments. These investigations and record searches resulted in the rejection of 72 job applicants and administrative actions against 332 employees. Internal Security also conducted 902 investigations of alleged employee misconduct, with 74 resulting in exoneration of the employees involved.

It's interesting to note that more bribery cases have been successfully prosecuted by the Internal Revenue Inspection Service than by all other federal investigative agencies combined.

To summarize, the investigative jurisdiction of the Inspection Service includes the areas of bribery, perjury, embezzlement, fraud, assault, conspiracy, collusion, extortion, forgery, unauthorized disclosure of information, and any acts that threaten the proper administration of IRS regulations. As an Internal Security Inspector, you will use physical force or firearms when necessary to apprehend and arrest suspected individuals.

Working Conditions

As an Internal Security Inspector, you may be assigned to workstations at the National Office of the Internal Revenue Service in Washington. D.C., or to one of the regional or district offices found throughout the United States. There are 58 IRS district offices with at least one in each of the 50 states. Regional offices are located in San Francisco, Dallas, Cincinnati, Chicago, Atlanta, Philadelphia, and New York. Internal Security Inspectors work on irregular schedules in excess of 40 hours a week and may have to travel to carry out their duties. They often work under stress and are subject to personal risks during certain assignments. Fringe benefits associated with this work include paid vacation and holidays, overtime pay, sick leave, low-cost medical and life insurance, financial protection in the event of job-related injury or death, and a retirement pension. As an Internal Security Inspector who has 20 years of service in criminal investigation activities, you are eligible to retire at 50 years of age.

Promotion Opportunities

Generally, the prospects for advancement in this field are favorable. Those Internal Security Inspectors who demonstrate the ability to assume more difficult and responsible tasks may compete for higher-level technical, supervisory, and managerial positions.

Duties of an Internal Revenue Service Special Agent

Special Agents of the Criminal Investigation Division (CID) of the IRS are responsible for investigating all criminal violations of the Internal Revenue Code except those relating to alcohol, tobacco, and firearms. Tax evasion and failure to file returns make up the majority of the violations IRS Special Agents investigate.

When agents uncover violations, they have to gather sufficient evidence to prove guilt beyond a reasonable doubt. Tax evaders often use clever methods to avoid tax payments, and their criminal acts often take place over a period of years. The numerous transactions that take place and the records that accumulate during those years can make the investigation difficult. The investigation process begins when the Criminal Investigation Division in a particular tax district receives reports about alleged tax violations. Typical sources of this information include IRS agents, tax technicians, and Revenue Officers; IRS Special Agents working on related cases; officers of other federal, state, and local law enforcement agencies; and informants. Supervisors evaluate the information and, if criminal violations are indicated, assign the case to a Special Agent of the Criminal Investigation Division. The Special Agent then interviews the subject, key witnesses, and other parties to the case to determine the true taxable income of the subject and whether a deliberate attempt was made to understate income or to avoid filing a tax return. The Special Agent carefully gathers, records, evaluates, and organizes the evidence. Special Agents have to be quite skilled at spotting tax frauds and uncovering unreported income or hidden assets. In cases where taxpayer records are withheld, lost, destroyed, or altered, agents are faced with the difficult task of reconstructing these records by locating alternative sources of information, such as bank records, canceled checks, brokerage accounts, and so on. These activities require a sound knowledge of accounting and tax-law procedures, rules of evidence, and the constitutional rights of individuals involved in the case.

In addition to gathering data, Special Agents engage in surveillance of suspects and are authorized to conduct searches and to arrest individuals, using physical force or firearms as necessary to protect human life. Once a case assignment is concluded, the Special Agent prepares detailed reports of all information gathered during the investigation process. These reports contain a complete history of the investigation and the agent's conclusions and recommendations. If the subject of the investigation is brought to trial, the Special Agent assists the U.S. Attorney in preparing the case and usually appears as a principal witness for the government.

Note

IRS Special Agents also investigate organized crime activities. Under federal law, income from illegal sources such as bootlegging, prostitution, and narcotics sales is subject to tax. As a result of IRS investigations, many crime figures have been prosecuted and convicted of tax evasion, resulting in substantial blows to the financial resources of criminal groups. As part of this effort, the Internal Revenue Service participates in the Federal Organized Crime Strike Force Program and works on a cooperating basis with other law enforcement agencies at all levels of government.

Working Conditions

As a Special Agent, you may be assigned to work locations at the National Office of the Internal Revenue Service in Washington, D.C., or to one of the 7 regional or 58 district offices located throughout the United States. As a Special Agent, you may be required to travel during the course of investigations. Working hours are sometimes irregular and in excess of 40 hours a week. You can expect the work to be stressful and, at times, physically risky. The fringe benefits you receive include paid vacation, sick leave, overtime pay, low-cost medical and life insurance, financial protection in the event of job-related injury or death, and a liberal retirement annuity. Special Agents with 20 years of service in criminal investigation activities can retire at age 50.

Promotion Opportunities

Prospects for advancement in this work are generally good. IRS Special Agents who demonstrate the skills needed to assume higher-level duties may move into supervisory or higher managerial positions.

Duties of a Customs Inspector

As members of the U.S. Customs Service law enforcement team. Customs Inspectors play a key role in enforcing numerous customs regulations through precise and thorough methods of examination, inspection, and questioning. Inspectors are responsible for cargoes and baggage; articles worn or carried by individuals; and vessels, vehicles, and aircraft entering or leaving the United States. When carriers such as ships, aircraft, or motor transport cross our borders, Customs Inspectors are authorized to go aboard to inspect, search, and determine the exact nature of the cargo. They review cargo manifests and baggage declarations, examine cargo containers, and oversee unloading activities to prevent smuggling, fraud, or cargo thefts. Customs Inspectors also weigh and measure imported merchandise to make certain that customs, neutrality, and commerce laws are followed.

Customs Inspectors are responsible for the examination of crew and passenger lists, health clearances, stores' lists, and ships' documents; they also issue required permits. They seal the holds of ships and compartments containing sea stores used by crew members as a way of preventing the illegal sale or smuggling of dutiable merchandise into the United States. In certain cases, where wrongdoing is suspected, they conduct body searches of crew members to check for contraband.

When assigned to baggage examination stations at points of entry in the United States, Customs Inspectors perform a variety of tasks. They classify, assess, and collect duties on articles being brought into the country and advise tourists about U.S. Customs regulations. If Customs Inspectors discover undeclared items in baggage, they must determine whether this is merely an oversight or deliberate fraud on the passenger's part. In most instances, these matters are settled immediately, but occasionally the articles are held and a U.S.

4

Customs hearing is scheduled to decide the case. Customs Inspectors fill a number of critical roles: They may question suspicious-looking individuals, explain Customs procedures and laws to tourists, and are authorized to search suspected individuals and seize contraband and undeclared merchandise. In addition, they may arrest or detain these individuals, using physical force or firearms if necessary.

In carrying out their responsibilities, Customs Inspectors often work in cooperation with other government agents, such as Customs Patrol Officers, Import Specialists, FBI Special Agents, and agents of the U.S. Immigration and Naturalization Service and the Food and Drug Administration. They prepare reports to submit to supervisors of findings, transactions, violations, and arrests that take place during their work tour. Customs Inspectors are also called upon to testify in court as government witnesses for cases in which they have been involved.

Working Conditions

The territory of the United States is divided into nine regions that include the 50 states, the District of Columbia, Puerto Rico, and the U.S. Virgin Islands. As a Customs Inspector, you may be assigned to any of the nearly 300 ports of entry along our land and sea borders, or you may work overseas. Where possible, the Customs Service places you in the work location of your choice. The typical work schedule is eight hours a day, five days a week, but it includes rotating shifts and weekend duty. The hours of the typical seaport or airport are often long and irregular, and remoteness characterizes the many one-man border ports where Custom Inspectors must often perform immigration and agricultural inspections in addition to regular duties.

For all this extra effort, you will be liberally compensated by special overtime privileges enacted by congressional legislation. As a Customs Inspector, you need to be aware that the job involves some physical risks: You may be required to seize and arrest people suspected of serious Customs violations. The fringe benefits you'll receive include paid vacations and sick leave; military leave; low-cost group hospitalization, medical, and life insurance; and retirement annuities covered by the Bureau of Retirement of the Office of Personnel Management.

Promotion Opportunities

After achieving permanent employment status, Customs Inspectors can qualify and compete for promotions to higher-level positions within the U.S. Customs Service. These may be supervisory positions or simply those at a higher grade level in the agency.

Duties of a Secret Service Special Agent

The primary responsibility of the Secret Service is protecting the president of the United States. In addition, Special Agents are authorized by law to protect the vice president; the immediate families of the president and vice president; the president-elect, vice president-elect, and their immediate families; a former president and his wife during his lifetime; the widow of a former president until her death or remarriage; minor children of a former president until age 16; major presidential and vice presidential candidates; and visiting heads of foreign governments.

Secret Service Special Agents use the same protective measures for every individual they're assigned to protect. Special Agents are responsible for planning, organizing, and enacting security arrangements well in advance of the person's arrival at a given location. Special Agents work with other agency staff to establish security perimeters and devise the security arrangements. These security arrangements may include the use of police patrols on the streets parallel to, adjacent to, or having access to the route to be taken, or the deployment of helicopters for surveillance purposes. If the person being protected is traveling on or near water routes, Special Agents may use U.S. Coast Guard and police patrol craft. Special Agents are assigned to advance-team duty and are also responsible for briefing and assigning personnel to duty posts and for selecting sites such as hospitals, evacuation routes, and relocation areas to be used in emergency situations.

Special Agents assigned to protective duty receive essential support from the Intelligence Division of the Secret Service. Intelligence Agents gather much of their information by developing and maintaining contacts with state and local law enforcement agencies as well as with such federal agencies as the Federal Bureau of Investigation, Central Intelligence Agency, Treasury Department, Department of State, Department of Defense, Drug Enforcement Administration, U.S. Postal Service, and the General Services Administration. In addition, Special Agents involved with gathering intelligence are responsible for overseeing electronic-security operations and keeping current with new developments in security measures.

Special Agents assigned to the permanent Secret Service detail that protects the president have a difficult and complicated mission. While charged with providing the Chief Executive with maximum protection, they have the impossible task of guarding against all the perils that can develop, particularly when national or international travel is involved. Presidents are often reluctant to follow any security measures that hinder their work activities or limit their contact with the general public. Providing maximum security without affecting the president's customary routine makes the agents' work a complex and challenging assignment.

4

In addition to protective responsibilities, Secret Service Special Agents have investigative functions as well. They investigate all cases that involve the counterfeiting of U.S. currency and securities and the forgery of U.S. Government checks, bonds, and securities. Each year, Special Agents seize and arrest thousands of people engaging in such illegal activities.

Regardless of the type of case assigned, working alone or in teams, Secret Service Special Agents collect and evaluate all the available data from other law enforcement agencies, informants, and the general public and plan the conduct of the investigation. They interview witnesses and suspects to obtain useful information and evidence in the case. When necessary, they work undercover, keep suspects under surveillance, and use court-approved listening devises to gather evidence and uncover others involved in the case. After gathering and analyzing all available data and evidence, Special Agents determine what investigative, arrest, or seizure activities are in order. Where the evidence indicates, they obtain warrants and seize, search, arrest, and take suspects into custody. Special Agents are highly skilled in the use of various types of firearms as well as in hand-to-hand defensive tactics; they use these skills as needed when apprehending suspects. Agents prepare detailed, written reports of all cases in which they take part and assist U.S. Attorneys in the preparation of cases for trial. They are also called on to give court testimony in cases in which they have participated.

Working Conditions

The Secret Service has district field offices throughout the United States; its headquarters is in Washington, D.C. As a Special Agent, you may be assigned to work locations anywhere in the United States and may travel frequently while performing your duties. In addition, you can expect frequent transfers and work reassignments throughout your career. You must be available for assignments at any time and often will work more than 40 hours per week. Your work will be stressful, and you'll be exposed to potential physical harm during the course of your protective or investigative duties. The fringe benefits you can expect include low-cost medical and life insurance, financial protection in the event of job-related injury or death, paid vacations, sick leave, overtime pay, and retirement annuities. Agents with 20 years of service may retire at age 50. Retirement is mandatory at age 55.

Promotion Opportunities

Secret Service Special Agents start at grade GS-5 or GS-7. The advancement prospects of Special Agents are quite favorable. If you demonstrate the ability to assume greater responsibilities, you are eligible to compete for supervisory or higher-level positions.

Q&A

Q: Aren't most federal law enforcement positions in Washington, D.C.?

A: Nothing could be further from the truth. As a matter of fact, very few federal law enforcement positions are in Washington, D.C. And for those that may be headquartered there (for example, the **FBI**), you will more than likely be assigned to a field office as you start your career and may very well remain in the field office.

Q: I'm interested in being a Secret Service Agent. Will that guarantee me a job protecting the president?

A: Not necessarily. Many Secret Service personnel are assigned to other areas, including security at National Monuments and other federal buildings.

A: Can I work as long as I want (without retiring) in federal law enforcement jobs?

Q: No. Many federal law enforcement jobs have mandatory retirement ages (usually at or around age 55).

A: I've been told that passing the training for a federal law enforcement position is much tougher than, say, passing the training for a local Police Officer. Is this true?

Q: That depends on how you define "tough." Certainly, if you have a relative who is a Police Officer for your hometown, and you also want to become a Police Officer there, you probably have a much better chance of securing that job as compared to other law enforcement positions. However, as with most everything else, it comes down to your willingness to acquire a specific job, your talents, and how much you want to sacrifice for the job (for example, your willingness to relocate).

4

The Hour in Review

- Jobs in federal law enforcement are quite varied and cover an incredible range of interests. If you are willing to make certain sacrifices (most notably, relocation), you should have no problem finding something in this area that appeals to you.

- Most training for federal law enforcement agencies takes place in specialized training facilities, such as the Federal Law Enforcement Training Center (FLETC) in Georgia. Also note that, with many federal agencies, there are considerable costs involved in both traveling to and from the training facility, as well as "extra" costs you may need to cover (such as the cost of your uniform). Note, however, that some positions cover traveling expenses, and others offer you reimbursement for your uniform. Make sure that you understand the requirements regarding cost for your position of choice.

- As with some other law enforcement positions, certain positions within federal law enforcement are "geography based." For example, working with the Border Patrol obviously requires you to work on a border and not in the middle of the country! Be sure that you understand the relocation requirements of these types of jobs. It is also a good idea to become thoroughly familiar with the area to which you will be moving to (or at least, to the best of your ability).

- You will benefit from knowing a second language in any field of law enforcement, but it can really pay off in a federal position. Take advantage of any opportunity you get to learn a second language (in fact, some positions, such as Border Patrol Agent, may require you to know a second language).

- Federal positions are as difficult to get and maintain as any other law enforcement position, even though some of them are not what you might think of as "typical" law enforcement. Be sure that you take each position seriously and consider it as difficult to obtain as any other position.

- Although relocation is a major issue in federal law enforcement, you probably won't work in Washington, D.C. The FBI, for example, has an extensive field office network. In fact, you will more than likely begin your career in one of these field offices.

Part II

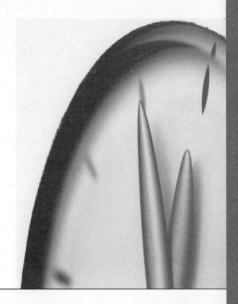

Learn What
It Takes to Get In

HOUR 5

Qualifying for Local Law Enforcement Positions

What You'll Learn in This Hour

All law enforcement positions require you to pass extensive qualifying examinations that test both your physical and mental stamina. In this hour, you will examine these qualification requirements for local law enforcement positions, including those of Police Officer, Correction Officer, and county law enforcement positions.

Make Connections

For general information about the role and duties of local law enforcement officers, see Hour 2, "Learn About Positions in Local Law Enforcement."

Hours 8 through 13 teach you more specific strategies for passing written examinations, as well as how these tests are presented and what they are testing you for. See Appendix B for information about preparing for the physical training programs.

Here's a list of your goals for this hour:

- Get an overview of local law enforcement qualifications
- Learn the physical qualifications for a local law enforcement officer
- Understand the written testing requirements

An Overview of Local Law Enforcement Qualifications

Each city or town sets its own standards for the law enforcement officers it employs. The only requirements that all federal and almost all state and local jurisdictions hold in common are U.S. citizenship and a high school education.

Tip

If you are a veteran of the U.S. Armed Forces, be sure to make this fact known. Veterans receive some form of employment preference when they apply for any government position at the local, state, or federal level.

The veteran's preference sometimes takes the form of points added to the examination score.

For some positions, the maximum age of entry is raised by the number of years served in the military.

Service-connected disability, if it is not disqualifying for the job, can add still more weight to the application.

In short, make sure that you make it known that you are a veteran!

Although some requirements for the positions of Police Officer, Sheriff, and Deputy Sheriff are similar, there are some differences. The following sections discuss the requirements for each position in more detail.

General Requirements for Qualifying as a Police Officer

Entry requirements for Police Officers vary to a certain degree among police agencies throughout the country. As a rule, however, applicants must be U.S. citizens between the ages of 20 and 35 at the time they join the force. Most police agencies require that you have a high school diploma or its equivalent, and some require that you also have com-

pleted a number of specified college credits. Other agencies consider only applicants who
have a college degree.

> **Tip**
> Secondary and postsecondary courses helpful in preparing for police work
> include government, English, psychology, sociology, American history, physics,
> and foreign languages. In addition, over 1,000 junior colleges, colleges, and
> universities offer programs in police science or criminal justice.

As mentioned in previous hours, newly hired Police Officers must successfully complete a
probationary period before they're assigned to permanent duty on the force. The length
and content of probation programs vary widely from agency to agency. In small departments, you can expect less formal instruction and more on-the-job training as a way of
developing skills. In large police agencies, formalized programs of instruction are the rule
and may last from several weeks to six months or more. Some departments combine
formal training with field experience to reinforce concepts learned in the classroom.

General Requirements for Qualifying as a Police Detective

"Detective" is a promotional title in most police agencies; in others, detectives hold the
same grade and salary level as Police Officers. Regardless, this job has status within
police circles, and competition for openings is always keen. Opportunities for entry into
the job vary depending on the size of the department.

Detectives in most local, county, and state police agencies are selected internally from the
ranks of Police Officers who meet specific requirements. The basic requirements for the
position of Police Detective usually include the following:

- A minimum (usually) of three years' experience as a uniformed Police Officer
- Demonstrated investigative talent
- In some agencies, the completion of a specified number of college credits

> **Tip**
> Usually, there are no specified courses you must take to qualify for appoint-
> ment as a detective. Because this is often considered a lateral move, there is
> no qualifying exam.

Most new detectives receive formal instruction in a police training facility. The length of this training varies among departments throughout the country, but it usually lasts from two weeks to a few months or more. Where formal training isn't available, candidates are trained on the job. Whether the training is formal, on the job, or a combination of both, new detectives are instructed in several areas, including the following:

- Rules of evidence
- Courtroom procedures
- Warrant and subpoena procedures
- Media relations
- Investigative techniques

Even if they have already served as permanent members of a police force, newly trained detectives have to go through a probationary period before they're permanently appointed as Police Detectives.

General Requirements for Qualifying as a Deputy Sheriff

The entry requirements for Deputy Sheriffs vary significantly among counties throughout the United States. As a rule, candidates must be U.S. citizens between the ages of 21 and 29 at the time of appointment. (Most agencies deduct *only some* of the time the candidate spent in military service from that candidate's chronological age.) Most sheriffs' agencies require completion of high school as the educational minimum, but more and more agencies are requiring that applicants hold college credits as well.

Every county has its own regulations or programs that control how it selects and employs Deputy Sheriffs. Some of those regulations are listed here:

- State and county civil service laws
- Merit board regulations
- Formal work agreements or contracts

Each of these regulations is unique, but most of them involve some kind of test-selection process (written or oral) or an evaluation of the candidate's previous work experience. In addition to meeting prescribed physical requirements (including standards of weight, height, and vision), candidates must also pass a comprehensive medical examination that may also include a psychological evaluation.

All newly trained Deputies go through some type of formal training before they're assigned to duty, but the length and nature of that training varies from agency to agency. Deputies in large agencies are likely to attend training academies where programs can last from two to six months. Deputies who work in smaller agencies may not go through formal training immediately, but may be sent to state or municipal training academies at a future time to develop their skills further. Regardless of how the training takes place, deputies usually receive instruction in the following subjects:

- Criminal law
- Arrest, search, and seizure procedures
- Methods of patrol, surveillance, and communications
- Accident prevention and traffic control
- Motor vehicle codes
- Laws of evidence
- Methods of self-defense
- Police ethics

After they've successfully completed training, candidates are placed on probation for a period ranging from 6 to 18 months, depending on the agency. During probation, candidates work with experienced Deputies. When they're skilled enough to work independently, the candidates are hired as Deputy Sheriffs on a permanent basis.

General Requirements for Qualifying as a Correction Officer

Most penal systems require that Correction Officer candidates have a high school diploma or its equivalent and are at least 21 years old and in good health. Many states require that applicants pass a civil service examination; other states require some experience in corrections or related work—for example, military service.

5

> **Note**
> If you apply for a position in the federal prison system, the U.S. Office of Personnel Management may allow you to substitute your post-high school education for general experience. Because many universities and community colleges now offer courses in criminal justice, this may be a viable option for you.

> **Tip**
> If you're interested in becoming a Correction Officer, you may give yourself a real employment edge by taking some college courses in areas such as psychology, sociology, English, communications, and foreign languages.

Most states require that applicants meet certain height and weight requirements and have good vision and hearing. You'll learn more about physical qualifications and testing later in this hour.

The American Correctional Association has established guidelines for training Correction Officers. Most federal and state (and even some local) correction departments base their training programs on those guidelines. Some states have special training academies for Correction Officers. All states and local departments of correction, however, provide informal on-the-job training. Experienced officers receive inservice training to keep abreast of new ideas and procedures.

Caution
More than any other law enforcement group, Correction Officers spend their workdays surrounded by convicted inmates. Because this is true, the Correction Officer must possess a certain higher level of mental stamina because the everyday conditions of prison life are obviously unique. The Correction Officer must be ready to deal with rapidly changing conditions and be prepared to use force (if necessary) to subdue rioting inmates or other violent situations that, unfortunately, are quite common in prisons across the country.

One final note on basic qualifications: Because Correction Officers are an important link in the offender rehabilitation process, people who are considering such employment should be tuned in to the needs of people in trouble and have a true interest in helping inmates overcome their problems. Although interviews, psychological testing, and examinations help gauge this quality in applicants, each individual is the best judge of whether he or she possesses it.

Physical Qualifications for a Position in Law Enforcement

Good physical health is a requirement for any position in law enforcement. But the qualifications go beyond what you may regard as being healthy. When you're an applicant for a job in local law enforcement, you must be agile, able to lift excessive weight, be in outstanding cardiovascular condition, and in general, have no physical condition (no matter how subtle) that would impede your performance in the role of law enforcement official.

The Medical Examination

The first physical requirement is that you successfully complete a medical examination. The following list was taken from one police department and lists specific requirements of the medical examination. Although this list may vary from department to department (including county positions and the role of Correction Officer), it should be taken as a good example of the potential rigorous medical examination you can expect.

Tip
The medical examination "checklist" provided here is pretty much a standard for most law enforcement agencies. You'll see it referenced again in later hours that deal with other areas of law enforcement.

- **Vision.** You must test 20/40 (Snellen) in both eyes without corrective lenses. Uncorrected vision must test at least 20/70 in each eye. Vision in each eye must be corrected to 20/20. In addition, you must have the ability to distinguish basic colors.

- **Hearing.** Without using a hearing aid, you must be able to hear the whispered voice at 15 feet with each ear. Using an audiometer for measurement, you should have loss of no more than 30 decibels in each ear at the 500, 1000, and 2000 levels.

- **Speech.** You must be able to speak clearly. Diseases or conditions resulting in indistinct speech are disqualifying.

- **Respiratory System.** Your respiratory system must work well enough that you can do the job you're applying for. If you have any chronic disease or condition that affects your respiratory system and that could impair your full performance of duties of the position, you'll be disqualified.

- **Cardiovascular System.** Organic heart disease (compensated or not), hypertension with repeated readings that exceed 150 systolic and 90 diastolic without medication, symptomatic peripheral vascular disease, and severe varicose veins are all disqualifying conditions.

- **Gastrointestinal System.** Chronic symptomatic diseases or conditions of the gastrointestinal tract and any conditions that require special diets are disqualifying.

- **Endocrine System.** You'll be disqualified if you have any history of a systemic metabolic disease, such as diabetes or gout.

- **Genito-Urinary Disorders.** Chronic, symptomatic diseases or conditions of the genito-urinary tract are disqualifying. Examples of such conditions might include chronic bladder or kidney problems, including the need for dialysis on a regular basis.

5

- **Extremities and Spine.** Any deformity or disease of your spine or limbs that would interfere with your range of motion or dexterity, or that is severe enough to limit your ability to fully perform the duties of the position, is disqualifying.

- **Hernias.** Inguinal and femoral hernias with or without the use of a truss are disqualifying.

- **Nervous System.** Applicants must possess emotional and mental stability with no history of a basic personality disorder. If you have a history of epilepsy or convulsive disorder, you must have been seizure free for the past two years without medication. Also, any neurological disorder that has decreased your neurological or muscular function is disqualifying.

Sample Physical Performance Test

Physical performance tests, like the medical examination requirements, can vary. Following are two examples of physical fitness tests that can be expected by candidates for many law enforcement positions.

Here's the first example of a typical physical fitness test:

1. Run up 3 flights of stairs, down 1 flight, and then 9 yards to a track.

2. Run 90 yards around the track.

3. Run approximately 5 yards to a maze of 6 cones set 3 feet apart; follow a prescribed course through the maze. *Penalty time:* 5 seconds for missing one or more turns in the maze.

4. Run 10 yards and go over a 5-foot wall. *Maximum time:* 30 seconds.

5. Run approximately 5 feet to a wood box with a weight of approximately 100 pounds. Push the box a distance of 10 feet. *Maximum time:* 30 seconds.

6. Run approximately 4 yards and jump across a 3-foot space. *Penalty time:* 15 seconds if you fail this task.

7. Run 7 yards and go over a 3-foot-high barrier. *Maximum time:* 15 seconds.

8. Run 5 yards and go through a maze of 6 cones set 3 feet apart; follow a prescribed course through the maze. *Penalty time:* 5 seconds for missing one or more turns in the maze.

9. Run 5 yards and lift or drag a 70-pound dummy 25 feet. *Maximum time:* 30 seconds.

10. Run 90 yards to the end of the course.

> **Tip**
> Although continuous running through all events is not mandatory, remember that you have only 2 minutes and 15 seconds to complete the entire course!

> **Note**
> Most of these types of physical fitness tests are timed. However, if you fail the first attempt, the examiners usually let you try a second time.

Here's an example of another type of physical fitness test and the requirements for it:

1. Run up approximately 40 steps.

2. Run approximately 40 yards following a designated path—including at least four 90-degree turns—to a sandbag.

3. Push the sandbag, weighing approximately 100 pounds, forward a distance of approximately 5 yards and then back to its original position.

4. Run approximately 10 yards to a 110-pound dummy, which is hanging by a ring from a metal pipe, with its lowest point approximately 3 feet above the floor.

5. Raise the dummy so as to lift the attached ring off the metal pipe. Allow the dummy to slide onto the floor or place it on the floor. You must not drop the dummy or throw it down.

6. Step up approximately 18 inches and walk across a 12-foot beam by placing one foot in front of the other until you reach the other end.

7. Run approximately 10 yards to the finish line.

5

> **Note**
> Another type of physical fitness test might consist of simply measuring the number of set exercises (for example, sit-ups, push-ups, and so on) you are able to complete in a set amount of time.

Written Tests for Law Enforcement Positions

In addition to physical requirements, most law enforcement positions also require you to pass written examinations. Although these types of exams vary greatly from position to position, most are similar in that they test for the following:

- Reading comprehension
- Visual memory
- Computation skills
- Investigative judgment and decision making
- General problem solving

More specific descriptions of these types of tests, as well as strategies for passing them, are discussed in later hours in this book.

> **Caution**
> Do not take the written exams lightly. Even though you may do very well on the physical exams and pass all medical requirements, a low score on the written exams can easily disqualify you from consideration for employment as a law enforcement officer.

Q&A

Q: I've heard that the only way to become a local law enforcement official is to know someone on the force. Is there any truth to this?

A: Put simply, having a relative or close friend who is employed with the same agency may give you some advantage, but only from the aspect of what inside knowledge they can impart to you. Ultimately, your mental abilities and physical health, along with various other factors, are the deciding factors, not whom you know.

Q: Will military service automatically get me a job?

A: No. Although military service can be of great value (and can help reduce the age qualification limit), other experiences can be of equal benefit, depending on what type of position you are interested in. For example, as a forensic expert, the appropriate schooling would obviously give you a major advantage over someone who is interested in the same job but who has no formal training.

Q: Is there any way I can prepare for the physical tests that all local law enforcement positions require?

A: Of course! As a matter of fact, you should begin a self-training program long before you take the physical examinations. Of course, certain health problems cannot be solved by exercising, but if you simply want to increase your physical health (especially your cardiovascular system and upper-body strength), you should most certainly engage in a training program. Note that a training program will also help you once you become employed because you will be expected to maintain a certain level of physical fitness throughout your law enforcement career.

The Hour in Review

- Local law enforcement requires you to pass strenuous mental and physical examinations. Don't think that local positions are easier to qualify for than state or federal positions!

- There are several general requirements for local positions. Although differences may (and do) occur, you should be in excellent physical health, have at least a high school diploma (and some college, if possible), and related experience.

- Some law enforcement agencies deduct time you've spent in the military from your age when calculating whether or not you meet the age qualifications. This can work for you, so check for this information on job postings and with the agency to which you're applying.

- Although there are some physical conditions that can be corrected and thus not disqualify you from service as a local law enforcement official, you should carefully consult local jurisdictions regarding physical defects or other health problems that may and can prevent you from serving as a local law enforcement official.

5

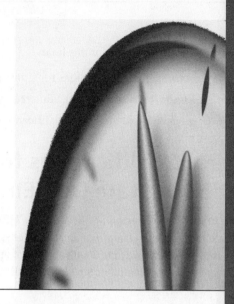

HOUR 6

Qualifying for State Law Enforcement Positions

What You'll Learn in This Hour

When you work in state law enforcement, you often work alone and without any direct supervision. Because of that, positions in this field bring with them a demand for self-discipline that may be unique in all of law enforcement. If you have the self-discipline to work as a State Police Officer or Trooper, it will serve you well as you prepare to take the physical and written examinations required to enter this field. This hour looks at the qualification requirements for the position of State Police Officer.

Make Connections

Later hours in this part of the book teach you more specific strategies for passing written examinations. Those discussions also explain how these tests are presented and what they are testing you for.

Here's a list of your goals for this hour:

- Understand the qualifications for a position in state law enforcement
- Learn about physical qualification requirements
- Learn about written testing qualifications

General Qualifications for a Position in State Law Enforcement

Candidates for the position of State Police Officer are selected according to civil service regulations that vary from state to state. Generally, applicants must be U.S. citizens between the ages of 21 and 29 at the time of appointment: service in the military may be deducted from the candidate's chronological age in meeting this age requirement.

Tip

If you are a veteran of the U.S. Armed Forces, be sure that you make this fact known. Veterans receive some form of employment preference when they apply for any government position at the local, state, or federal level. For example, some agencies add points to your examination score if you're a veteran. For some positions, the maximum age of entry is raised by the number of years served. A service-connected disability, if it isn't disqualifying, can add still more weight to your application.

In short, make sure that you make it known that you are a veteran!

As a rule, most state police agencies require that applicants have a high school diploma or its equivalent, but if you have college training, you have a distinct advantage. Secondary and postsecondary courses considered useful in preparing for this work include the following:

- Government
- English
- Psychology
- Physics
- Chemistry
- Foreign languages (increasingly important because more of the population consists of citizens who are bilingual or who have a language other than English as their native tongue)

> **Tip**
> You must pass a civil service examination as well as receive a qualifying rating on an interview conducted by a police board of examiners to be considered for the position of State Police Officer.

In addition to these requirements, you must pass a comprehensive medical examination. In some states, you may have to undergo psychological and psychiatric testing to determine your emotional stability and suitability for this type of work. Also, you will take tests that measure your physical capabilities such as strength, stamina, and agility.

> **Note**
> As with all law enforcement positions, a thorough background check is conducted for every applicant interested in the field of State Police Officer. Your driver's license and driving record are included in this check—make sure that they're clean and up to date!

The Selection Process for State Police Officers

When a state agency knows it's going to have a number of vacancies, a group of prospective State Police Officers is selected from the civil service list. These recruits enter training school on a probationary basis. They must complete an intensive training program of approximately 12 to 16 weeks. Instruction is given in a variety of subjects, including these:

- Criminal law
- State motor vehicle code
- Laws of evidence, arrest, search, and seizure
- Methods of patrol, surveillance, and communications
- Accident prevention and traffic control
- Crime prevention and criminal investigation methods
- Police ethics
- Use of firearms
- Self-defense

6

> **Make Connections**
> For more information on State Police Officer training, see Appendix B, "Preparing for Training Programs."

Candidates who successfully conclude this training are assigned to duty on a probationary basis for a period ranging from six months to one year or longer, depending on state police policy. Candidates work with experienced Troopers until they are skilled enough to function independently and receive permanent employment status after completing the probationary period.

Physical Qualifications

Sound health and physical condition are required of all candidates because the physical activities of the job often demand extreme exertion in emergency situations. A medical examination will be given before your appointment. During the exam, the following characteristics will be determined:

- Vision
- Hearing
- Weight
- Dental condition
- General fitness

> **Make Connections**
> In addition to the medical examination, the physical tests can be quite extensive and can vary significantly from agency to agency. See the section entitled, "Learn About the Physical Qualifications for a Position in Law Enforcement" in Hour 5, "Qualifying for Local Law Enforcement Positions," for a complete description of these tests, as well as a more detailed description of what is determined in a typical medical examination.

Here are some general requirements of the preceding characteristics:

- Visual acuity can be no worse than 20/40 in each eye (uncorrected) and must be correctable to 20/20.
- Color-perception deficiency is disqualifying.
- There is no minimum or maximum height standard.

- Weight must be in proportion to height and build.
- Candidates may be required to provide blood or urine samples for analysis to determine use of dangerous or illegal drugs.

Sample Medical Examination

The first physical requirement is that you successfully complete a medical examination. The following list was taken from a local police department but is standard for state police agencies, as well; it lists specific requirements of the medical examination. Although this list may vary from state to state, it should be taken as a good example of the potential rigorous medical examination you can expect.

- **Vision.** You must test 20/40 (Snellen) in both eyes without corrective lenses. Uncorrected vision must test at least 20/70 in each eye. Vision in each eye must be corrected to 20/20. In addition, you must have the ability to distinguish basic colors.
- **Hearing.** Without using a hearing aid, you must be able to hear a whispered voice at 15 feet with each ear. Using an audiometer for measurement, you should have loss of no more than 30 decibels in each ear at the 500, 1000, and 2000 levels.
- **Speech.** You must be able to speak clearly. Diseases or conditions resulting in indistinct speech are disqualifying.
- **Respiratory System.** Your respiratory system must work well enough that you can do the job you're applying for. If you have any chronic disease or condition that affects your respiratory system and could impair your full performance of duties of the position, you'll be disqualified.
- **Cardiovascular System.** Organic heart disease (compensated or not), hypertension with repeated readings that exceed 150 systolic and 90 diastolic without medication, symptomatic peripheral vascular disease, and severe varicose veins are all disqualifying conditions.
- **Gastrointestinal System.** Chronic symptomatic diseases or conditions of the gastrointestinal tract and any conditions that require special diets are disqualifying.
- **Endocrine System.** You'll be disqualified if you have any history of a systemic metabolic disease, such as diabetes or gout.
- **Genito-Urinary Disorders.** Chronic symptomatic diseases or conditions of the genito-urinary tract are disqualifying. Examples of such conditions might include chronic bladder or kidney problems, including the need for dialysis on a regular basis.
- **Extremities and Spine.** Any deformity or disease of your spine or limbs that would interfere with your range of motion or dexterity, or that is severe enough to limit your ability to fully perform the duties of the position, is disqualifying.

6

- **Hernias.** Inguinal and femoral hernias with or without the use of a truss are disqualifying.
- **Nervous System.** Applicants must possess emotional and mental stability with no history of a basic personality disorder. If you have a history of epilepsy or convulsive disorder, you must have been seizure free for the past two years without medication. Also, any neurological disorder that has decreased your neurological or muscular function is disqualifying.

Sample Physical Performance Test

Physical performance tests, like the medical examination requirements, can vary. Following are two examples of physical fitness tests that can be expected by candidates for many law enforcement positions.

Here's the first example of a typical physical fitness test:

1. Run up 3 flights of stairs, down 1 flight, and then 9 yards to a track.
2. Run 90 yards around the track.
3. Run approximately 5 yards to a maze of 6 cones set 3 feet apart; follow a prescribed course through the maze. *Penalty time:* 5 seconds for missing one or more turns in the maze.
4. Run 10 yards and go over a 5-foot wall. *Maximum time:* 30 seconds.
5. Run approximately 5 feet to a wood box with a weight of approximately 100 pounds. Push the box a distance of 10 feet. *Maximum time:* 30 seconds.
6. Run approximately 4 yards and jump across a 3-foot space. *Penalty time:* 15 seconds for failing to complete this task.
7. Run 7 yards and go over a 3-foot-high barrier. *Maximum time:* 15 seconds.
8. Run 5 yards and go through a maze of 6 cones set 3 feet apart; follow a prescribed course through the maze. *Penalty time:* 5 seconds for missing one or more turns in the maze.
9. Run 5 yards and lift or drag a 70-pound dummy 25 feet. *Maximum time:* 30 seconds.
10. Run 90 yards to the end of the course.

> **Tip**
> Although continuous running through all events is not mandatory, remember that you have only 2 minutes and 15 seconds to complete the entire course!

> **Note**
> Most of these types of physical fitness tests are timed. However, if you fail the first attempt, the examiners usually let you try a second time.

Here's an example of another type of physical fitness test and the requirements for it:

1. Run up approximately 40 steps.

2. Run approximately 40 yards following a designated path—including at least four 90-degree turns—to a sandbag.

3. Push the sandbag, weighing approximately 100 pounds, forward a distance of approximately 5 yards and then back to its original position.

4. Run approximately 10 yards to a 110-pound dummy, which is hanging by a ring from a metal pipe, with its lowest point approximately 3 feet above the floor.

5. Raise the dummy so as to lift the attached ring off the metal pipe. Allow the dummy to slide onto the floor or place it on the floor. You must not drop the dummy or throw it down.

6. Step up approximately 18 inches and walk across a 12-foot beam by placing one foot in front of the other until you reach the other end.

7. Run approximately 10 yards to the finish line.

> **Note**
> Another type of physical fitness test might consist of simply measuring the number of set exercises (for example, sit-ups, push-ups, and so on) you are able to complete in a set amount of time.

Written Testing

6

In addition to physical requirements, most law enforcement positions also require you to pass written examinations. Although these types of exams vary greatly from position to position, most are similar in that they test for the following:

- Reading comprehension
- Visual memory
- Computation skills
- Investigative judgment and decision making
- General problem solving

More specific descriptions of these types of tests, as well as strategies for passing them, are discussed in later hours in this book.

> **Caution**
> Do not take the written exams lightly. Even though you may do very well on the physical exams and pass all medical requirements, a low score on the written exams can easily disqualify you from consideration for employment as a law enforcement officer.

Q&A

Q: What is a good way to begin preparing for a career in law enforcement at a young age?

A: Some state police agencies have cadet programs for high school graduates under the age of 21 who are interested in a law enforcement career. Cadets work as civilian employees performing nonenforcement duties and also receive instruction in the various facets of police work. Some of these cadets attend colleges offering programs in law enforcement and criminal justice as preparation for a police career. Cadets who successfully complete this program may receive an appointment as State Police Officer after reaching the age of 21.

Q: Other than general physical requirements, are there other physical defects or health problems I should be aware of that might keep me from qualifying?

A: In addition to the general requirements listed in this chapter, any other medical problem deemed by the Division Physician to be disqualifying for service as a State Trooper will be grounds for rejection.

Q: Do law enforcement positions perform randomized drug testing?

A: On unannounced occasions while you are in the State Police Academy Basic School and during the probationary period following graduation from the Basic School, appointees *may* be required to provide urine samples for analysis to determine the presence of illegal drugs, controlled substances, and/or marijuana. Confirmed positive tests are grounds for discharge from employment.

The Hour in Review

- You must be prepared to have yourself evaluated both on a mental level and on a physical level to become a state law enforcement official. Don't assume that one requirement is more important than the other; everything you are tested on is considered in assessing whether or not you should be accepted for employment.

- Many state law enforcement agencies require some postsecondary education. Suggested course work includes government, English, psychology, physics, chemistry, and foreign languages.

- Although there are some physical conditions that can be corrected and thus not disqualify you from service as a state law enforcement official, you should carefully consult local jurisdictions regarding physical defects or other health problems that may and can prevent your employment.

- State Police Officers are selected from the civil service list. These recruits enter training school on a probationary basis. Candidates must complete an intensive training program of approximately 12 to 16 weeks.

6

HOUR 7

Qualifying for Federal Law Enforcement Positions

What You'll Learn in This Hour

As you learned in Hour 4, "Learn About Positions in Federal Law Enforcement," there's a tremendous variety of positions available in federal law enforcement. Many of these positions call for an even wider variety of educational and experiential backgrounds. From agriculture to drug enforcement, the field of federal law enforcement offers nearly limitless possibilities. In this hour, you'll examine the qualifications required in some of the major concentrations of interest. This chapter also gives you a brief overview of the requirements of these challenging fields.

> **Make Connections**
> Later chapters in this part of the book teach you more specific strategies for
> passing written examinations, as well as how these tests are presented and
> what they are testing you for.

Here is a list of your goals for this hour:

- Get an overview of the qualifications for federal law enforcement positions
- Learn about qualifying for employment as a Bureau of Alcohol, Tobacco, and Firearms Special Agent
- Learn about qualifying for employment as a Drug Enforcement Administration Special Agent
- Learn about qualifying for employment as an FBI Special Agent
- Learn about qualifying for employment as a Border Patrol Agent
- Learn about qualifying for employment as a Secret Service Special Agent

Federal Law Enforcement Qualifications—An Overview

Candidates for positions in the field of federal law enforcement must have a good idea of what area they are particularly interested in because the qualifications, job criteria, working conditions, and general aspects of the various positions vary greatly from field to field. However, whether you are interested in becoming a Special Agent for the Bureau of Alcohol, Tobacco, and Firearms or an Internal Security Inspector for the IRS, you must be aware that, as with all federal agencies, you will often work in close cooperation with state and local authorities to ensure the most comprehensive enforcement of the law.

Throughout this chapter, as we discuss each of the various positions within federal law enforcement, each section will touch on these six primary "qualification components" of federal law enforcement:

- Age/citizenship/legal status requirements
- Academic/job experience requirements
- Written testing requirements
- Physical testing requirements
- Panel review/qualifying interview
- Training/academy and probation requirements

> **Make Connections**
> Be sure to refer to Appendix B, "Preparing for Training Programs," which gives you an excellent general overview of each of these six "requirements." Note that Appendix B applies to all areas of law enforcement, not just those positions at the federal level.

> **Tip**
> If you are a veteran of the U.S. Armed Forces, be sure to make this fact known. Veterans receive some form of employment preference when they apply for any government position, whether that be local, state, or federal.

Each of the following sections gives you a brief overview of some of the major areas of federal law enforcement, along with the general physical and written requirements (and any other unique requirement to that area) for each position.

Qualifying as a Bureau of Alcohol, Tobacco, and Firearms Special Agent

Applicants for the job of BATF Special Agent must be U.S. citizens between the ages of 21 and 37 at the time of appointment of duty. Other requirements include a bachelor's degree in a field of major study from an accredited college or university, or three years of work experience—including at least two years of criminal investigation activity.

> **Note**
> As with many federal law enforcement positions, postsecondary education is a requirement for BATF Special Agents. See Hour 4, "Learn About Positions in Federal Law Enforcement," for more information on the duties and responsibilities of this job and the academic areas that will best prepare you for it.

In addition to these academic requirements, applicants must get a qualifying score of at least 70 on the Treasury Enforcement Agent (TEA) Examination.

7

> **Make Connections**
> Hour 22, "Sample TEA Problems for Investigation Exam," contains a sample of the Treasury Enforcement Agent examination and provides the information you need to prepare for it.

If you have completed accredited courses in police science or police administration, you may have extra points added to your qualifying score on the TEA examination. Those who qualify on the exam are placed on a certified list of eligible candidates. The people on that list with the highest scores are then further evaluated by the BATF. The BATF holds extensive panel interviews with selected applicants, during which time the panel rates the candidates on such factors as these:

- Appearance
- Poise
- Communication skills
- Interpersonal skills
- Analytical ability

Applicants who reach the panel interview stage are also required to pass a qualifying medical examination to determine their physical and mental fitness for normal work and training activities.

> **Make Connections**
> For more detailed information on physical requirements, see Hour 5, "Qualifying for Local Law Enforcement Positions."

> **Caution**
> No waiver on these requirements for the position of BATF Special Agent will be granted.

Newly hired Special Agents enter an intensive training and development program that provides the special knowledge and skills demanded by the BATF. The program combines classroom study with closely supervised on-the-job training. New agents first receive about eight weeks of intensive training at the consolidated Federal Law Enforcement Training Center in Georgia.

Qualifying as a Drug Enforcement Administration Special Agent

As you prepare to begin your actual work in the field as a DEA Special Agent, you will need to have at least three years of general law enforcement experience and one year of specialized experience.

General experience must show progressively responsible activities, which have required you to work and deal effectively with individuals or groups of people, show your skill in collecting and assembling pertinent facts, emphasize your ability to prepare clear and concise reports, and demonstrate your ability and willingness to accept responsibility.

> **Note**
> There is no written examination for this position! In lieu of a written examination, applicants meeting minimum experience or educational substitution requirements are evaluated on the quality of their job-related experience, education, and special skills.

When you compete for a job as a DEA Special Agent, you're competing with candidates from across the nation. Applicants who rank the highest (based on previous experience. education, and skills) are scheduled for a panel interview. The panel recommends a list of candidates for further consideration by the DEA. Those candidates the DEA selects from this list are given a qualifying medical examination to determine physical and mental fitness. Here are the requirements of the physical and mental fitness tests.

- Candidates must be free of any impairment that would interfere with normal work performance.

- Vision requirements for Special Agents are 20/40 in both eyes without corrective lenses for distance vision and 20/20 in one eye and 30/30 in the other with corrective lenses permitted.

- Candidates are also further evaluated through personal interviews. They are rated on such factors as appearance, poise, and communication skills.

> **Note**
> The physical examination and all travel for interviews are at the applicant's own expense.

7

Shortly after appointment, Special Agent trainees attend a formal 12- to 15-week training program at the Federal Law Enforcement Training Center in Georgia.

When new agents have completed their training programs, they're assigned to DEA field offices, where they work with experienced personnel until they can function independently. Special Agents continue to receive periodic training throughout their careers to keep them current with the developments in their field of work.

Qualifying as an FBI Special Agent

Candidates for the position of FBI Special Agent are screened by the Federal Bureau of Investigation. The FBI considers only those applicants who are U.S. citizens between the ages of 23 and 37 and willing to accept assignment anywhere within the United States and Puerto Rico.

Caution
Although you *could* be asked to relocate in any law enforcement position, you must *expect* relocation when you work as an FBI Special Agent. If you don't like the idea of moving, you may want to consider another field of law enforcement.

To compete successfully for an entrance position with the FBI, you should have a solid professional background that demonstrates your logical reasoning ability and that shows you have received (in general) broad academic training in a variety of subjects.

The following list describes each of the five entrance programs under which you can qualify for possible appointment to FBI Special Agent:

- **Law.** You must be a graduate of a state-accredited resident law school with at least two years of resident, undergraduate college work.
- **Accounting.** You must possess a four-year resident college degree with a major in accounting.
- **Language.** You must have a four-year resident college degree and fluency in a foreign language.
- **Modified.** You need three years of full-time work experience in addition to a four-year resident college degree, or two years of such work experience if you possess an advanced degree.
- **Science.** Many options are available here, with qualifications based on backgrounds in electrical engineering, metallurgy, physics, chemistry, biological science, and mathematics, to name a few.

> **Note**
> You must submit college transcripts and detailed resumes that show your experience to qualify for consideration under the Science program.

All candidates must qualify on batteries of written and oral examinations designed to measure emotional stability, resourcefulness, interpersonal skills, and the ability to apply analytical methods to work assignments. Because Special Agents must be able to use firearms and defensive tactics to participate in dangerous assignments and raids, each individual must pass a physical examination.

Applicants who receive appointments as Special Agents undergo training at the FBI academy located on the U.S. Marine Corps Base at Quantico, Virginia. For a period of about 15 weeks, they receive intensive training in defensive tactics, judo, and the use of various types of firearms. After successful completion of training, new Special Agents are appointed on a probationary basis. They are assigned to FBI field offices and initially teamed with experienced agents under actual field conditions. After one year of satisfactory performance, they receive permanent employment as FBI Special Agents.

Qualifying as a Border Patrol Agent

You must be a U.S. citizen between the ages of 21 and 37 at the time of appointment to qualify for the position of Border Patrol Agent. The age limitation may be waived for applicants with current or previous federal law enforcement work experience.

> **Tip**
> The applicant may substitute a full four-year course of college undergraduate study for experience, provided that the college work indicates the ability to learn the activities of a Border Patrol Agent.

> **Tip**
> Good working knowledge of Spanish gives a real competitive edge to the Border Patrol Agent applicant! Knowledge of Spanish can also make the training period a little less arduous. *Spanish proficiency is mandatory for appointment to a duty station.*

A passing grade on the written Border Patrol Agent exam and a qualifying rating from a panel of interviewers are also required. You must also submit to a complete medical examination to determine physical and mental fitness for this work. Vision requirements

7

for this job are binocular vision of 20/40 in each eye without corrective lenses, and uncorrected vision of at least 20/70 in each eye. In addition, corrected vision must be 20/20, and you must also have the ability to distinguish basic colors.

Note
The physical examination is performed by a government physician at government expense, but travel to the physical examination is the responsibility of the applicant.

Make Connections
For more information on training requirements (both physical and academic), make sure that you check out Appendix B, "Preparing for Training Programs."

For more information on strategies and tips regarding written examinations, check out the chapters in Parts II and III that cover specific exam questions and provide strategies for achieving the highest possible score.

Newly hired agents undergo 18 weeks of training at the Border Patrol Academy located in Georgia. The course consists of training in the following areas:

- Immigration and naturalization
- Criminal law
- Laws of evidence and court procedures
- Border patrol methods and operations
- Methods of tracking and surveillance
- Patrol vehicle operation
- Care and use of firearms
- Spanish language instruction

Border Patrol trainees must wear full uniform in all classes and at official functions, and the trainees must purchase the uniforms at their own expense. The initial cost for the training academy is approximately $300; the cost for the first year's uniforms is in excess of $1,200.

Note
When you become a Border Patrol Agent, your department will help with the cost of your uniforms. Each new Border Patrol Agent receives $480 toward the cost of uniforms and then receives $480 annually for the maintenance and replacement of uniforms.

The trainee's progress and work performance are reviewed by a panel of two top-level sector supervisors. The decision to hire is based on recommendations of these probationary examining boards.

As a new agent, your first appointment will be on a conditional basis (that is, you have to meet certain requirements during an initial probationary period). This conditional appointment leads to a permanent career appointment after three years of continuous and satisfactory service.

Qualifying as a Secret Service Special Agent

Applicants for positions with the Secret Service are carefully selected according to the agency's very strict and rigid standards. Some general requirements include the following:

- You must be a U.S. citizen between the ages of 21 and 37 at the time of appointment.
- You must possess either a bachelor's degree in a major field of study, three years of work experience (two of these years involving criminal investigation), or a suitable combination of education and work experience.
- You must achieve a qualifying grade on the Treasury Enforcement Agent (TEA) examination.
- You must also pass a qualifying medical examination to determine physical and mental fitness and freedom from any disabilities that would interfere with normal work.

> **Caution**
> As is true for candidates for most law enforcement positions, a background check is performed on the applicant to the position of Secret Service Special Agent. However, the background check for this position is especially detailed. Because agents receive a top-secret security clearance, general character, honesty, and loyalty to the U.S. government are extremely important.

Candidates who meet all these requirements undergo intensive training at the Federal Law Enforcement Training Center in Georgia and specialized training at the U.S. Secret Service training facilities in Washington, D.C. New agents receive on-the-job training to supplement classroom courses and continue to receive instruction throughout their careers.

After successful completion of all training, new agents are assigned to Secret Service field offices on a probationary basis. They work with experienced Special Agents and, after satisfactory performance during the probationary period, receive permanent appointments.

7

Q&A

Q: Are federal law enforcement positions harder to procure than local or state law enforcement positions?

A: Although every law enforcement position brings with it unique and challenging requirements, federal positions often require more from an applicant. That is, positions in federal law enforcement often require a greater degree of postsecondary education as well as the requirement that you be willing to relocate.

Q: If I become an **FBI** or Secret Service Special Agent, will I work in Washington, D.C.?

A: Not necessarily. Both the FBI and the Secret Service (along with most federal law agencies) have field offices throughout the country (some, such as the FBI, have offices in other provinces such as Puerto Rico).

The Hour in Review

- Most federal law enforcement agencies require applicants to qualify by meeting specific physical, educational, training, and probation standards.

- Many federal law enforcement agencies conduct panel interviews of applicants who have passed the first level of screening.

- Many federal law enforcement positions require you to first complete a conditional or probationary period before you are granted a permanent position.

- You should be aware that some federal law enforcement positions require you to have a specific academic background. For example, to qualify as a Special Agent with the FBI, you are required to have completed one of five college-level degrees (some of which require you to complete academic work at the graduate level as well—such as attending law school).

- The vast majority of federal law enforcement positions require you to relocate. You must consider this fact—and how it affects your personal beliefs as well as your career goals.

- Although there is great variety in the field of federal law enforcement, successful entrance to and completion of a training program is as competitive as it is for any other law enforcement field.

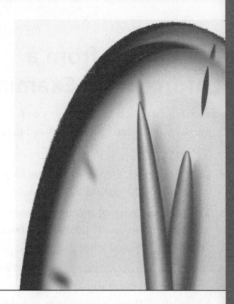

HOUR **8**

Learn What's Tested on Written Exams

What You'll Learn in This Hour

In this hour, you'll focus on the different types of questions you are likely to find on any law enforcement written exam. Although some of the question types may seem specific to one area of law enforcement (for example, Police Officer versus Secret Service Special Agent), the skills that are tested by the written exams are essential—and universal—to any position in law enforcement.

Here's a list of your goals for this hour:

- Know the general format of law enforcement exams
- Understand practical and investigative judgment questions
- Understand reading comprehension questions
- Understand observation and memory questions
- Understand general mathematical questions

What to Expect from a Law Enforcement Examination

Law enforcement exams take a variety of forms. Their content and length vary according to the agency administering the exam and the demands of the job they're testing for, but some generalities apply to all the exams.

- **They are timed.** Depending on the length and make-up of the exam, you can expect to spend anywhere from 50 minutes to 3 1/2 hours on the test.

- **They are made up of multiple-choice questions.** You are given an answer sheet (similar to those you'll see in later hours of this book), and you provide answers by filling in the circled letter that represents your choice for each question.

- **Questions are categorized.** The questions typically fall into the categories of practical and/or investigative judgment, reading comprehension and/or verbal reasoning, arithmetic reasoning, and observation and memory.

- **No knowledge of special or "secret" information is required.** None of the tests assumes that you have in-depth knowledge of law enforcement rules, practices, or procedures. None of them expects you to be a math, science, or psychology wizard! A well-rounded education, a clear head, common sense, and the confidence you'll gain by working through the information in this book are all you need to succeed on a law enforcement exam.

The sections that follow take a closer look at each of the question categories you'll encounter on a law enforcement exam. Later hours in this book walk you through each of these categories in more detail—and give you plenty of practice in mastering these question types!

Understanding Practical and Investigative Judgment Questions

What would you do if....

This is the essential form of the judgment question on law enforcement exams. Assume that you are a Police Officer. Here is a given situation. How would you respond to it? This is a very subtle and efficient method of testing how well officers can apply their knowledge of the law to the situation at hand to achieve the best outcome.

Judgment questions are often based on actual situations. Consider this example:

What would you do if you saw a man walking down the street dressed only in a sheet and leading a dog on a leash? Arrest him? On what charge? Take the dog to an animal shelter? Take the man to a doctor?

This is a true story. *What would you do?*

Although this type of question might have originated with the Police Officer in mind, it is commonly found—in various permutations—on many law enforcement position written exams.

Note
Early Police Officer examinations were a strange mixture of questions covering municipal government, municipal geography, spelling, grammar, first aid—in short, everything that every person should know something about but very little that was specific to measuring the ability of future Police Officers to do their jobs well. So the emphasis shifted from factual to actual exams. "Let the questions supply the facts," the examiners reasoned, "and let the aspiring officers display their judgment in choosing the correct answers."

Often, you are placed in a peculiar position by these types of questions in that the correct answers are often influenced by specific departmental or agency policy. As an applicant, you aren't expected to know the policies. The fact is that test makers often assume that these policies are "common sense" rules. In Hour 12, "Teach Yourself Practical and Investigative Judgment Strategies," you get a good "cram-course" in the common sense of law enforcement that will help you be prepared for these questions.

Tip
As mentioned in several places throughout this book, if you have a relative or know someone who is involved in the field of law enforcement, it will greatly benefit you to spend some time talking with that person. Often, you can pick up valuable "insider knowledge" dealing with procedures and techniques that may help you on the exams.

Understanding Reading-Based Questions

The reading comprehension question asks you to quickly and accurately read a short paragraph and then choose the best answer (from a set of answers) to questions related to the paragraph. Reading comprehension exams can fall into the following formats:

- Some exams include classic reading comprehension questions that present a passage and then ask questions on the details of the passage (and perhaps its meaning, too).

- Other exams require you to indicate proper behavior based on your reading of printed procedures and regulations.

- Still another type of reading-based question requires you to reason and choose "next steps" on the basis of information presented in a reading passage. These reading comprehension questions are typically labeled "verbal reasoning" because they draw from your abilities to comprehend written information *and* make reasonable decisions based on what you've read.

Reading-based questions can take a number of different forms. In general, here are some of the most common forms:

- **Question of fact or detail.** You may have to mentally rephrase or rearrange, but you should find the answer stated in the body of the selection.

- **Best title or main idea.** The answer may be obvious, but the incorrect choices to the "main idea" question are often half-truths that can be easily confused with the main idea. They may misstate the idea, omit part of the idea, or even offer a supporting idea quoted directly from the text. The correct answer is the one that covers the largest part of the selection.

- **Interpretation.** This type of question asks you what the selection *means*, not just what it says.

- **Inference.** This is the most difficult type of reading comprehension question. It asks you to go beyond what the selection says and to predict what might happen next. You might have to choose the best course of action to take based on given procedures and a fact situation, or you may have to judge the actions of others. To answer this type of question, you must understand the author's point of view and then make an inference from that viewpoint based on the information in the selection.

- **Vocabulary.** Some reading sections directly or indirectly ask the meanings of certain words as used in the selection.

The reading comprehension question is one of the most common question types for any law enforcement exam. Quite often, it is also the most devious: Test makers like to "stack" your answer choices with at least one answer that, to the unwary test taker, immediately appears to be correct. Although this "pseudo" answer is often partially true, the key word here is *partially*—there is always an answer that is more thorough, and thus is the correct answer. This device is used to test your ability to pay attention to details. The key is to read both the question and *all* answer choices carefully.

Between now and the test day, you should work to improve your reading concentration and comprehension. Give some thought to your reading habits and skills. Of course, you already know how to read, but...

- How well do you read?
- Do you concentrate?
- Do you get the point on your first reading?
- Do you notice details?

Your daily newspaper provides excellent material to improve your reading comprehension. Make a point of reading all the way through any article that you begin. Do not be satisfied with the first or second paragraph. Read with a pencil in hand. Underscore details and ideas that seem to be crucial to the meaning of the article. When you have finished, summarize it for yourself by asking yourself these questions:

- Do you know the purpose of the article?
- Do you know the main idea presented?
- Do you know the attitude of the writer?
- Do you know the points over which there is controversy?
- Did you find certain information lacking?

As you answer these questions, skim back over what you have underlined. Did you focus on important words and ideas? Did you read with comprehension? As you repeat this process day after day, you will find that your reading will become more efficient. You will read with greater understanding, and you will get more from your newspaper.

Tip

Strange as it may seem, it's a good idea to approach reading comprehension questions by reading the questions—not the answer choices, just the questions themselves—before you read the selection.

Next, skim the selection very rapidly to get an idea of its subject matter and its organization.

Then read the selection carefully with comprehension as your main goal.

Finally, return to the questions. Eliminate the obviously incorrect answers. Then skim the passage once more, focusing on the underlined segments. By now, you should be able to conclude which answer is the best.

Understanding Observation and Memory Questions

In any law enforcement position, you must possess a keen memory for details if you are to function effectively. You must constantly be on the alert for physical characteristics that can help identify key people, places, or things, thereby leading to the apprehension of a criminal or the solution to a criminal investigation.

Most people (and many things) have distinguishing features that are difficult to disguise: the contour of a face; the size, shape, and position of the ears; the shape of the mouth. Any of these may be sufficient for a law enforcement officer to detect an individual wanted for criminal activities. On the other hand, the color or style of an individual's hair, or the first impression of his or her face may change drastically with the addition of a wig, mustache, or beard. In addition, eye color can be altered with tinted contact lenses. Therefore, the law enforcement officer must focus attention on those physical features that can't be changed easily and that can serve as the basis for a positive identification of that person at some time in the future.

Note
Observation is not limited to the act of *seeing*. In addition, you must learn to recognize and recall distinctive features of people, places, and things. An official record in the memorandum book may serve as a reminder for the facts stored in a law enforcement officer's mental record; but a law enforcement officer without a sharp sense of recall cannot perform his or her duties effectively.

Make Connections
In Hour 11, "Teach Yourself Observation and Memory Strategies," you gain important practice in observing scenes and people and then noting and recalling the important details of what you've seen. Hour 11 teaches you to sort through many pieces of "observable" information to focus on the details most important to law enforcement operations.

Law enforcement exams test you on how well you've mastered the skills of observation and memory. The usual format for memory questions is to present you with a picture or other illustration, give you a set amount of time to study the illustration, and then ask you questions related to the illustration.

8

These illustrations can consist of a photograph, a set of hand drawings (often depicting a typical "Wanted" poster, listing a criminal suspect, his or her physical attributes, and a description of the crime, as well as whom to contact if you see the person), or any other visual representation that can then be used as the basis for testing your memory for details. After you study the illustration, you are given a set amount of time to answer the questions without referring back to the illustration. By using the practice exams in this book, you should be familiar with the question format so that you don't have any surprises on test day.

Observation questions are often framed in a similar format to reading comprehension questions in that they ask you to first study a short selection (which is packed full of details) and then choose a "best" answer from a set of possible answers that describe and summarize key details from the selection.

Often, observation questions test your ability to summarize information that you see. Sound confusing? The basis of this question type is to see how well and (this is important) *how quickly* you can absorb numerous facts and then accurately summarize those facts for others.

> **Caution**
> Unlike the memory questions (where you are first given a set amount of time to study an illustration and another amount of time to answer questions related to it), observation questions usually require you to do both tasks in the same amount of time. You have to work quickly (but, as always, accurately!) to get through all the questions in the time allotted.

Understanding General Mathematical Questions

Is there any word in our language that puts more fear into the hearts of test takers than *math?* Probably not!

However, you should not be overly concerned with the mathematical sections on your law enforcement exam. Because the exams must assume a generalized knowledge of the subject, you don't have to worry about understanding calculus or other advanced mathematical theorems and techniques. However, you should have a fairly strong knowledge of basic algebra because several math exam questions ask you to manipulate relationships between numbers (or *variables*, which are placeholders for actual values) to find the correct answer.

Tip
Manipulate what between how? Don't let the "complex" wording of math sections scare you. Basically, you just have to be aware that you will be asked to do a little "factoring" to find the answers. For example, x + 4 = 8 is a good example of how you may have to "manipulate" a number placeholder (again, a *variable*) to find the correct answer.

If you can answer this simple problem, you've already come a long way in understanding the "complex" math you have to be familiar with on law enforcement exams.

Make Connections
Be sure to check out the sample math exams in Part III of this book. They provide lots of sample questions (and answers!) for the various types of math questions you are likely to encounter.

Generally speaking, you are asked to answer math questions in the following categories:

- **Ratio and proportion.** These questions test your ability to recognize the relationship between two (or more) quantities in terms of numbers.

- **Work problems.** In work problems, there are three items involved: the number of people working, the time, and the amount of work done. You are asked to find the "missing" element (that is, the number of people working, the time, or the amount of work done) in these problems, usually using some simple algebra and lots of common sense.

- **Distance problems.** This type of problem simply asks you to find the "missing" quantity (just as work problems do), which is usually how far something has traveled, how fast it traveled, or how long it took to get there.

- **Interest problems.** Interest problems ask you to figure out the price paid for the use of money (which is a good description of interest, by the way!). Use the following basic interest "formula":

$I = prt$

In this formula, I is interest, p is the principal (or the amount of money bearing interest), r is the interest rate, and t is the time the principal is used. You are asked to find the "missing" element (again). If you've ever had a loan, you should find these questions quite familiar.

8

> **Note**
> You may also encounter other money-type problems, such as questions dealing with taxation and profit and loss. However, if you understand the interest problem, and feel comfortable doing the simple math calculations (again, finding that "missing" element), you should have no problem with these other types of questions.

- **Formula questions.** Formula questions ask you to find (you guessed it) the "missing" element by both manipulating just letters and manipulating actual number values presented in a "story problem" format. In both cases, the questions test your ability to logically "factor" what is being asked and then use your deductions to find the best answer.

> **Tip**
> *Story problems? Factor?* Again, don't let these "complex" terms frighten you. Almost everyone who has gone through high school algebra groans at the thought of a story problem ("If two trains leave different stations at 10:00 P.M., and one train is traveling 60 mph while the other train is traveling 70 mph..."). Remember that the law enforcement exams can only test you on fairly basic mathematical concepts. It is the reasoning skill you bring to the table that is more important!
>
> In short, when you approach these questions, do so with the attitude that you can easily solve them (which you can!) by simply reading the question carefully and reducing your answer choices through some simple calculations.

Q&A

Q: Is there anything I can do to improve my memory skills?

A: Although some people are inherently better "memorizers" than others, you can practice (and possibly enhance) your memory by taking note of your surroundings and then trying to recall what you saw at a later time.

Q: Is common sense is all I need to do well on written exams?

A: Although this may be true (to some extent) of the judgment questions, other types of questions, such as reading comprehension, require you to analyze and interpret the meaning of a passage, often on a analytical level. In addition, you may be asked to define the meanings of words, a task that obviously goes far beyond simple common sense.

Q: If I do well on the physical tests and pass all related physical requirements for my field of interest, do I have to worry about scoring well on the written exams?

A: Yes. A good law enforcement officer is one who is trained in both mind and body. Although not everyone is a good test taker—and a poor score on a test may not reflect the abilities of the test taker—a good score goes a long way in presenting yourself in the most attractive way. In addition, competition for many law enforcement positions is often quite intense. A good score on the written examinations can greatly enhance your prospects of being selected from the field of applicants, many of whom may be as qualified as yourself.

The Hour in Review

- Reading comprehension questions test your ability to study a short paragraph (or sometimes a short phrase) and then answer a set of questions based on the passage you have just read. By quickly skimming through the passage, seeking first important details and then rereading the passage after you've viewed the questions, you should be able to find the correct answers.

- Verbal reasoning questions are a form of the reading comprehension type of question. These questions demand that you read a block of information and accurately interpret that information to arrive at reasonable conclusions or decisions for action.

- Observation and memory questions test—you guessed it—your observation and memory skills. They provide you with a picture or other type of illustration or present you with a set of details and then test how well you can recall the details of what you've seen or read. These questions are intended to test your ability to quickly and accurately remember important details surrounding an event.

- Practical and investigative judgment questions ask you to make decisions based on a given situation. Although you aren't expected to have "insider knowledge" (for example, you don't have to know agency-specific procedures for dealing with a given situation), you'll benefit from some grounding in the "common sense" of law enforcement. In addition to the information on this subject provided in Hour 11, "Teach Yourself Observation and Memory Strategies," take advantage of any opportunity you have to discuss this question type with friends or acquaintances in law enforcement.

8

- General math questions will also come your way on law enforcement exams. The good news is that by knowing basic mathematical concepts (and a little bit of high school algebra) and by applying that to lots of common sense, you should be able to do very well on these types of questions. Don't let your possible fear of math diminish your confidence with these questions. The actual mathematical concepts are very general (as they must be, because few of us have Ph.D.s in mathematics). Read each question carefully (as you would any law enforcement question) and proceed to "factor out" the incorrect answers.

HOUR 9

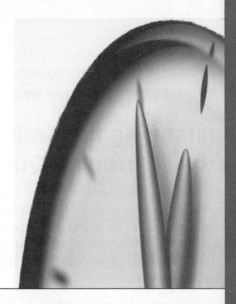

Teach Yourself Verbal Reasoning Strategies

What You'll Learn in This Hour

This hour teaches you to prepare for the verbal reasoning section of the law enforcement exams. In this hour, you'll learn how these questions differ from the usual reading comprehension questions. You'll also learn how to prepare for them. You'll look at some sample verbal reasoning questions from a law enforcement exam, and then you'll review some exercises that will help you learn to draw logical conclusions based on information you are supplied. By working through these exercises and carefully reviewing the answers and explanations to each question, you'll learn how to tackle verbal reasoning questions on law enforcement exams.

Here is a list of your goals for this hour:

- Understand the basics of the verbal reasoning question
- Learn and practice verbal reasoning skills

- Learn and practice logical reasoning
- Practice verbal reasoning with paragraph-format questions
- Review the answers and answer explanations

Understanding the Basics of Verbal Reasoning Questions

The verbal reasoning questions are similar to reading comprehension questions, but with a twist. The passages are short, but the questions are tricky. The questions require that you read and reread them with careful consideration of what each is really asking. You must be aware that two negatives make a positive, and that the third negative in the same sentence makes it negative again. Sound confusing? Not really, once you understand how the questions are structured.

Here is an example of a typical verbal reasoning question:

George is older than Bob. Fred is younger than George. Bob is older than Fred. If the first two statements are true, the third statement is:

A.   True
B.   False
C.   Uncertain

What's the answer? We know only that George is the oldest.

There is no way to tell whether Bob is older than Fred or Fred than Bob. So, the correct answer is C.

Tip

Verbal reasoning questions make up one of three parts in the Treasury Enforcement Agency (TEA) examination. On that exam, you're given 50 minutes to read and answer 25 verbal reasoning questions.

Although these types of questions are specific to the Treasury Enforcement Agency examination, you should take some time to review these types of questions, no matter which law enforcement exam you're preparing for. They offer excellent practice in brushing up on your logical reasoning, a skill that will greatly benefit you on nearly every other type of law enforcement exam question.

These types of questions demand logical reasoning ability as much as they require reading proficiency. Although you don't need a formal logic course to prepare for this question type, practicing your logical reasoning skills can be helpful.

As you approach each question in these exercises, read carefully, think carefully, and then circle the letter of the answer you choose. When you have completed an exercise, study the answers and explanations following the questions.

Practice Verbal Reasoning Skills

The following questions help you hone your logic and reasoning skills, although you may not see this specific question format on many actual law enforcement exams. In these exercises, you learn to respond only to the facts presented in text passages. If you cannot arrive at a True or False response based on the information supplied, you must choose Uncertain. By learning to read and respond solely to the facts, you're preparing yourself for critical investigative and reporting law enforcement functions.

Example: The black horse jumped over more hurdles than the spotted horse. The white horse jumped over more hurdles than the spotted horse. The white horse jumped over more hurdles than the black horse. If the first two statements are true, the third statement is

    A.   True
    B.   False
    C.   Uncertain

Explanation: From the first two statements, we know that both the black and white horse jumped over more hurdles than the spotted horse. This is all we know. The first two statements don't give us any information about how the black horse's performance compared to that of the white horse. The answer, therefore, must be C. Based on the information given in the first two statements, we can't confirm or deny the third statement.

> **Caution**
> Don't assume anything when you're answering verbal reasoning questions! Base your answers strictly on the information presented in the question, even if it contradicts something that you know from your own experience.

Workshop I

DIRECTIONS: Answer the questions below by circling the correct response. Base your response solely on the information provided.

1. George is older than Bob. Fred is younger than George. Bob is older than Fred. If the first two statements are true, the third statement is:

    A. True
    B. False
    C. Uncertain

2. Group A sings higher than Group C. Group B sings lower than Group C. Group A sings higher than Group B. If the first two statements are true, the third statement is:

    A. True
    B. False
    C. Uncertain

3. Percolator coffee is weaker than electric drip coffee. Extractor coffee is stronger than electric drip coffee. Electric drip coffee is stronger than extractor coffee. If the first two statements are true, the third statement is:

    A. True
    B. False
    C. Uncertain

4. Red kites fly higher than yellow kites. Yellow balloons fly higher than red kites. Yellow kites fly higher than yellow balloons. If the first two statements are true, the third statement is:

    A. True
    B. False
    C. Uncertain

5. The New York team lost fewer games than the Boston team. The Boston team won more games than the Baltimore team but not as many games as the New York team. The Baltimore team lost the fewest games. If the first two statements are true, the third statement is:

    A. True
    B. False
    C. Uncertain

6. The history book has more pages than the poetry book but fewer pages than the math book. The math book has more pages than the science book but fewer pages than the English book. The poetry book has the fewest pages. If the first two statements are true, the third statement is:

    A. True
    B. False
    C. Uncertain

7. Bill runs faster than Mike. Jeff runs faster than Bill. Jeff is not as fast as Mike. If the first two statements are true, the third statement is:

    A. True
    B. False
    C. Uncertain

8. Ann reads faster than Sue. Karen reads faster than Ann. Karen reads more slowly than Sue. If the first two statements are true, the third statement is:

    A. True
    B. False
    C. Uncertain

9. Paul is taller than Peter. Peter is shorter than John. Paul is taller than John. If the first two statements are true, the third statement is:

A. True
B. False
C. Uncertain

10. Harry is more intelligent than George. Sam is more intelligent than Ralph. Harry is more intelligent than Ralph. If the first two statements are true, the third statement is:

A. True
B. False
C. Uncertain

Practice Logical Reasoning Skills

The following exercise gives you an opportunity to further flex your abilities in reading comprehension and interpretation of information. Whereas in the preceding workshop you had the option of choosing *Uncertain*, in the following exercises, you are asked to interpret all the information you've been given and choose an answer that is supported, if not specifically spelled out, by that information. Although you will be making some assumptions, you are in fact arriving at a logical conclusion based on your comprehension and interpretation of the material.

Example: The little red house on our block is very old. It was once used as a church, and Abraham Lincoln may have worshipped there. It also served as a schoolhouse.

A.   At one time, schools were used for worship.
B.   Abraham Lincoln prayed in school.
C.   The house has an interesting history.
D.   Red is a popular color for schools.

Explanation: Take one statement at a time. Choice A can't be supported by the paragraph: The paragraph states that the house was once used as a church, not that it was once used as a church and a school at the same time. Choice B also can't be supported by the information in the paragraph: If Lincoln worshipped in the house, he did so when it was a church. (Although Lincoln may have prayed in a school as a child, the paragraph doesn't give us that information.) Choice C is clearly correct. The house does have a long and interesting history; it dates back to or before the Civil War and has been at various times a church, a school, and a house. Choice D makes a statement of fact that may be true in its own right, but not one that is supported by the information in the passage. You must therefore choose answer C.

Workshop II

DIRECTIONS: For each question, find the statement that must be true according to the given information. Circle the letter that precedes the correct answer.

---

1. Mr. Stonehill worked in the corporate headquarters of a large corporation. Another company acquired Mr. Stonehill's company and sold off the operating divisions one by one. There can be no corporate headquarters without any operating divisions. Mr. Stonehill is:

    A. Unemployed.
    B. Working for one of the operating divisions.
    C. No longer working in corporate headquarters.
    D. Working for the new company.

2. Mr. Moffitt is a high school chemistry teacher. As a young man, Mr. Moffitt worked in the textile dyes division of a chemical company. In addition to teaching chemistry, Mr. Moffitt operates a business cleaning Oriental carpets.

    A. Mr. Moffitt changes jobs often.
    B. Mr. Moffitt teaches students how to clean carpets.
    C. Mr. Moffitt is a wealthy man.
    D. Mr. Moffitt is well qualified for the work he does.

Tip

Take another look at question 2. Does it seem sort of silly? If you answer yes, don't be alarmed.

The point of these questions is to test your reasoning skill on very convoluted questions. If you find yourself frustrated at the insanity of some of the questions, you're probably thinking too hard and falling into a common trap of question designers—getting you to speculate on information that is in no way related to what is being asked.

If you start imagining yourself in the role of Mr. Moffitt (!), take a deep breath and try to focus on just what is being asked. If you treat these questions as statements of fact, you will have a much better chance of approaching them objectively—which is the cornerstone of reasoning and logic to begin with!

---

3. Sally and Susie are twins. Sally lives near her parents in a Chicago suburb with her husband and children. Susie lives in a remote area of Alaska and raises dogs.

    A. Susie does not get along with her parents.
    B. Twins may have different interests and tastes.
    C. Sally does not like dogs.
    D. There are special bonds between twins.

4. The baby woke and cried in the middle of the night. Molly Davis changed the baby's diaper, gave him a warm bottle, and put him back to bed.

    A. The baby woke because it was time for his bottle.
    B. The baby's mother is Molly Davis.
    C. The baby woke with a wet diaper.
    D. After his bottle, the baby went back to sleep.

5. Eight children went trick-or-treating together. Each child carried a lighted flashlight and a big bag. Jill and Mary did not wear masks.

    A. The children went trick-or-treating at night.
    B. Six children wore masks.
    C. The bags were heavy.
    D. The youngest children were Jill and Mary.

6. Julie is in second grade. Laura is in third grade. Julie's sister Anne rides a tricycle.

    A. Laura is smarter than Julie.
    B. Anne is physically handicapped.
    C. Julie is behind Laura in school.
    D. Julie and Laura are sisters.

7. Jeffrey is a law student. On Monday evenings, he plays the violin in an orchestra. On Tuesdays and Thursdays, he goes square dancing. On Friday afternoons, Jeffrey fiddles for a children's folk dancing group.

    A. Jeffrey plays the violin at least twice a week.
    B. Jeffrey likes music better than law.
    C. Jeffrey dances three times a week.
    D. Musicians are good dancers.

8. Debbie took the written Foreign Service Officer examination in December. Today, Debbie received an appointment date for the Oral Assessment. Debbie is very happy.

    A. Debbie failed the written exam.
    B. Debbie is now a Foreign Service Officer.
    C. Everyone who takes the Foreign Service exam must take an oral exam as well.
    D. Debbie is still under consideration for appointment as a Foreign Service Officer.

9

Practice Verbal Reasoning with Paragraph-Format Questions

The paragraph-format question type represents the same type of verbal reasoning skills you have been working on earlier in this hour, they are just in a different format. Each of these questions provides a paragraph that contains all the information necessary to infer the correct answer. Choose your answer based solely on the information provided in the paragraph. Don't speculate or make assumptions that go beyond this information.

> **Tip**
> Assume that all information given in the paragraph is true, even if it conflicts with some fact known to you.

Here are some general strategies for these types of questions:

- Pay special attention to negated verbs (for example. "are not") and negative prefixes (for example, *"incomplete"* or *"disorganized"*).

- Pay special attention to quantifiers such as "all," "none," and "some." For example, from a paragraph in which it is stated that "it is not true that all contracts are legal," you can validly infer that "some contracts are not legal," or that "some contracts are illegal," or that "some illegal things are contracts," but you cannot validly infer that "no contracts are legal."

- Keep in mind that, in some tests, universal quantifiers such as "all" and "none" often give away incorrect response choices. That is not the case in this test. Some correct answers refer to "all" or "none" of the members of a group!

- Be sure to distinguish between essential information and unessential, peripheral information. That is to say, in a real test question, information such as "all contracts are legal" and "all contracts are two-sided agreements" would appear in a longer, full-fledged paragraph. It is up to you to separate the essential information from its context and then to realize that a response choice that states, "some two-sided agreements are legal" represents a valid inference, and thus the correct answer.

The questions that follow look like ordinary reading questions, but be careful! There is a twist to each.

Workshop III

DIRECTIONS: Answer each of the following questions based solely on the information provided in the reading passages. Circle the letter that precedes the correct answer.

1. Life is very complicated, and it is art's business to simplify it. The artist must find the common denominator—that which is similar among all of us—and draw on that to produce a work that not only unites us but also separates us. Each of us must be able to see something different in the work, although the underlying thing we grasp in it is the same.

With which of the following statements is the author most likely to agree?

A. All art imitates nature.

B. Every man is an artist.

C. Because we cannot see it, music is not art.

D. The artist must simplify and then complicate.

E. No great art was ever created without tears.

2. Through advertising, manufacturers exercise a high degree of control over consumers' desires. However, the manufacturer assumes enormous risks in attempting to predict what consumers will want and in producing goods in quantity and distributing them in advance of final selection by the consumers.

The paragraph best supports the statement that manufacturers

A. Can eliminate the risk of over-production by advertising.

B. Distribute goods directly to the consumers.

C. Must depend on the final consumers for the success of the undertakings.

D. Can predict with great accuracy the success of any product they put on the market.

E. Are more concerned with advertising than with the production of goods.

9

3. For a society to function properly, everyone must function with everyone else. Individual effort is great—for the individual. Social scientists should devote less time to figuring out how and why the individual does what he or she does and should spend more time figuring out how to get people to do more of what everybody should do: cooperate.

The author of this statement probably would approve most of

A. A psychological study of the determinants of behavior.
B. A sociological study of why people go to war.
C. A historical study of the communes that have failed.
D. An increase in the number of social scientists.
E. A psychological study of what makes people cooperative or antisocial.

4. For the United States, Canada has become the most important country in the world, yet there are few countries about which Americans know less. Canada is the third-largest country in the world; only Russia and China are bigger. The area of Canada is more than a quarter of the whole British Commonwealth.

The paragraph best supports the statement that

A. The British Commonwealth is smaller than Russia or China.
B. The territory of China is greater than that of Canada.
C. Americans know more about Canada than about Russia or China.
D. The United States is the most important nation in the world as far as Canada is concerned.

5. Because the government can spend only what it obtains from the people, and this amount is ultimately limited by the people's capacity and willingness to pay taxes, it is very important that the people be given full information about the work of the government.

The paragraph best supports the statement that

A. Government employees should be trained not only in their own work but also in how to perform the duties of other employees in their agency.
B. Taxation by the government rests on the consent of the people.
C. The release of full information on the work of the government will increase the efficiency of governmental operations.
D. The work of the government, in recent years, has been restricted because of reduced tax collection.
E. The foundation of our government is abhorrence of the principle of taxation without representation.

Answer Key

Here are the answers to Workshop I:

1.	C		6.	C
2.	A		7.	B
3.	B		8.	B
4.	B		9.	C
5.	C		10.	C

Here are the answers to Workshop II:

1.	C		5.	A
2.	D		6.	C
3.	B		7.	A
4.	C		8.	D

Here are the answers to Workshop III:

1. D
2. C
3. E
4. B
5. B

Answer Explanations

Workshop I

1. **(C)** We know only that George is the oldest. There is no way to tell whether Bob is older than Fred or Fred than Bob.

2. **(A)** Group A sings the highest of the three.

3. **(B** Extractor coffee is the strongest; electric dip comes next; and percolator coffee is the weakest.

4. **(B)** Yellow balloons fly higher than red or yellow kites.

5. **(C)** We know for certain that Baltimore won the fewest games, but without information about how many games were played, we can't know how many games Baltimore lost.

6. **(C)** The English book has the most pages, followed by the math book. The history book has more pages than the poetry book, but we don't have enough information to rank the science book: It may have more or fewer pages than the poetry book.

7.   **(B)** If the first two statements are true, Jeff runs faster than both Bill and Mike.

8.   **(B)** Because the first two statements are true and Karen reads faster than Ann, she must also read faster than Sue.

9.   **(C)** The first two statements only tell us that Peter is the shortest of the three boys. We can't determine the relationship between Paul and John.

10.   **(C)** The first two statements indicate no relationship between Harry and Ralph, therefore, the third statement is uncertain.

Workshop II

1.   **(C)** There is no information about whether or not Mr. Stonehill is now working, nor for whom. However, if the operating divisions have been sold, there is no corporate headquarters, so we can be certain that Mr. Stonehill does not work there.

2.   **(D)** With the credentials required of all schoolteachers and with his specialized experience in a chemical company, Mr. Moffitt is clearly qualified to teach high school chemistry. The training he received working in the textile dyes division applies beautifully to his sideline operation, cleaning Oriental carpets. The other choices, although all possible, are in no way supported by the paragraph.

3.   **(B)** The only statement definitely supported by the paragraph is that twins may have different interests and tastes.

4.   **(C)** Nobody changes a dry diaper in the middle of the night. The other choices are possibilities but not certainties. The baby may have awakened for any number of reasons: Molly Davis may be a baby-sitter; the baby may have played happily in his crib once dry and fed.

5.   **(A)** If all eight children carried lighted flashlights, we can be pretty sure that it was dark. The information that Jill and Mary did not wear masks *implies* that the other children did but does not prove it. (Some of the others may have worn sheets over their heads or painted their faces.) Jill and Mary were not necessarily the youngest.

6.   **(C)** The only certainty is that Julie is behind Laura in school. The fact that Laura is ahead in school does not necessarily mean that she is smarter, possibly only older. Anne may well be a normal, healthy two-year old. Julie and Anne are sisters, but Laura's relationship to them is not given.

7.   **(A)** Jeffrey definitely plays violin at least twice a week. Although we know that he enjoys both music and dancing, we have no way of knowing if he prefers either of these activities to the study of law. From this paragraph, you can't tell how often he dances.

8.   **(D)** Chances are that Debbie did not fail the written exam because she is about to go for an Oral Assessment. Surely the per-

son who failed the first step would not be called for the second. Likewise, we can assume that only people who pass the written exams take the oral. Otherwise, both exams could be scheduled in advance. If Debbie were already a Foreign Service Officer, she would not need to go for an Oral Assessment. You can assume from the paragraph that Debbie is happy because she passed the exam and is still under consideration.

Workshop III

1. **(D)** The passage begins by saying that the artist must simplify and find the common denominator. It then says that the artist must draw on the common denominator to produce something that separates us. This act of separation presumably involves adding to the common denominator and thus may be considered as a complicating act. Answers A, B, and E have no relation to the passage. Answer C is presumably derived from the statement that "each of us must be able to see something different in the work." This statement uses *see* in a broader sense than mere visual perception.

2. **(C)** The correct answer, C, is supported by the paragraph's statement that although advertising gives manufacturers considerable control over the consumer's demand for their products, there are still big risks involved in producing and distributing their goods in advance of the consumers' final selection. This implies that the manufacturers' ultimate success depends on the consumers.

3. **(E)** Answer E suggests what the author is most in favor of: finding out how to make people cooperate. Clearly, finding out why people are cooperative or antisocial is a crucial part of this research undertaking.

4. **(B)** The paragraph states that Russia and China are larger than Canada. No other answer to this question is correct. Choice C makes a statement in direct contradiction to the paragraph. Choice A is wrong because the paragraph compares the size of Canada with that of Russia and China, not the size of the British Commonwealth with Russia and China. It is entirely possible that the United States is the most important nation in the world as far as Canada is concerned, but choice D is not directly supported by the paragraph.

5. **(B)** According to the paragraph, the government can spend only what it obtains from the people. The government obtains money from people by taxation. If the people are unwilling to pay taxes, the government has no source for funds.

The Hour in Review

This hour presented you with the verbal reasoning question and all its delightful permutations. In tackling this type of question, remember the following:

- It is absolutely necessary to read verbal reasoning questions slowly because the use of two or three negatives can be quite confusing.

- Be sure to watch for the use of special clues in the questions themselves. For example, negated verbs (such as "are not") and negative prefixes (such as "*incomplete*") can help you understand what the question is looking for (or is not looking for).

- Try to determine what is essential information and what is nonessential information. Often, these types of questions include material that is completely irrelevant to what is being asked.

- Remember to assume that all "factual" information presented in the question is true, even if the information goes against what you personally know to be true. In short, you must suspend your "outside knowledge" and focus specifically on the facts presented in the question.

- Don't read too much into the questions. One of the tricks used by question designers is to get you thinking/inferring/speculating about information that is not related to the question (and for that matter, the correct answer).

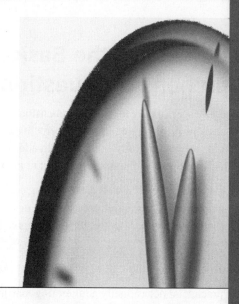

HOUR **10**

Teach Yourself Reading Comprehension Strategies

What You'll Learn in This Hour

The key to success in reading questions is not speed but, naturally, comprehension. If you are reading with comprehension, your mind will not wander, and your speed will be adequate. However, success in reading questions depends on more than reading comprehension. You must also know how to draw the answers from the reading selection and be able to distinguish the best answer from a number of answers that all seem to be good ones, or from a number of answers that all seem to be wrong. In this hour, you'll learn about this type of question and some strategies for tackling these questions. You'll also practice answering some sample reading comprehension questions.

Here is a list of your goals for this hour:

- Understand the basics of the reading comprehension question
- Answer some sample reading comprehension questions
- Review the answers and explanations

Understanding the Basics of Reading Comprehension Questions

Generally speaking, reading comprehension questions can be combined with other types of questions on any given law enforcement exam, so you should be prepared to encounter them in various locations on test day. In addition, you should expect to see at least two reading comprehension questions "back to back."

What does this mean? The typical reading comprehension question first asks you to read a paragraph of text and is followed by four or five multiple-choice questions related to that text. You should expect to see two paragraphs "back to back," or roughly 8 to 10 questions in a row.

Following is an example of a typical reading comprehension question:

The practice of occasionally adulterating marijuana complicates analysis of the effects of marijuana use in noncontrolled settings. Behavioral changes attributed to the use of marijuana may actually derive from the adulterants or from the interaction of tetrahydro-cannabinols and adulterants. Similarly, in today's society, marijuana is often used simulta-neously or sequentially with other psychoactive drugs. When drug interactions occur, the simultaneous presence of two or more drugs in the body can exert effects that are more than those that would result from the simple addition of the effects of each drug used separately. Thus, the total behavioral response may be greater than the sum of its parts. For example, if a given dose of marijuana induced two units of perceptual distortion, and a certain dose of LSD given alone induced two units of perceptual distortion, the simulta-neous administration of these doses of marijuana and LSD may induce not four but five units of perceptual distortion.

1.   According to the paragraph, the concurrent presence of two drugs in the body can

   A.   Compound the effects of the drug
   B.   Reduce perceptual distortion
   C.   Simulate psychotic symptoms
   D.   Be highly toxic

2.   On the basis of the paragraph, it is most reasonable to assume that tetrahydrocannabinols are

   A.   Habit-forming substances
   B.   Components of marijuana
   C.   Similar to quinine or milk-sugar
   D.   Used as adulterants

3. Based on the paragraph, it is most reasonable to state that marijuana is

   A. Most affected by adulterants when used as a psychoactive drug
   B. Erroneously considered to be less harmful than other drugs
   C. Frequently used in conjunction with other mind-affecting drugs
   D. Occasionally used as an adjunct to LSD in order to reduce bad reactions

Answers and Explanations

1. **(A)** "The simultaneous presence of two or more drugs in the body can exert effects that are more than would result from the simple addition of the effect of each drug used separately."

2. **(B)** Adulterants interact with tetrahydrocannabinols, so tetrahydrocannabinols must be components of marijuana.

3. **(C)** The whole point of the passage is to discuss the problems created by the practice of using marijuana with other mind-affecting drugs.

    Reading comprehension questions may take a number of different forms. In general, some of the most common forms are as follows:

    - **Question of fact or detail.** You may have to mentally rephrase or rearrange, but you should find the answer stated in the body of the selection.

    - **Best title or main idea.** The answer may be obvious, but the incorrect choices to the "main idea" question are often half-truths that are ideas (or even offer a supporting idea) quoted directly from the text. The correct answer is the one that covers the largest part of the selection.

    - **Interpretation.** This type of question asks you what the question *means*, not just what it says.

    - **Inference.** This is the most difficult type of reading comprehension question. It asks you to go beyond what the selection says and to predict what might happen next. Your answer must be based on what the information provided may have said about that subject. A variation of the inference question can be stated as, "The author would expect that...." To answer this question, you must understand the author's point of view and then make an inference from that viewpoint based on the information in the selection.

    - **Vocabulary.** Some law enforcement exams, directly or indirectly, ask the meaning of certain words as used in the selection.

> **Tip**
> Your daily newspaper provides excellent material to improve your reading concentration and comprehension. Read with a pencil in hand. Underscore details and ideas that seem to be crucial to the meaning of an article. Notice points of view, arguments, and supporting information. When you have finished the article, summarize it for yourself. Do you know the purpose of the article? the main idea presented? the attitude of the writer? the points over which there is controversy? Did you find certain information lacking? As you answer these questions, skim back over what you underlined. Did you focus on important words and ideas? Did you read with comprehension?
>
> As you repeat this process day after day, you will find that your reading will become more efficient. You will read with greater understanding, and you will "get more" from your newspaper.

Strange as it may seem, it's a good idea for you to approach reading comprehension questions by reading the **questions**—not the answer choices, just the questions themselves—before you read the selection. The questions will alert you to look for certain details, ideas, and points of view. Use your pencil. Underscore key words in the question. These words will help you direct your attention as you read. Next, skim the selection very rapidly to get an idea of its subject matter and its organization. Then read the selection carefully. Finally, return to the questions and be sure that you understand what they ask.

Workshop I

DIRECTIONS: Read the following selection. In the questions that follow, circle the letter of the correct answer.

If we are to study crime in its widest social setting, we will find a variety of conduct which, although criminal in the legal sense, is not offensive to the moral
(5)   conscience of a considerable number of persons. Traffic violations, for example, do not brand the offender as guilty of moral offense. In fact, the recipient of a traffic ticket is usually simply the subject
(10) of some good-natured joking by friends. Although there may be indignation among certain groups of citizens against gambling and liquor law violations, these activities are often tolerated, if not openly
(15) supported, by the more numerous residents of the community. Indeed, certain social and service clubs regularly conduct gambling games and lotteries for the purpose of raising funds. Some communities
(20) regard violations involving the sale of liquor with little concern if it results in profit from increased license fees and taxes paid by dealers. The thousand-and-one forms of political graft and corruption that
(25) infest our urban centers only occasionally arouse public condemnation and official action.

1. According to the passage, all types of illegal conduct are

   A. Condemned by all elements of the community.
   B. Considered a moral offense, although some are tolerated by a few citizens.
   C. Violations of the law, but some are acceptable to certain elements of the community.
   D. Found in a social setting and therefore not punishable by law.

2. According to the passage, traffic violations are generally considered by society to be

   A. Crimes requiring the maximum penalty set by the law.
   B. More serious than violations of liquor laws.
   C. Offenses against the morals of the community.
   D. Relatively minor offenses requiring minimum punishments.

3. According to the passage, a lottery conducted for the purpose of raising funds for a church

   A. Is considered a serious violation of the law.
   B. May be tolerated by a community that has laws against gambling.
   C. May be conducted under special laws demanded by the more numerous residents of a community.
   D. Arouses indignation in most communities.

10

4. On the basis of the passage, the most likely reaction in the community to a police raid on a gambling casino would be

A. More an attitude of indifference than interest in the raid.

B. General approval of the raid.

C. A condemnation of the raid by most people.

D. A demand for further action because the raid is not sufficient to end gambling.

5. The one of the following that best describes the central thought of this passage and would be most suitable as a title is

A. "Crime and the Police"

B. "Public Condemnation of Graft and Corruption"

C. "Gambling Is Not Always a Vicious Business"

D. "Public Attitude Toward Law Violations"

Workshop II

DIRECTIONS: Read the following selection. In the questions that follow, circle the letter of the correct answer.

Cotton fabrics treated with XYZ Process have features that make them far superior to any previously known flame-retardant cotton fabrics. XYZ Process-treated
(5) fabrics are durable to repeated laundering and dry cleaning; are glow resistant as well as flame resistant; when exposed to flames or intense heat, they form tough, pliable, and protective chars; are inert physiologically
(10) to persons handling or exposed to the fabric: are only slightly heavier than untreated fabrics: and are susceptible to further wet and dry finishing treatments. In addition, the treated fabrics exhibit little
(15) or no adverse change in feel, texture, and appearance and are shrink resistant, rot resistant, and mildew resistant. The treatment reduces strength only slightly. Finished fabrics have "easy care" properties
(20) in that they are wrinkle resistant and dry rapidly.

1. It is most accurate to state that the author in the proceeding selection presents

A. Facts and reaches a conclusion concerning the value of this process.

B. A conclusion concerning the value of the process and presents the facts to support that conclusion.

C. A conclusion concerning the value of the process unsupported by facts.

D. Neither facts nor conclusions; the author merely describes the process.

2. The one of the following articles for which the XYZ Process would be most suitable is

A. Nylon stockings

B. Woolen shirt

C. Silk tie

D. Cotton bedsheet

3. The one of the following aspects of the XYZ Process that is not discussed in the preceding selection is its effects on

A. Costs
B. Washability
C. Wearability
D. The human body

4. The main reason for treating a fabric with the XYZ Process is to

A. Prepare the fabric for other wet and dry finishing treatment.
B. Render it shrink resistant, rot resistant, and mildew resistant.
C. Increase its weight and strength.
D. Reduce the chance that it will catch fire.

5. Which of the following is considered to be a minor drawback of the XYZ Process?

A. Forms chars when exposed to flame.
B. Makes fabrics mildew resistant.
C. Adds to the weight of the fabric.
D. Is compatible with other finishing treatments.

10

Workshop III

DIRECTIONS: Read the following selection. In the questions that follow, circle the letter of the correct answer.

Language performs an essentially social function: It helps us to get along together, to communicate, and to achieve a great measure of concerted action. Words are
(5) signs that have significance by convention; those people who do not adopt the conventions simply fail to communicate, They do not "get along," and a social force arises that encourages them to
(10) achieve the correct associations. By "correct" we mean "as used by other members of the social group." Some of these vital points about language are brought home to a British visitor to America (and
(15) vice versa) because our vocabularies are nearly the same—but not quite.

1. As defined in the preceding selection, use of a word is "correct" when it

A. Is defined in standard dictionaries.
B. Is used by the majority of persons throughout the world who speak the same language.
C. Is used by the majority of educated persons who speak the same language.
D. Is used by other persons with whom we are associating.

2. In the preceding selection, the author is concerned primarily with the

A. Meaning of words.
B. Pronunciation of words.
C. Structure of sentences.
D. Origin and development of language.

3. According to the proceeding selection, the main language problem of a British visitor to America stems from the fact that a British person

A. Uses some words that have different meanings for Americans.
B. Has different social values from Americans.
C. Has had more exposure to non-English-speaking persons than Americans have had.
D. Pronounces words differently from Americans.

Answer Key

Here are the answers to Workshop I:

1. C
2. D
3. B
4. A
5. D

Here are the answers to Workshop II:

1. B
2. D
3. A
4. D
5. C

Here are the answers to Workshop III:

1. D
2. A
3. A

> **Note:** You have undoubtedly noticed the varied subject matter in these three exercises. This variety is common to all reading comprehension tests and should be expected.

Answer Explanations

Workshop I

1. **(C)** Because this is exactly what the passage implies, choice C is correct. Answer A is not true; the passage indicates that certain violations of laws are more or less accepted by the citizenry (for example, traffic violations, liquor laws, and so on). Answer B is not true; the passage indicates that traffic violators are usually *not* deemed guilty of a moral offense. And nothing in the passage indicates that answer D is true.

2. **(D)** Because answer D is the exact inference of the passage, it is the correct choice. Nothing in the passage indicates that answer A is correct. In fact, the passage states that traffic violators are usually only subject to good-natured joking by their friends. Answer B is not true; the implication in the passage is that violators of liquor laws are probably frowned on more than are traffic violators. Answer C is not true; the passage states exactly the opposite.

3. **(B)** Answer B is the correct choice as supported by the contents of the passage. There is nothing in the passage to indicate that answer A is true. Answer C is not true; there is nothing in the passage to support this choice. Answer D is not true; the passage supports the opposite point of view.

4. **(A)** Answer A is the correct choice. Answer B is not correct: the community, in general, would not approve of a raid on an activity that it favors. Answer C is not correct; the community's reaction would be that the police could better busy themselves with other areas of crime prevention. Answer D is not true; there is nothing in the passage to support this choice.

5. **(D)** Answer D is the correct choice; this title describes the main focus of the passage. Answer A is not suitable; this title is too broad. The passage deals specifically with certain kinds of crime. Answer B is not suitable; the passage makes the point that the public does not always condemn crime and corruption. Answer C is not suitable; this title is too narrow because crimes other than gambling are discussed.

10

Workshop II

1. **(B)** Answer B combines the main idea and the interpretation question. If you cannot answer this question readily, reread the selection. The author clearly thinks that XYZ Process is terrific and says so in the first sentence. The rest of the selection presents a wealth of facts to support the initial claim.

2. **(D)** At first glance, you might think that this is an inference question requiring you to make a judgment based on the few drawbacks of the process. Closer reading, however, shows that there is no contact for the correct answer here. This is a simple question of fact: XYZ Process is a treatment for *cotton* fabrics.

3. **(A)** Your underlined passages should help you with this question of fact. Cost is not mentioned: all other aspects of the XYZ Process are. If you are having trouble finding mention of the effect of the XYZ Process on the human body, add to your vocabulary list the words *inert* and *physiologically*.

4. **(D)** This is a main-idea question. You must distinguish between the main idea and the supporting and incidental facts.

5. **(C)** Obviously, a *drawback* is a negative feature. The selection mentions only two negative features: The treatment reduces strength slightly, and it makes fabrics slightly heavier than untreated fabrics. Only one of these negative features is offered among the answer choices.

Workshop III

1. **(D)** The answer to this question is stated in the next to last sentence of this selection.

2. **(A)** This main-idea question is an easy one to answer. Hopefully, you readily eliminated all the wrong choices.

3. **(A)** This is a question of fact. The phrasing of the question is quite different from the phrasing of the last sentence, but the meaning is the same. You may have found this reading selection more difficult to absorb than some of the others, but you probably had no difficulty answering this question by eliminating the wrong answers.

The Hour in Review

- Reading comprehension questions are perhaps the most common type of question you will encounter on law enforcement exams. Unfortunately, they are often the most insidious, too, because many people erroneously perceive them as the "easiest" (which is often not the case). Remember to read each question carefully, also remembering that a good strategy is to read the questions first, so that you have an idea of what section of the paragraph is being referenced.

- Test designers often provide a "too good to be true" answer. In other words, they will provide as an answer an option that seems to directly answer the question. Often, these "answers" are given to trick the hurrying test-taker. Be careful to read each answer thoroughly; don't jump at the first answer that seems to be "perfect."

- Be aware of the different "types" of reading comprehension questions. Although the format may appear different, all reading comprehension questions test your ability to quickly read a paragraph of text and to then be able to apply the details of that paragraph to a set of questions. Read each question closely: read the answers even more closely.

- You can "practice" for reading comprehension exams by reading your daily newspaper and looking for the important details. Try to remember the details after reading the story for the first time. As you repeat this process day after day, you will find that your reading will become more efficient. You will read with greater understanding, and you will "get more" from your newspaper.

10

HOUR **11**

Teach Yourself Observation and Memory Strategies

What You'll Learn in This Hour

Although observation and memory skills aren't things that can really be "taught," the skills and practice in this hour can help you prepare for the memory and observation sections of law enforcement tests. In this hour, you become familiar with how these questions are presented on the exams, and you learn some strategies for honing your memory and observation skills to note the types of specific information on which you may be tested. That information and those strategies, in combination with the practice exercises you work through in this hour, can help increase your chances of doing well on these exams.

Here is a list of your goals for this hour:

- Understand the basics of observation and memory questions
- Sharpen your skills in observation and memory
- Complete Exercise I: Practice your observation skills
- Complete Exercise II: Practice your memory skills
- Review your answers and the answer explanations

Understanding the Basics of Observation and Memory Questions

In any law enforcement position, you need a keen memory for details if you are to function effectively. You're constantly on the alert for physical characteristics that can help you identify key people, places, or things, thereby leading to the apprehension of a criminal or to the solution to a criminal investigation.

> **Note**
> Many dangerous criminals have been arrested by virtue of a law enforcement officer's keen observation. A good officer observes and remembers the people, places, and things on his or her post, as well as the routine activities that go on there. That way, the officer can quickly spot a stranger, an unusual activity, or anything that seems out of the ordinary and that may signal trouble.

Because most law enforcement positions require a good memory for details and a good sense of recall, law enforcement examinations frequently contain sections that evaluate memory and observation skills.

A typical memory question asks you to study a diagram for a set period of time (this diagram can also be a photograph). Alternatively, you may be asked to study drawings that represent the faces of suspected criminals. Whatever you are presented with, the idea is to try to retain as many details about the diagram(s) or illustration(s) as possible in the allotted amount of time. Then, when you turn the page in your exam booklet, you are asked a series of questions that test your ability to memorize the details of the illustrations/diagrams/pictures you've just seen. For example, if the illustration is that of a storefront on a busy street, one question may ask you how many people were photographed walking into the store.

A typical observation question most likely presents you with a set of information about an individual (for example, a profile for a suspected criminal) that lists his or her physical attributes, suspected crime, where he or she was last seen, and whom that person was seen with. Another example might present you with a police report of a criminal activity (listing the time the event took place, the evidence gathered, information from witnesses, and so on). The questions ask that you study this information and then pick the best answers to questions based on the information. Similar in some regards to reading comprehension, observation questions test your ability to study a set of facts and then pick the answer that best summarizes the information presented to you.

> **Note**
> Observation questions are usually presented in sets of four or five questions; unlike the memory questions, where you are first given a set period of time to study the illustration and then answer questions, observation questions ask you to do *both* tasks in a set period of time.

Sharpen Your Observation and Memory Skills

Good observation is a matter of training and knowledge. To best sharpen your memory and sense of recall, *you must practice using these skills!* You can work on these skills just by walking around your neighborhood and observing. Keep your eyes open to everything you see. Later, try to recall details of buildings or people you saw. Recall is an essential element of observation. Test yourself by trying to accurately describe a man or woman you encountered casually or try to remember the details on a billboard you passed. Remember that your environment is your study aid—virtually any place you go, you can practice observing and recalling details.

> **Caution**
> You can't be observant just by "looking around." Be deliberate and methodical in your observations and don't omit details. Don't let preconceived notions, prejudice, or emotions "fill in the blanks" of your observations and don't exaggerate. See all things equally and as they are. Finally, be alert—if you're absentminded or careless, you'll miss something.

> **Tip**
> Although psychologists estimate that roughly 85 percent of our knowledge is obtained through the sense of sight, remember that you observe with all *five* of your senses. The sounds and smells you observe in your environment also provide you with valuable information, and you should note them.

Observation is of little use to law enforcement unless it's accompanied by keen memory. Memory is a very individualized skill. Some people remember details of what they see and hear; others remember only the obvious facts. Memory can be clouded by imagination, emotional stress, or prejudice. Memories of one incident may become mixed with those of another. Although everyone has a unique capacity for memory, you can train yourself to better remember details.

You can enhance your memory and observation skills by trying to arrange some sort of meaningful grouping of people and activities, which can help secure the description, the activities, and the interactions in your mind. Whether the material is pictorial or narrative, try to organize it in some meaningful way.

You can improve your memory by exercising and training it. *Association* is a memory aid that many people find very effective. To recall a detail—for example, a person's name or distinguishing characteristics, a location, or a color—you can associate the item or feature with something familiar to you. For example, you may note that someone has a scar, and to help you recall the exact appearance and location of the scar, you associate it with a scar you remember on a childhood friend. You may better remember a car's make and model by mentally associating it with something it reminds you of—an animal, a place, a person. By practicing association when you're memorizing information, you sharpen your abilities to recall details. It's a memory device that can help you.

Caution
This book can't really teach you how to memorize, but the information and exercises in this hour, and the practice test in Hour 16, "Sample Correction Officer Reading Comprehension Exam," can help you be better prepared to deal with observation and memory questions on the law enforcement exams.

Exercise I: Practice Your Observation Skills

This exercise measures your ability to observe and recognize the basic differences and similarities in the faces of people. When people are being pursued by the law, they often attempt to disguise their appearance (facial features, hair color, even body shape) to make it difficult for officers to apprehend them. Most people have distinguishing features that are difficult to disguise—the contour of a face; the size, shape, and position of the ears; the shape of the mouth. Barring surgery, these features aren't easy to change. On the other hand, people can change their hair color or hair style, wear tinted contact lenses, or use a wig, mustache, or beard to dramatically alter their general appearance. Therefore, law enforcement officers focus attention on those physical features that can't be changed easily and that can serve as the basis for a positive identification of that person at some time in the future.

Observation Quiz A

DIRECTIONS: Answer the following 10 questions by selecting the face (labeled A, B, C, or D) that is most likely to be the same as that of the suspect on the left. You are to assume that no surgery has taken place since the sketch of the suspect was made. Only observation and recognition are factors in this exercise. Do not try to memorize features of these faces. Circle the letter of the face you choose. Explanations follow the last question.

11

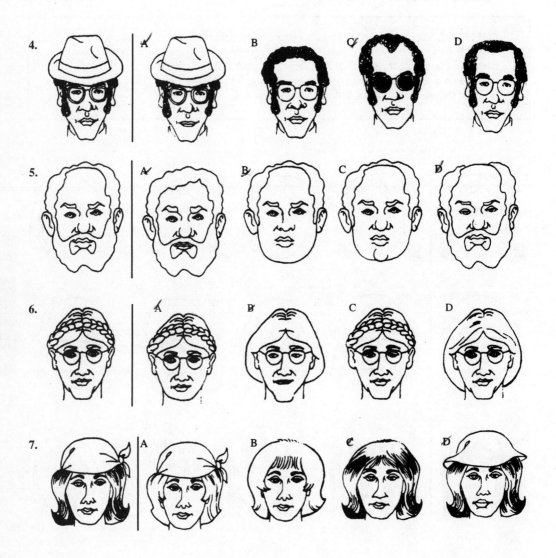

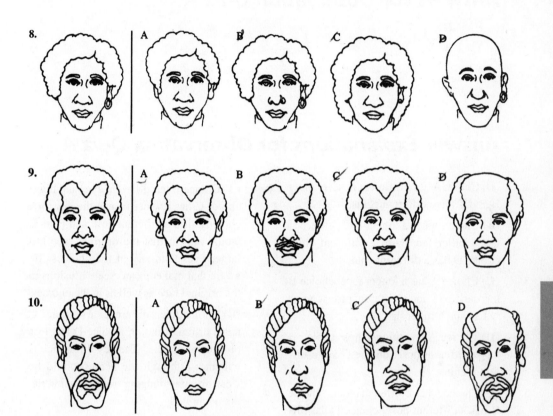

Answers for Observation Quiz A

1. D
2. B
3. C
4. D
5. C

6. D
7. B
8. A
9. B
10. A

Answer Explanations for Observation Quiz A

1. **(D)** Choice A has a different nose; choices B and C have different chins.

2. **(B)** Choice A has a longer face; choice C has a fuller face with a different chin; choice D has a different chin.

3. **(C)** Choice A has a longer face; choice B has dark eyes and a different nose; choice D has much fuller lips.

4. **(D)** Choice A has thinner lips: choice B has a different nose; choice C has a different chin.

5. **(C)** Choice A has a different mouth; choice B has a different nose; choice D has different eyes.

6. **(D)** Choice A has a different chin; choice B has a different mouth; choice C has different eyes.

7. **(B)** Choice A has different eyes; choice C has a different nose; choice D has a different mouth.

8. **(A)** Choice B has different eyes and nose; choice C has a wider face at the jaw line; choice D has a different nose and chin. It would appear that the original face has larger eyes than any of the choices. Be aware that makeup can create illusions in the original face as well as in the choices.

9. **(B)** Choice A has different ears; choice C has a different mouth; choice D has less prominent nostrils. The key difference is hairline; although the person could be wearing a wig, judging from his hairstyle, that is unlikely.

10. **(A)** Choice B has a different nose; choice C has different ears; choice D has different eyes and the hairline of the original face looks natural, where the hairline in choice D suggests a wig.

Observation Quiz B

DIRECTIONS: Answer the following questions on the basis of the following sketches. The face on top is a sketch of an alleged criminal based on witnesses' descriptions at the crime scene. One of the four sketches below that face is the way the suspect might look after changing his or her appearance. Assume that no surgery has been done on the suspect's face. Circle the letter of the face you choose. The answers and explanations follow the last set of sketches.

1.

2.

(A)

(A)

(C)

(C)

(B)

(D)

(B)

(D)

11

Answers for Observation Quiz B

1.   B
2.   B
3.   D
4.   C
5.   B

Answer Explanations for Observation Quiz B

1.   **(B)** The suspect in choice A has larger eyes; the suspect in choice C has different ears; the suspect in choice D has a fuller face.

2.   **(B)** The suspect in choice A has a smaller nose; the suspect in choice C has a fuller face and fuller lips; the suspect in choice D has lighter eyes and thinner lips.

3.   **(D)** The suspect in choice A has a different nose; the suspect in choice B has different ears; the suspect in choice C has an entirely different head and face shape.

4.   **(C)** The suspect in choice A has a much finer nose; the suspect in choice B has a narrower jaw structure; the suspect in choice D has different ears.

5.   **(B)** The suspect in choice A has a smaller nose; the suspect in choice C has lighter eyes and a wider mouth; the suspect in choice D has a fuller face and thinner lips.

Exercise II: Practice Your Memory Skills

The following exercise provides you with good practice in anticipating the type of memory questions you will be asked on the typical law enforcement exam. Because you usually have very little time to finish these sections on the exam (usually about 10 minutes or so), try to look over the information presented as quickly as you can.

DIRECTIONS: You will be given 10 minutes to study the following six "Wanted" posters. Try to remember as many details as you can. You may not take any notes during this time.

11

Wanted for Assault

Name: John Markham

Age: 27

Height: 5'11"

Weight: 215 lbs.

Race: Black

Hair Color: Black

Eye color: Brown

Complexion: Dark

Identifying marks: Eagle tattoo on back of right hand; very hard of hearing

Suspect is a former boxer. He favors brass knuckles as his weapon.

Wanted for Rape

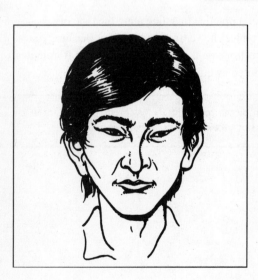

Name: Arthur Lee

Age: 19

Height: 5'7"

Weight: 180 lbs.

Race: Asian

Hair color: Black

Eye color: Brown

Complexion: Medium

Identifying marks: None

Suspect carries a pearl-handled knife with an eight-inch curved blade. He tends to attack victims in subway passageways.

Wanted for Armed Robbery

Name: Antonio Gomez

Age: 31

Height: 5'6"

Weight: 160 lbs.

Race: Hispanic

Hair color: Brown

Eye color: Brown

Complexion: Medium

Identifying marks: Missing last finger of right hand; tattoo on back says, "Mother"; tattoo on left biceps says, "Linda"; tattoo on right biceps says, "Carmen"

Suspect was seen leaving the scene in a stolen yellow 1987 Corvette. He carries a gun and must be considered dangerous.

11

Wanted for Car Theft

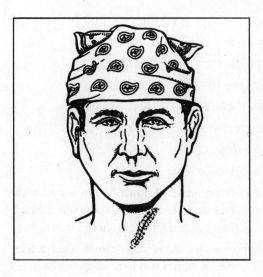

Name: Robert Miller

Age: 24

Height: 6'3"

Weight: 230 lbs.

Race: White

Hair color: Brown

Eye color: Blue

Complexion: Light

Identifying marks: Tracheotomy scar at base of neck; tattoo of dragon on right upper arm

Suspect chain smokes unfiltered cigarettes. He always wears a red head scarf.

Wanted for Murder

Name: Janet Walker

Age 39

Height: 5'10"

Weight: 148 lbs.

Race: Black

Hair color: Black

Eye color: Black

Complexion: Dark

Identifying marks: Large hairy mole on upper left thigh; stutters badly

Suspect has frequently been arrested for prostitution. She often wears multiple ear and nose rings.

Wanted for Arson

Name: Margaret Pickford

Age: 42

Height: 5'2"

Weight: 103 lbs.

Race: White

Hair color: Red

Eye color: Green

Complexion: Light

Identifying marks: Known heroin addict with track marks on forearms; walks with decided limp because left leg is shorter than right

Suspect has a child in foster care in Astoria. She usually carries two large shopping bags.

Memory Questions

1. Which of the following suspects may have committed a crime in order to support a drug habit?

A

C

B

D

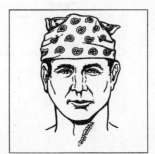

11

2. Which one of the following is missing a finger? The suspect wanted for

   A. Rape

   B. Assault

   C. Murder

   D. Armed robbery

3. Which of the suspects is most likely to be found in the subway?

   A. John Markham

   B. Margaret Pickford

   C. Arthur Lee

   D. Robert Miller

4.   Which of these suspects has a dragon tattoo?

A

C

B

D
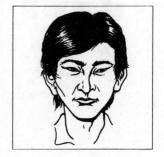

5.   Which is an identifying mark of this suspect?

   A.   Deafness

   B.   A large mole

   C.   A tattoo that reads "Mother"

   D.   Needle tracks

6.   Which of the following is considered to be the most dangerous?

A

C

B

D

11

7.   Which of these suspects is known to be a parent?

    A.   The suspect who stutters

    B.   The former boxer

    C.   The smoker

    D.   The suspect who limps

8.   Which of these suspects escaped the scene of the crime in a stolen car?

A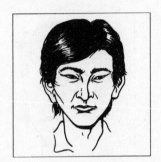

C

B

D

9.   Which of these suspects would have the hardest time running from the police?

A.   The heroin addict

B.   The suspect who is nearly deaf

C.   The suspect who wears lots of jewelry

D.   The suspect with brass knuckles in his pocket

10.   Which of these suspects is wanted for rape?

A

C

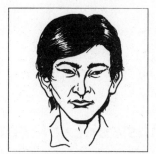

B

D

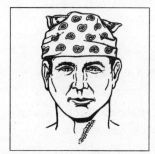

11

Answer Key for Memory Quiz

1.	B		6.	B
2.	D		7.	D
3.	C		8.	C
4.	A		9.	A
5.	B		10.	C

Answer Explanations for Memory Quiz

1. **(B)** Margaret Pickford is a known heroin addict.

2. **(D)** Antonio Gomez is wanted for armed robbery. He is missing the last finger of his right hand.

3. **(C)** Arthur Lee often attacks his victims in subway passageways.

4. **(A)** Robert Miller has a tattoo of a dragon on his right upper arm.

5. **(B)** Janet Walker has a large hairy mole on her upper left thigh.

6. **(B)** Antonio Gomez carries a gun. Although Arthur Lee carries a wicked looking knife, Lee is not offered among the choices.

7. **(D)** Margaret Pickford, who walks with a limp because her left leg is shorter than her right, has a child in foster care, so obviously she is a parent.

8. **(C)** Antonio Gomez escaped from the scene of a recent armed robbery in a stolen yellow 1987 Corvette.

9. **(A)** Margaret Pickford, who is a drug addict, has a severe limp because one leg is shorter than the other. She would have a hard time running from the police.

10. **(C)** Arthur Lee is wanted for rape.

The Hour in Review

In this hour, you learned more about the observation and memory questions from law enforcement exams. You also got some practice in answering this type of question. Here are the important details to remember from this hour:

- Observation and memory questions test your ability to observe people and events and to recall the details of what you've seen that are most important to law enforcement operations.

- Observation questions present you with information and a series of 4 or 5 questions that draw from your recall of that information. The test gives you a set amount of time to both study the information and respond to the questions.

- Memory questions are similar to observation questions but give you a specific time (often 10 minutes) to study a set of visual and written information. You then are asked to answer questions based on that information without referring back to the information or visuals. When you take the practice quizzes, don't cheat by flipping back to the original information. You won't be able to do that on test day!

- Observation and memory questions demand that you pay close attention to details— the *right* details. By noting unchangeable physical features and characteristics, you record the information that is vital to identifying suspects.

- You can hone your observation and memory skills by practicing. Observe the people and events that surround you daily and then make a habit of "quizzing" yourself to see how well you recall the specific details of those people and events.

11

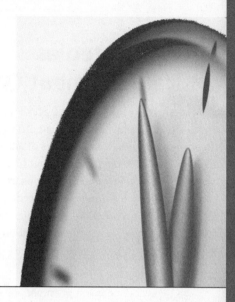

Teach Yourself Practical and Investigative Judgment Strategies

What You'll Learn in This Hour

Practical and investigative judgment questions are a typical component of Police, State Police, and some Treasury Enforcement Agency exams. In this hour, you learn some of the basic tenets on which these agencies base practical and investigative judgment questions. You also learn some strategies for analyzing and correctly answering these questions on the exam. We'll also look at plenty of sample questions so that you can become familiar with the question format and learn what to expect.

Here's a list of your goals for this hour:

- Teach yourself test-taking strategies for judgment questions.
- Work through some sample judgment exercises.
- Work through some investigative problem exercises.

Test-Taking Strategies
for Practical Judgment Questions

Practical judgment questions typically take the form of a paragraph or statement that describes a situation a law enforcement officer may encounter, a question that asks how the officer should respond, and a series of answers from which you can choose. The question type itself is straightforward but finding the answer takes a bit of skill. Practical judgment questions on law enforcement exams can place you in a peculiar position: As an applicant taking the exam, you're not expected to know the agency's procedures and policies. On the other hand, test-makers often assume that these polices and procedures are just common sense, and the exam questions may reflect that assumption.

> **Note**
> Practical judgment questions are an important component of Police Officer and State Trooper examinations, so in this section, we concentrate on techniques for tackling this section of those exams.

To do well, you must understand the basics of what most law enforcement agencies view as "common sense" so that you can supply the answer that best fits with that view.

In a nutshell, the common sense of law enforcement—particularly at the local and state police level—revolves around three basic principles: the police role, the priorities of responsibilities within that role, and the minimum use of force. Your best strategies for tackling practical judgment questions on the Police and State Trooper exams are to commit these "common sense" listings to memory and to use them when determining the best answer to "common sense" questions on the exam.

Remember the "Common Sense" of the Police Role

In previous hours, you learned that every law enforcement agency has unique demands and plays a unique role, depending on the size of the agency, the location it serves, and the needs that result from those factors. However, the following lists contain some "common sense" ideas that should guide you when you're answering judgment questions that reflect your understanding of the police role:

- Police Officers are professionals; they avoid emotional responses, biased behavior, and becoming indebted to people on their beat.
- Police Officers aren't parents, doctors, or private security guards for people on their beat. In an emergency, officers provide other assistance (such as medical aid) to the best of their ability; where time isn't as pressing, they leave nonpolice roles to others.

- Police Officers assist endangered people 24 hours a day. They're prepared to assist in keeping the peace at any time, and they take initiative in urgent situations. On exam questions, however, think of the role of an off-duty officer as one of "peace keeper" first and as "arresting officer" only in emergencies.

Remember the "Common Sense" Hierarchy of Police Priorities

All law enforcement officers have a number of responsibilities that fall into a distinct hierarchy. In most local and state police agencies, the officers' responsibilities share the same order of priority:

1. Assist endangered people
2. Keep the peace
3. Enforce the law
4. Assist people who aren't in immediate danger but who need help
5. Maintain order on the beat

When you encounter questions that ask you "what is your first responsibility in this situation?" or "what should your first action be?" look for the answer that fits the hierarchy in the preceding list.

Remember the Rule of Minimum Necessary Force

Finally, practical judgment questions may pose situations in which use of force is required, and then ask you to determine the level of force with which the officer should respond. Remember that, in nearly every law enforcement agency, the rule of force is that officers should always resolve problems with *the minimum amount of force necessary*. The officer's action should never cause greater harm than what is presented by the problem he or she is trying to resolve. A simple concept—but a critical one for many practical judgment questions.

12

> **Tip**
> When assessing the amount of force necessary to resolve a situation, consider the physical setting (are bystanders likely to be hurt?), the actions and intentions of the people involved, and the intent of the law. Never choose an answer that recommends more force than the problem deserves.

Test-Taking Strategies for Investigative Judgment Questions

Investigative judgment questions are usually presented in three parts. First, a paragraph of text describes a given situation that is under investigation. Next comes a series of numbered statements, representing the statements of witnesses or sources gathered in the investigation. Last are the questions that ask you to interpret or otherwise assess those statements.

How well you do on investigation problems depends on how well you understand what you read. Reading speed is not crucial for these questions. For example, the Treasury Enforcement Agent (TEA) exam usually gives you 60 minutes to read, ponder, and answer 30 questions. Clear thinking and total concentration are the keys to doing well on this very significant portion of a law enforcement exam. Because you will have some time to contemplate these questions, you should try to arrive at the true meaning and the implications of each statement. Ask yourself the following things about each situation:

- Is this a fact? Can the fact be substantiated?
- Is the statement based on hearsay?
- Is the statement pure conjecture?
- How reliable is the source of the evidence?
- Does the person have a motive for making this statement?

> **Tip**
> As you try to determine which statements support the questions, take note of time sequences and the interrelationships of events. Also consider interpersonal relationships.

As you read the paragraphs, remain cool, detached, and strictly analytical. You may disagree with the actions taken by the law enforcement official in regard to handling evidence or questioning witnesses, but don't let those opinions influence your responses to the questions. Concentrate on the description of the events as they are reported, the statements made by witnesses, and the questions that must be supported by statements. In short, be analytical, objective, and very careful!

Workshop I: Practical Judgment Exercises

> **DIRECTIONS:** Carefully read each of the following questions and then choose the correct answer to each by circling the letter that precedes your choice.

1. An off-duty Police Officer was seated in a restaurant when two men entered, drew guns, and robbed the cashier. The officer made no attempt to prevent the robbery or apprehend the criminals. Later, he justified his conduct by stating that an officer, when off duty, is a private citizen with the same duties and rights as all private citizens. The officer's conduct was

   A. Wrong. A Police Officer must act to prevent crimes and apprehend criminals at all times.

   B. Right. The Police Officer was out of uniform at the time of the robbery.

   C. Wrong. He should have obtained the necessary information and descriptions after the robbers left.

   D. Right. It would have been foolhardy for him to intervene when outnumbered by armed robbers.

2. While you are on traffic duty, a middle-aged man crossing the street cries out with pain, presses his hand to his chest, and stands perfectly still. You suspect that he may have suffered a heart attack. You should

   A. Help him cross the street quickly in order to prevent his being hit by moving traffic.

   B. Permit him to lie down flat in the street while you divert traffic.

   C. Ask him for the name of his doctor so that you can summon the physician.

   D. Request a cab to take him to the nearest hospital for immediate treatment.

3. Assume that you have been assigned to a traffic post at a busy intersection. A car bearing out-of-state license plates is about to turn into a one-way street going in the opposite direction. You blow your whistle and stop the car. You should then

   A. Hand out a summons to the driver in order to make an example of him because out-of-town drivers notoriously disregard our traffic regulations.

   B. Pay no attention to him and let him continue in the proper direction.

   C. Ask him to pull over to the curb and advise him to get a copy of the latest New York City traffic regulations.

   D. Call his attention to the fact that he was violating a traffic regulation and permit him to continue in the proper direction.

12

4. A Police Officer, walking his beat at 3 A.M., notices heavy smoke coming out of a top floor window of a large apartment house. Of the following, the action the officer should take first is to
A. Make certain that there really is a fire.
B. Enter the building and warn all the occupants of the apartment house.
C. Attempt to extinguish the fire before it gets out of control.
D. Call the fire department.

5. You notice that a man is limping hurriedly, leaving a trail of blood behind him. You question him, and his explanation is that he was hurt accidentally while he was watching a man clean his gun. You should
A. Let him go because you have no proof that his story is not true.
B. Have him sent to the nearest city hospital under police escort so that he can be questioned further after treatment.
C. Ask him whether the man has a license for his gun.
D. Ask him to lead you to the man who cleaned his gun so that you can question him further about the accident.

6. Law enforcement officials are instructed to pay particular attention to anyone apparently making repairs to an auto parked in the street. The most important reason for this rule is that
A. The person making the repairs may be stealing the car.
B. The person making the repairs may be obstructing traffic.
C. Working on autos is prohibited on certain streets.
D. Many people injure themselves while working on their cars.

7. In dealing with children, law enforcement official should
A. Treat them the same as adults.
B. Instill in them a fear of the law.
C. Secure their confidence.
D. Impress them with the rights of the law to punish them for their wrongdoing.

8. Ten percent of the inmates released from a certain prison are arrested as parole violators. It follows that
A. 90 percent have been reformed.
B. 10 percent have been reformed.
C. None have been reformed.
D. None of the foregoing are necessarily true.

9. The best attitude for a law enforcement officer is to
A. Be constantly on alert.
B. Be hostile.
C. Vary watchfulness with the apparent need for it.
D. Regard tact as the most effective weapon for handling any degree of disorder.

10. A criminal is typically someone who
A. Has a suspicious appearance.
B. Exhibits a most degenerate kind of behavior.
C. Is an intelligent, well-educated person.
D. Looks like other people.

Workshop II: Investigative Problem Exercises

DIRECTIONS: Read the paragraph and statements carefully. Then answer the questions that follow the investigative situation. You may refer to the paragraph and statements as often as needed.

The area had recently been plagued by a rash of cargo pilfering and large-scale hijacking, so when the giant container ship docked, security was especially tight. At night, city Police Officers, accompanied by dogs, patrolled the piers and adjacent warehouses. One night, a stray dog in the area began to act very strangely and erratically. A guard dog sniffed the stray, then led its handler to a crate with a liquid seeping from one corner. Analysis proved that the liquid was whiskey.

In the course of the investigation, the following statements were made:

1. Police Officer Caleb Hill stated that he had seen the puddle earlier in the evening, but had assumed it was water. He further stated that his guard dog has been well trained and that it eats and drinks only when it is served by its handler.

2. Customs Inspector Hank Harker stated that cargo on the dock consisted of automobile parts sent from a manufacturing plant in Europe to an assembly plant in the United States.

3. Crane operator Manny Fargoli stated that he did not notice anything unusual in the offloading of this particular cargo.

4. Longshoreman Nathan Bullwick stated that every container ship carries some sort of smuggled goods.

5. DEA Officer Tim Green stated that his dogs had sniffed the cargo for narcotics and had found nothing.

6. Gunnar Gustafon, the shipping company representative, stated that there was one more container on the dock right now than had been officially loaded.

7. Seaman Tom Tripp stated that Seaman Bill Crooker had told him that he (Crooker) had seen a truck back up to the ship in the night in its European berth and had seen someone handing money to Gunnar Gustafon.

8. Police Officer Helen Hanson stated that ship's officer Martin Blight seemed to spend more time wandering among the containers than was usual practice for ships' officers.

9. Longshoreman Jim Dunn stated that Gunnar Gustafon's assistant, Thorpe Nichols, seemed excessively agitated when a forklift operator dropped the box now identified as contraband.

10. First Mate Nelson Sparrow stated that this ship appeared to have an exceptionally hard-drinking crew.

12

1. Which statement is hearsay?

    A. Statement 2

    B. Statement 4

    C. Statement 7

    D. Statement 9

    E. Statement 10

2. Which two statements explain why the dogs did not independently lead police officers to the whiskey?

    A. Statements 1 and 3

    B. Statements 1 and 5

    C. Statements 4 and 5

    D. Statements 4 and 10

    E. Statements 5 and 10

3. Which statement, along with statement 8, seems to implicate "management" in the smuggling of whiskey?

    A. Statement 2

    B. Statement 4

    C. Statement 6

    D. Statement 9

    E. Statement 10

4. Which statement might be an attempt to divert the investigation?

    A. Statement 1

    B. Statement 4

    C. Statement 5

    D. Statement 6

    E. Statement 10

5. Which two statements indicate that law enforcement officials might not have been as thorough as they ought to have been?

    A. Statements 1 and 2

    B. Statements 1 and 5

    C. Statements 2 and 5

    D. Statements 3 and 5

    E. Statements 5 and 8

6. Which statement might represent an attempt by the speaker to eliminate himself from suspicion?

    A. Statement 1

    B. Statement 3

    C. Statement 5

    D. Statement 6

    E. Statement 10

7. Which two statements, along with statement 4, have no real bearing on this investigation?

    A. Statements 1 and 2

    B. Statements 2 and 3

    C. Statements 5 and 7

    D. Statements 5 and 10

    E. Statements 7 and 10

8. Which statement suggests that a ship's officer was doing more than minding official business?

    A. Statement 3

    B. Statement 6

    C. Statement 7

    D. Statement 8

    E. Statement 9

Answer Key

Answers for Workshop I are as follows:

1.   A
2.   A
3.   D
4.   D
5.   B
6.   A
7.   C
8.   D
9.   A
10. D

Answers for Workshop II are as follows:

1.   C
2.   B
3.   D
4.   E
5.   A
6.   D
7.   D
8.   D

Answer Explanations

Workshop I

1. **(A)** A Police Officer is always a Police Officer, even when not officially on duty. Off-duty status does not relieve a Police Officer from fulfilling the police role.

2. **(A)** The first thing to do is to protect the man's life by escorting him out of danger. Securing medical assistance should then follow.

3. **(D)** Obviously, going the wrong way down a one-way street creates a dangerous situation for many people. It would be wise to point out to the individual exactly how one-way streets are marked in your town. By stopping the driver, you have averted the danger.

4. **(D)** A Police Officer is not a firefighter. It is the job of firefighters to ascertain whether or not there really is a fire and, if one exists, to put it out.

5. **(B)** Your first consideration must be protecting life and limb. Get the man to the hospital for medical help but have him escorted for further questioning. Gunshot wounds should always be investigated.

6. **(A)** The owner may indeed be caring for his car, in which case the owner can prove ownership. An open hood can also be a sign of a car theft by means of jump-start.

7. **(C)** In police exams, older children are generally referred to as *juveniles. Children* means "young children." In dealing with children, whether protecting them or arresting them, the Police Officer must secure their confidence to get maximum cooperation.

8. **(D)** If 10 percent of the inmates released from a prison are arrested as parole violators, the only fact-based conclusion is that

12

10 percent have violated parole and have been caught. The statement gives no basis for any other conclusions.

9. **(A)** The Police Officer must be alert at all times.

10. **(D)** A Police Officer cannot allow his or her professional judgment to be influenced in any way by misinformation or personal prejudice.

Workshop II

1. **(C)** Tom Tripp is simply repeating a statement made to him.

2. **(B)** Guard dogs are trained to accept food and drink only from their handlers. The purpose of this training is to protect the dog from poisoned bait. Statement 1 implies that the officer's dog did not investigate the puddle on its own because it knew not to drink a standing liquid. Once sensitized to the odor, the dog led the officer to the liquid. The dog in statement 5 was trained to sniff out only narcotics, not alcohol.

3. **(D)** As Gustafon's assistant, Thorpe Nichols was part of a management group. Nichols's agitation as the crate that contained the whiskey was dropped implies that he knew of the contents and the smuggling scheme.

4. **(E)** The First Mate's mentioning that the crew of the ship did a lot of drinking might be a diversionary tactic, an attempt to suggest that the crew was transporting liquor for its own use or for sale to a stateside contact.

5. **(A)** The puddle deserved the officer's attention. He should have checked out its nature and not simply assumed that it was water. The Customs Inspector should not have flatly stated what the cargo consisted of without fully checking it out.

6. **(D)** Gustafon's indication of surprise that there was an extra box on the dock, one more box than he had loaded, is his way of clearing himself.

7. **(D)** The gratuitous statement that every container ship carries some smuggled goods is completely useless to this investigation. Equally irrelevant is the statement that the DEA dogs did not sniff out any narcotics. The oblique suggestion that a hard-drinking crew had a hand in smuggling a large crate of whiskey is so outlandish as to have no real bearing on this investigation.

8. **(D)** After the ship has docked and the cargo has been offloaded, the ship's officers have no further responsibility for the cargo. A ship's officer spending a great deal of time wandering among the crates must raise suspicions that the officer has some personal interest beyond those of his assigned duties.

The Hour in Review

- Practical and investigative judgment questions are important components of most local and state police exams. Investigative judgment questions are included in every TEA exam.

- Practical judgment questions assume that you possess a certain law enforcement "common sense"; your best strategy for tackling these questions is to become familiar with the basic principles of the officer's role, the hierarchy of the officer's responsibilities, and the rule of minimum force.

- Read practical and investigative judgment questions slowly and completely. Think them through before you answer. Remember that these questions test your ability to apply your judgment, so take the time you need to do so.

- Investigative judgment questions demand that you evaluate both the information people give and the reliability of that information. As you read the statements, remember to judge their reliability in terms of the motivations of the individuals who make the statements. You normally have ample time to analyze and answer these questions, so don't rush through your responses.

- Carefully review the sample questions and answer explanations you worked through in this chapter, even those you answered correctly. By reviewing the responses to practical and investigative judgment questions, you'll be better prepared to tackle them on test day.

12

HOUR 13

Teach Yourself Arithmetic Reasoning Strategies

What You'll Learn in This Hour

The two words "arithmetic reasoning" strike terror into the hearts of people who have been out of school for a while or who have concentrated their studies in the humanities.

Have no fear! With respect to the various law enforcement exams, your fear of arithmetic is unfounded. The arithmetic reasoning tested on law enforcement exams doesn't require you to understand intricate mathematical procedures or to have memorized complicated formulas. In this hour, you will learn strategies and techniques for taking the bite out of these problems. (Yes, their bark is far, far worse than their bite!)

Here is a list of your goals for this hour:

- Teach yourself ratio and proportion strategies
- Teach yourself work problem strategies

- Teach yourself distance problem strategies
- Teach yourself interest problem strategies
- Teach yourself taxation problem strategies
- Teach yourself profit-and-loss problem strategies
- Teach yourself payroll problem strategies
- Teach yourself formula problem strategies
- Complete some sample exam questions
- Check your answers and review the explanations

Ratio and Proportion Problem Strategies

A *ratio* expresses the relationship between two (or more) quantities in terms of numbers. The mark used to indicate ratio is the colon (:) and is read "to" (for example, 3:2 is read "three to two"). A ratio also represents division. Therefore, any ratio of two terms can be written as a fraction, and any fraction can be written as a ratio. Here are some examples:

$$3:4 = \frac{3}{4}$$

$$\frac{5}{6} = 5:6$$

To simplify any complicated ratio of two terms containing fractions, decimals, or percents, perform one of these steps:

- Divide the first term by the second
- Write the ratio as a fraction in lowest terms
- Write the fraction as a ratio

Simplify the ratio $\frac{5}{6} : \frac{7}{8}$

Solution: $\frac{5}{6}$ divided by $\frac{7}{8} = \frac{5}{6} \times \frac{8}{7} = \frac{20}{21}$

$\frac{20}{21}$ is also equal to 20:21

To solve problems in which the ratio is given, follow these steps:

1.   Add the terms in the ratio.
2.   Divide the total amount to be put into the ratio by this sum.
3.   Multiply each term in the ratio by this quotient.

Here's an example:

The sum of $360 is to be divided among three people according to the ratio 3:4:5. How much does each one receive?

This question says that $360 is to be divided among three people: One of those people gets 3 parts, another gets 4 parts, and the last gets 5 parts of the money. You can find the solution by following these steps:

1.   Add the terms in the ratio:

   $3 + 4 + 5 = 12$

2.   Divide the total amount to be put into the ratio by this sum:

   $360 \div 12 = 30

3.   Multiply each term in the ratio by this quotient:

   $30 \times 3 = 90

   $30 \times 4 = 120

   $30 \times 5 = 150

Answer: The money is divided this way: $90, $120, $150.

A *proportion* indicates the equality of two ratios. In a proportion, the two outside terms are called the *extremes* and the two inside terms are called the *means*.

Proportions are often written in a fractional form. In any proportion, the product of the means equals the product of the extremes. If the proportion is in fractional form, the products may be found by cross-multiplication. The product of the extremes divided by one mean equals the other mean; the product of the means divided by one extreme equals the other extreme. Here's an example:

The scale on a map shows that 2 cm represents 30 miles of actual length. What is the actual length of a road that is represented by 7 cm on the map?

Solution: The map lengths and the actual lengths are in proportion; that is, they have equal ratios. If *m* stands for the unknown length, the proportion is as follows:

$$\frac{2}{7} = \frac{30}{m}$$

13

As the proportion is written, m is an extreme and is equal to the product of the means divided by the other extreme:

$$m = \frac{7 \times 30}{2}$$

$$m = \frac{210}{2}$$

$$m = 105$$

Many problems in which three terms are given and one term is unknown can be solved by using proportions. To solve such problems, follow these steps:

1. Formulate the proportion very carefully according to the facts given. If any term is misplaced, the solution will be incorrect. Any symbol can be used in place of the missing term.

2. Determine by inspection whether the means or the extremes are known. Multiply the pair that has both terms given.

3. Divide this product by the third term given to find the unknown term.

Here's another example of a proportion problem:

If a moneybag containing 500 nickels weighs 6 pounds, how much will a moneybag containing 1600 nickels weigh?

Solution: The weights of the bags and the number of coins in them are proportional. Suppose that w represents the unknown weight. The proportion is as follows:

$$\frac{6}{w} = \frac{500}{1600}$$

The unknown is a mean and is equal to the product of the extremes, divided by the other mean:

$$w = \frac{6 \times 1600}{500}$$

$$w = 19.2$$

Caution
Arithmetic reasoning questions are a common component of the TEA exam. On the actual exam, you are always given a choice E, "none of the above." This choice means that you shouldn't estimate answers. Perform the calculation; if none of the choices matches your answer, choose E.

Work Problem Strategies

In work problems, there are three items involved: the number of people working, the time spent working, and the amount of work done. The number of people working is *directly proportional* to the amount of work done; that is, the more people on the job, the more work will be done, and vice versa. The number of people working is *inversely proportional* to the time; that is, the more people on the job, the less time it will take to finish the job, and vice versa. Finally, the time expended on the job is directly proportional to the amount of work done; that is, the more time expended on a job, the more work that is done, and vice versa.

Work at Equal Rates

When given the time required by a number of people working at equal rates to complete a job, multiply the number of people by their time to find the time required by one person to complete the job. For example:

> If it takes 4 people working at equal rates 30 days to finish a job, then one person will take 30 x 4, or 120, days to finish the job.

When given the time required by one person to complete a job, you can find the time required by a number of people working at equal rates to complete the same job by dividing the time by the number of people. For example:

If 1 person can do a job in 20 days, it will take 4 people working at equal rates $\frac{20}{4}$, or 5, days to finish the job.

To solve time problems involving people who work at equal rates, multiply the number of people by their time to find the time required by one person. Then divide this time by the number of people required, as in this example:

> Four workers can do a job in 48 days. How long will it take 3 workers to finish the same job?

Solution: One worker can do the job in 48 x 4, or 192 days; 3 workers can do the job in $\frac{192}{3}$ = 64 days.

In some work problems, the rates, although unequal, can be equalized by comparison. To solve such problems, first determine how many equal rates there are. Then multiply this number of equal rates by the time given. Finally, divide this product by the number of equal rates. Here's an example:

13

Three workers can do a job in 12 days. Two of the workers work twice as fast as the third. How long would it take one of the faster workers to do the job by himself or herself?

Solution: There are two fast workers and one slow worker. Therefore, there are actually five slow workers working at equal rates.

1 slow worker will take 12 x 5, or 60, days.

Because 1 fast worker = 2 slow workers, the fast worker will take $\frac{60}{2}$, or 30, days to complete the job.

> **Note**
> There are several variations of these sample work problems. The key to successfully answering them is to read each question carefully and look for proportional measurements that can be made with the information given you, thus making your calculations—and your chance of getting the right answer—much easier and more accurate.

Distance Problem Strategies

In distance problems, there are usually three quantities involved: the distance (in miles), the rate (in miles per hour), and the time (in hours).

- To find the *distance*, multiply the rate by the time.
- The *rate* is the distance traveled in unit/time. To find the rate, divide the distance by the time.
- To find the *time*, divide the distance by the rate.

Combined Rates

When two people or objects are traveling toward each other, the rate at which they are approaching each other is the sum of their respective rates.

When two people or objects are traveling in directly opposite directions, the rate at which they are separating is the sum of their respective rates.

To solve problems involving combined rates, determine which of the three factors is to be found. Combine the rates and find the unknown factor. Here's an example:

A and B are walking toward each other over a road 120 miles long. A walks at a rate of 6 miles an hour, and B walks at a rate of 4 miles an hour. How soon will they meet?

Solution: The factor to be found is the time. Remember that *time = distance ÷ rate*. You know two of the factors in this problem: The distance is 120 miles, and the rate is 6 + 4, which equals 10 miles an hour. So:

$$\text{time} = \frac{120}{10} = 12 \text{ hours}$$

To find the time it takes a faster person or object to catch up with a slower person or object, determine how far ahead the slower person or object is. Then subtract the slower rate from the faster rate to find the gain rate per unit of time. Finally, divide the distance that has been gained by the difference in rates. Take a look at this example:

> Two automobiles are traveling along the same road. The first one, which travels at the rate of 30 miles an hour, starts out 6 hours ahead of the second one, which travels at the rate of 50 miles an hour. How long will it take the second one to catch up with the first one?

Solution: The first automobile starts out 6 hours ahead of the second. Its rate is 30 miles an hour. Therefore, it has traveled 6 x 30, or 180, miles by the time the second one starts. The second automobile travels at the rate of 50 miles an hour. Therefore, its gain is 50 - 30, or 20, miles an hour. The second auto must cover 180 miles. Therefore, it will take $\frac{180}{20}$, or 9, hours to catch up with the first automobile.

Average of Two Rates

In some problems, two or more rates must be averaged. When the times are the same for two or more different rates, add the rates and divide by the number of rates.

When the terms are not the same, but the distances are the same, follow these steps:

1. Assume that the distance is a length you can easily calculate.
2. Find the time at the first rate.
3. Find the time at the second rate.
4. Find the time at the third rate, if any.
5. Add all the distances and divide by the total time to find the average rate.

When the times are not the same, and the distances are not the same, follow these steps:

1. Find the time for the first distance.
2. Find the time for the second distance.
3. Find the time for the third distance, if any.
4. Add all the distances and divide by the total time to find the average rate.

Interest Problem Strategies

Interest (or *I*) is the price paid for the use of money. There are three items considered in calculating interest:

- The *principal (p)*, which is the amount of money on which interest must be paid.
- The *interest rate (r)* expressed in percent on an annual basis.
- The *time (t)* during which the principal is used, expressed in terms of years.

The basic formulas used in interest problems are listed here:

- $I = prt$
- $p = \dfrac{I}{rt}$
- $r = \dfrac{I}{pt}$
- $t = \dfrac{I}{pr}$

For most interest problems, the year is considered to have 360 days. Months are considered to have 30 days, unless a particular month is specified.

To use the interest formulas, time must be expressed as part of a year (for example, 1 year and 3 months is expressed as $\dfrac{15}{12}$ year).

Note
In reference to time, the prefix *semi-* means "every half." The prefix *bi-* means "every two." Therefore, *semiannual* means "twice in one year"; *biannual* means "once every two years."

There are two types of interest problems:

- *Simple interest*, in which the interest is calculated only once over a given period of time.
- *Compound interest*, in which interest is recalculated at given time periods based on previously earned interest.

Taxation Problem Strategies

We're all familiar with taxes! Taxation problems require special calculations, and you have to approach them with these two factors in mind:

- Taxes can be expressed as a percent or in terms of money based on certain denominations.

- A *surtax* is an additional tax imposed above the regular tax rate.

In taxation, there are usually three items involved: the amount taxable (called the *base*), the tax rate, and the tax itself.

To find the tax when given the base and the tax rate in percent, change the tax rate to a decimal and multiply the base by the tax rate. For example:

How much would be realized on $4,000 if taxed 15%?

Solution: 15% = .15
$4,000 x .15 = $600
Tax = $600

To find the tax rate in percent form when given the base and the tax, divide the tax by the base then convert to a percent, as in this example:

Find the tax rate at which $5,600 would yield $784.

Solution: $784 ÷ $5,600 = .14
.14 = 14%

Note

There are many variations on taxation problems. Just remember to convert to a percentage or convert to a base first, so that it's easier to visualize what you are trying to calculate.

Profit-and-Loss Problem Strategies

Profit-and-loss problems aren't difficult to solve, but they do have their own terminology. Here are some of the terms you may encounter in profit-and-loss problems and the definitions of those terms:

- The *cost price* of an article is the price paid by a person who wants to sell it again.

- There may be an *allowance* (a deduction from the cost because of some specific situation or some other prequalifying condition) or a *trade discount* (a deduction from cost because of existing materials) on the cost price.

- The *list price*, or *marked price*, is the price at which the article is listed or marked to be sold.

13

- There may be a discount or series of discounts on the list price.
- The *selling price*, or *sales price*, is the price at which the article is finally sold.
- If the selling price is greater than the cost price, there has been a *profit*.
- If the selling price is lower than the cost price, there has been a *loss*.
- If the article is sold at the same price as the cost, there has been no profit or loss.
- Profit or loss can be stated in terms of dollars and cents, or in terms of percent.
- *Overhead expenses* include such items as rent, salaries, and so on. Overhead expenses can be added to cost price to determine the total cost when calculating profit or assigning a selling price.

The basic formulas used in profit and loss are listed here:

Selling price = cost price + profit

Selling price = cost price - loss

Other types of basic formulas you should be aware of include these:

- To find the profit in terms of money, subtract the cost price from the selling price: Selling price - cost price = profit
- To find the selling price if the profit or loss is expressed in percent based on cost price, multiply the cost price by the percent of profit or loss to find the profit or loss in terms of money. Then add this product to the cost price if a profit is involved, or subtract for a loss.
- To find the cost price when given the selling price and the percent of profit or loss based on the selling price, multiply the selling price by the percent of profit or loss to find the profit or loss in terms of money. Then subtract this product from the selling price if a profit is involved, or add the product to the selling price for a loss.
- To find the percent of profit or percent of loss based on cost price, find the profit or loss in terms of money, divide the profit or loss by the cost price, and then convert to a percent.
- To find the percent of profit or percent of loss based on the selling price, find the profit or loss in terms of money, divide the profit or loss by the selling price, and then covert to a percent.
- To find the cost price when given the selling price and the percent of profit based on the cost price, establish a relation between the selling price and the cost price and then solve to find the cost price.
- To find the selling price when given the profit based on the selling price, establish a relation between the selling price and the cost price and then solve to find the selling price.

Payroll Problem Strategies

Some law enforcement arithmetic reasoning exams contain payroll problems. Although on the surface these problems seem pretty straightforward, there are a few pieces of information you need to arm yourself with when tackling these questions:

- Salaries are computed over various time periods: hourly, daily, weekly, biweekly (every 2 weeks), semimonthly (twice each month), and yearly.

- Overtime is usually computed as "time and a half"; that is, each hour in excess of the number of hours in the standard workday or workweek is paid at 1 1/2 times the regular hourly rate. Some companies pay "double time"— twice the regular hourly rate—for work on weekends and holidays.

- In occupations such as retail sales, real estate, and insurance, earnings may be based on *commission*, which is a percentage of the sales or a percentage of the value of the transactions that are completed. Earnings may be from straight commission, from salary plus commission, or from a commission that is graduated according to transaction volume.

- *Gross pay* refers to the amount of money earned from salary, commission, or both before any deductions are made.

- Several deductions are usually made from gross pay. These include *withholding tax*—the amount of money withheld for income tax. Withholding tax is based on wages, marital status, and the number of exemptions claimed by the employee. The withholding tax is found by referring to tables supplied by the federal, state, or city government.

Formula Problem Strategies

Formula questions appear in two distinct forms. Those described as "literal" questions are expressed mainly in terms of letters. The problem itself is written with no numbers (or very few numbers), and the multiple-choice answer must be chosen from a list of formulas that involve the manipulation of those letters.

13

> **Tip**
> Many individuals, including accountants and other professionals who deal intimately with numbers, have no trouble computing with numbers but panic at the sight of letters. This panic, although understandable, is unnecessary. The letters simply represent the numbers used in a particular problem.

If you understand the concepts of the problem, you should be able to apply those concepts equally to the manipulation of representative letters or to the computation of actual numbers. Understanding the concept is the key. As literal questions become more complex, they require greater concentration and reasoning. And, of course, basic arithmetic knowledge comes into play as well.

> **Tip**
> The best approach to literal multiple-choice questions is to solve the problem before looking at the choices offered. If you understand the concept, you are more likely to arrive at the correct answer by not allowing yourself to be influenced by other suggestions (that is, incorrect answers).

The other type of formula question gives the appearance of a routine arithmetic reasoning question. The stem of the question describes a situation and presents a mathematical problem that must be solved. The question itself is full of numbers. The answer choices, however, are not *final* answers. The question does not ask what the answer is, but rather asks you how you should *find* the answer. In other words, the question seeks the process rather than the results. The answer is a mathematical (not an algebraic) formula.

> **Tip**
> Careful reading and meticulous construction of the problem are key to solving these questions—as indeed they are to all arithmetic reasoning problems!

The subject matter of formula questions parallels that of traditional numerical questions: ratio and proportion, work, distance and gasoline problems, interest and discounts, and so on. Approach the questions in exactly the same way you approach numerical questions. Setting up the problem requires the same reasoning; the only differences are the use of symbolic letters in literal questions and the stopping point for choosing formula answers.

Practice Your Arithmetic Reasoning Skills

Use the information and strategies you've learned in the first part of this hour to answer the workshop questions that follow. Do all the questions with pencil on scratch paper. You won't be permitted to use a calculator at the exam, so you can use these sample questions to get used to working without one. Answer the questions by circling the letter of your choice. Answer keys and explanations follow the workshops.

Workshop I

1. Aluminum bronze consists of copper and aluminum, usually in the ratio 10:1 by weight. If an object made of this alloy weighs 77 pounds, how many pounds of aluminum does it contain?

   A. 7.7

   B. 7.0

   C. 70.0

   D. 62.3

2. It costs 31 cents a square foot to lay vinyl flooring. To lay 180 square feet of flooring it will cost

   A. $16.20

   B. $18.60

   C. $55.80

   D. $62.00

3. If a per-diem worker earns $352 in 16 days, the amount that worker will earn in 117 days is most nearly

   A. $3,050

   B. $2,574

   C. $2,285

   D. $2,080

4. A stenographer transcribes notes at the rate of 1 line typed in 10 seconds. At this rate, how long (in minutes and seconds) will it take to transcribe notes, which will require 7 pages of typing, 25 lines to the page?

   A. 29 minutes 10 seconds

   B. 17 minutes 50 seconds

   C. 40 minutes 10 seconds

   D. 20 minutes 30 seconds

5. A group of five clerks has been assigned to insert 24,000 letters into envelopes. The clerks perform this work at the following rates of speed: Clerk A, 1,100 letters an hour; Clerk B, 1,450 letters an hour; Clerk C, 1,200 letters an hour; Clerk D, 1,300 letters an hour; Clerk E, 1,250 letters an hour. At the end of two hours of work, Clerks C and D are assigned to another task. From the time that Clerks C and D were taken off the assignment, the number of hours required for the remaining clerks to complete the assignment is

   A. Less than 3 hours

   B. 3 hours

   C. More than 3 hours, but less than 4 hours

   D. More than 4 hours

6. If a certain job can be performed by 18 workers in 26 days, the number of workers needed to perform the job in 12 days is

   A. 24

   B. 30

   C. 39

   D. 52

7. A car began a trip with 12 gallons of gasoline in the tank and ended with 7 1/2 gallons. The car traveled 17.3 miles for each gallon of gasoline. During the trip, gasoline was bought for $10.00, at a cost of $1.25 per gallon. The total number of miles traveled during this trip was most nearly

   A. 79

   B. 196

   C. 216

   D. 229

13

8. A man travels a total of 4.2 miles each day to and from work. The traveling consumes 72 minutes each day. Most nearly, how many hours would he save in 129 working days if he moved to another residence so that he would travel only 1.7 miles each day, assuming that he travels at the same rate?

A. 92.11

B. 93.62

C. 95.35

D. 98.08

9. A man can travel a certain distance at the rate of 25 miles an hour by automobile. He walks back the same distance on foot at the rate of 10 miles an hour. What is his average rate for both trips?

A. $14 \frac{2}{7}$ mph

B. $15 \frac{1}{3}$ mph

C. $17 \frac{1}{2}$ mph

D. 35 mph

Workshop II

1. The scholarship board of a certain college lent a student $200 at an annual rate of 6% from September 30 until December 15. To repay the loan and accumulated interest, the student must give the college an amount closest to which one of the following?

A. $202.50

B. $203.00

C. $203.50

D. $212.00

2. If $300 is invested at simple interest so as to yield a return of $18 in 9 months, the amount of money that must be invested at the same rate of interest so as to yield a return of $120 in 6 months is

A. $3,000

B. $3,300

C. $2,000

D. $2,300

3. When the principal is $600, the difference in one year between simple interest at 12% per annum and interest compounded semi-annually at 12% per annum is

A. $2.16

B. $21.60

C. $0.22

D. $0.00

4. A piece of property is assessed at $22,850 and the tax rate is $4.80 per thousand. What is the amount of tax that must be paid on the property?

A. $109

B. $112

C. $109.68

D. $112.68

5. $30,000 worth of land is assessed at 120% of its value. If the tax rate is $5.12 per $1,000 assessed valuation, the amount of tax to be paid is

A. $180.29

B. $184.32

C. $190.10

D. $192.29

6. Of the following real estate tax rates, which is the largest?

A. $31.25 per $1,000

B. $3.45 per $100

C. $.32 per $10

D. $.03 per $1

7. A stationer buys note pads at $.75 per dozen and sells them at $.25 apiece. The profit based on the cost is

A. 50%

B. 300%

C. 200%

D. 100%

8. An article costing $18 is to be sold at a profit of 10% of the selling price. The selling price will be:

A. $19.80

B. $36.00

C. $18.18

D. $20.00

9. A calculating machine company offered to sell a city agency 4 calculating machines at a discount of 15% from the list price and to allow the agency $85 for each of two old machines being traded in. The list price of the new machines is $625 per machine. If the city agency accepts this offer, the amount of money it will have to provide for the purchase of these 4 machines is

A. $1,785

B. $2,295

C. $1,955

D. $1,836

13

Workshop III

1. Sam Richards earns $1,200 monthly. The following deductions are made from his gross pay monthly: federal withholding tax, $188.40; FICA tax, $84.60; state tax, $36.78; city tax, $9.24; savings bond, $37.50; pension plan, $5.32; repayment of pension loan, $42.30. His monthly net pay is

    A. $795.86

    B. $797.90

    C. $798.90

    D. $799.80

2. A salesman is paid a straight commission that is 23% of his sales. What is his commission on $1,260 of sales?

    A. $232.40

    B. $246.80

    C. $259.60

    D. $289.80

3. In a foreign-language school, 64% of the students are studying Spanish, 52% are studying French, and 28% are studying a language other than Spanish or French. What percent of the students at the school is studying both Spanish and French?

    A. (100 - 28) - [(72 - 64) + (72 - 52)]

    B. 100 - (64 + 52)

    C. (100 - 28) + 64 + 72

    D. (64 + 52 + 28) - [(100) - (100 - 72)]

4. What is the average of a student who received 90 in English, 84 in Algebra, 75 in French, and 76 in Music, if the subjects have the following weights: English 4, Algebra 3, French 3, and Music 1?

    A. $\frac{4(90+84+75+76)}{4+3+3+1}$

    B. $\frac{4(90)+6(84+75)+76}{4\times3\times3}$

    C. $\frac{\frac{90+84+75+76}{4}}{4+3+3+1}$

    D. $\frac{(90\times4)+(84\times3)+(75\times3)+(76\times1)}{4+3+3+1}$

5. A dealer mixes a lbs. of nuts worth b cents per pound with c lbs. of nuts worth d cents per pound. At what price should he sell a pound of the mixture if he wants to make a profit of 10 cents per pound?

    A. $\frac{ab+cd}{a+c+10}$

    B. $\frac{ab+cd}{a+c+.10}$

    C. $\frac{b+d}{a+c+10}$

    D. $\frac{b+d}{a+c+.10}$

Answer Keys

Here are the answers to Workshop I:

1.	B	4.	A	7.	C
2.	C	5.	B	8.	A
3.	B	6.	C	9.	A

Here are the answers to Workshop II:

1.	A	4.	C	7.	B
2.	A	5.	B	8.	D
3.	A	6.	B	9.	C

Here are the answers to Workshop III:

1.	A	4.	D
2.	D	5.	A
3.	A		

Answer Explanations

Workshop I

1.   **(B)** Because only two parts of a proportion are known (77 is the total weight), the problem must be solved by the ratio method. The ratio 10:1 means that if the alloy were separated into equal parts, 10 of those parts would be copper and 1 would be aluminum, for a total of 10 + 1 = 11 parts.

$$\frac{77}{11} = 7 \text{ lbs. per part}$$

The alloy has 1 part aluminum

7 x 1 = 7 lbs. aluminum

2.   **(C)** The cost (c) is proportional to the number of square feet:

$$\frac{\$.31}{c} = 1/180$$

$$c = \frac{\$.31 \times 180}{1}$$

$$c = \$55.80$$

3.   **(B)** The amount earned is proportional to the number of days worked. If a is the unknown amount:

$$\frac{352}{a} = \frac{16}{117}$$

$$a = \frac{\$352 \times 117}{16}$$

$$a = \$2,574$$

13

4.   **(A)** The stenographer must type 7 x 25 = 175 lines. At the rate of 1 line per 10 seconds, it will take 175 x 10 = 1,750 seconds.

$$\frac{1{,}750 \text{ seconds}}{60} = 29\frac{1}{6} \text{ minutes}$$

= 29 minutes 10 seconds

5.   **(B)** Let's set up this comparison chart:

Clerk	Number of Letters per Hour
A	1,100
B	1,450
C	1,200
D	1,300
E	1,250
Total per hour:	6,300

All 5 clerks working together process a total of 6,300 letters per hour. After 2 hours, they have processed 6,300 x 2 = 12,600 letters. Of the original 24,000 letters there are 24,000 - 12,600 = 11,400 letters remaining.

Clerks A, B, and E working together process a total of 3,800 letters per hour. It will take them $\frac{11{,}400}{3{,}800}$ = 3 hours to process the remaining letters.

6.   **(C)** The job could be performed by 1 worker in 18 x 26 days = 468 days. To perform the job in 12 days, you need $\frac{468}{12}$ = 39 workers.

7.   **(C)** The car used

$$12 - 7\frac{1}{2} = 4\frac{1}{2} \text{ gallons, } plus$$

$$\frac{\$10.00}{\$1.25 \text{ per gallon}} = 8 \text{ gallons}$$

for a total of $12\frac{1}{2}$ gallons, or 12.5 gallons.

12.5 gallons x 17.3 mpg = 216.25 miles

8.   **(A)** 72 min = $\frac{72}{60}$ hr = 1.2 hr

$$\text{Rate} = \frac{4.2 \text{ mi}}{\frac{1}{2} \text{ hr}} = 3.5 \text{ mph}$$

At this rate, it would take $\frac{1.7 \text{ mi}}{3.5 \text{ mph}} = .486$ hours (approx.) to travel 1.7 miles.
The daily savings in time is
1.2 hr - .486 hr = .714 hr
.714 hr x 129 days = 92.106 hr

9.   **(A)** Assume a convenient distance, say, 50 miles.

$$\text{Time by automobile} = \frac{50 \text{ mi}}{25 \text{ mph}} = 2 \text{ hours}$$

$$\text{Time walking} = \frac{50 \text{ mi}}{10 \text{ mph}} = 5 \text{ hours}$$

Total time = 7 hours

Total distance = 100 mi

$$\text{Average rate} = \frac{100 \text{ mi}}{7 \text{ hrs}}$$

$$\text{Average rate} = 14\frac{2}{7} \text{ mph}$$

Workshop II

1. **(A)** For this problem, we know the following:

    Principal = $200

    Rate = .06 = $\frac{6}{100}$

    Time from September 30 until December 15 is 76 days (31 days in October, 30 days in November, 15 days in December)

    76 days = $\frac{76}{360}$ year

    Interest = $200 x $\frac{6}{100}$ x $\frac{76}{360}$

    Interest = $\frac{\$152}{60}$ = $2.53

    $200 + $2.53 = $202.53

2. **(A)** For this problem, we know the following:

    Principal = $300

    Interest = $18

    Time = $\frac{9}{12}$ years = $\frac{3}{4}$ year

    $300 x $\frac{3}{4}$ = $225

    $\frac{\$18}{\$225}$ = .08

    Rate is 8%

    To yield $120 at 8% in 6 months,

    Interest = $120

    Rate = .08

    Time = $\frac{1}{2}$ year

    .08 x $\frac{1}{2}$ = .04

    $\frac{\$120}{.04}$ = $3,000 must be invested

3. **(A)** To calculate the simple interest:

    Principal = $600

    Rate = .12

    Time = 1

    Interest = $600 x .12 x 1

    Interest = $72.00

    To calculate the compound interest:

    Principal = $600

    Period of compounding = $\frac{1}{2}$ year

    Rate = .12

    For the first period,

    Interest = $600 x .12 x $\frac{1}{2}$

    Interest = $36

    New principal = $600 + $36

    New principal = $636

    For the second period,

    Interest = $636 x .12 x $\frac{1}{2}$

    Interest = $38.16

    New principal = $636 + $38.16

    New principal = $674.16

    Total interest = $74.16

    Difference = $74.16 - $72.00

    Difference = $2.16

4. **(C)** For this problem, we know the following:

    Base = $22,850

    Denomination = $1,000

    Tax rate = $4.80 per thousand

    $\frac{\$22,850}{\$1,000}$ = 22.85

    22.85 x $4.80 = $109.68

13

5.	**(B)** For this problem, we know the following:

Base = Assessed valuation

$\qquad$ = 120% of $30,000

$\qquad$ = 1.20 x $30,000

$\qquad$ = $36,000

Denomination = $1,000

Tax rate = $5.12 per thousand

$\frac{\$36,000}{\$1,000} = 36$

36 x $5.12 = $184.32

6.	**(B)** Express each tax rate as a decimal:

$31.25 per $1,000 = $\frac{31.25}{1,000}$ = .03125

$3.45 per $100 = $\frac{3.45}{100}$ = .0345

$.32 per $10 = $\frac{.32}{10}$ = .0320

$.03 per $1 = $\frac{.03}{1}$ = .0300

The largest decimal is .0345

7.	**(B)** Each dozen note pads cost $.75 and is sold for

12 x $.25 = $3.00

The profit is $3.00 - $.75 = $2.25

Profit based on cost = $\frac{\$2.25}{\$.75}$ = 3

$\qquad$ =300%

8.	**(D)** If profit = 10% of selling price, then cost = 90% of selling price:

$18 = 90% of selling price

Selling price = $\frac{\$18}{90\%}$

$\qquad$ = $\frac{\$18}{.90}$

$\qquad$ = $20

9.	**(C)** Discount for each new machine:

15% of $625 = .15 x $625 = $93.75

Each new machine will cost

$625 - $93.75 = $531.25

Four new machines will cost

$531.25 x 4 = $2,125

But there is an allowance of $85 each for 2 old machines:

$85 x 2 = $170

Final cost to city:

$2,125 - $170 = $1,955

Workshop III

1. **(A)** Deductions:

    $188.40

      84.60

      36.78

       9.24

      37.50

       5.32

    + 42.30

    $404.14

    = $1,200.00 - $404.14 = $795.86

2. **(D)** 23% of $1,260 = .23 x $1,260 = $289.80

3. **(A)** First you must define your universe:

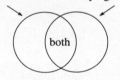

Studying Spanish 64% ⟶ Studying French 52%

both

⟶ Studying neither 28%

The population with which you are concerned excludes the 28%, so 100% - 28% = 72%

With this awareness, you can label the circles and flesh out the formula:

(100 - 28) - [(72 - 64) + (72 - 52)]

4. **(D)** Let's start with this simple chart:

Subject	Grade	Weight
English	90	4
Algebra	84	3
French	75	3
Music	76	1

$$\frac{\text{Sum of weighted grades}}{\text{Sum of weights}} = \frac{(90\times4)+(84\times3)+(75\times3)+(76\times1)}{4+3+3+1}$$

5. **(A)** The a lbs. of nuts are worth a total of ab cents. The c lbs. of nuts are worth a total of cd cents. The value of the mixture is $ab + cd$ cents. Because there are $a + c$ pounds, each pound is worth $\frac{ab+cd}{a+c \text{ cents}}$.

    Because the dealer wants to add 10 cents to each pound for profit, and the value of each pound is in cents, we add 10 to the value of each pound:

$$\frac{ab+cd}{a+c+10}$$

13

The Hour in Review

In this hour, we assuaged your fear of the various types of arithmetic questions you are likely to encounter on the law enforcement exams. Here are some important facts to remember:

- Arithmetic reasoning questions appear on some law enforcement exams—most commonly, on the Treasury Enforcement Examination.

- In most cases, you aren't allowed to use a calculator, so practice working problems on scratch paper.

- Arithmetic reasoning questions rarely require you to memorize long lists of formulas, but they do require that you have a few basic math skills and terms under your belt on test day.

- Read the questions thoroughly and then determine what calculations you have to perform to reach the answer. If you're totally stumped, mark the question, move on, and return to it later.

- Don't estimate your answers—if none of the answers matches the figure you arrive at, choose answer E, "None of the above."

- Remember to stay calm and don't let the numbers and letters scare you. All the types of arithmetic questions you will see can be solved quite easily with a little bit of concentration and simple logic.

Part III

Practice the Exam Questions

Hour **14**

Sample State Trooper Reading Comprehension Exam

What You'll Learn in This Hour

In this hour, you'll test your ability to tackle reading comprehension questions. Follow all the directions closely, marking the best answer to each question. An answer key and detailed answer explanations follow the exam questions.

Here's a list of your goals for this hour:

- Complete the sample exam
- Check your answers and review the answer explanations

Although the questions presented here are actual exam questions, they represent only part of an exam. When you're finished answering questions, carefully check your answers against those provided in the answer key. Then read over all the answer explanations (even the ones you got right—you might find strategies included in the explanations that can help you on other questions you missed).

Answer Sheet

1. Ⓐ Ⓑ Ⓒ Ⓓ   9. Ⓐ Ⓑ Ⓒ Ⓓ   17. Ⓐ Ⓑ Ⓒ Ⓓ

2. Ⓐ Ⓑ Ⓒ Ⓓ   10. Ⓐ Ⓑ Ⓒ Ⓓ   18. Ⓐ Ⓑ Ⓒ Ⓓ

3. Ⓐ Ⓑ Ⓒ Ⓓ   11. Ⓐ Ⓑ Ⓒ Ⓓ   19. Ⓐ Ⓑ Ⓒ Ⓓ

4. Ⓐ Ⓑ Ⓒ Ⓓ   12. Ⓐ Ⓑ Ⓒ Ⓓ   20. Ⓐ Ⓑ Ⓒ Ⓓ

5. Ⓐ Ⓑ Ⓒ Ⓓ   13. Ⓐ Ⓑ Ⓒ Ⓓ   21. Ⓐ Ⓑ Ⓒ Ⓓ

6. Ⓐ Ⓑ Ⓒ Ⓓ   14. Ⓐ Ⓑ Ⓒ Ⓓ   22. Ⓐ Ⓑ Ⓒ Ⓓ

7. Ⓐ Ⓑ Ⓒ Ⓓ   15. Ⓐ Ⓑ Ⓒ Ⓓ

8. Ⓐ Ⓑ Ⓒ Ⓓ   16. Ⓐ Ⓑ Ⓒ Ⓓ

Sample Exam

> **DIRECTIONS:** Carefully read the following paragraphs. Using the answer sheet, mark the correct answers to the questions that follow each paragraph. Base your answers solely on the information supplied in the paragraphs. Allow 50 minutes to complete the exam.

Answer questions 1 through 4 on the basis of the information given in the following passage.

The public often believes that the main job of a uniformed officer is to enforce laws simply by arresting people. In reality, however, many of the situations an
(5) officer deals with do not call for the use of the power of arrest. In the first place, an officer spends much of his or her time preventing crimes from happening by spotting potential violations or suspicious
(10) behavior and taking action to prevent illegal acts. In the second place, many of the situations in which officers are called on for assistance involve elements such as personal arguments, husband and wife
(15) quarrels, noisy juveniles, or emotionally disturbed persons. The majority of these problems do not result in arrests and convictions, and often they do not even involve illegal behavior. In the third place,
(20) even in situations where there seems to be good reason to make an arrest, an officer may have to exercise very good judgment. There are times when making an arrest too soon could touch off a riot,
(25) could result in the detention of a minor offender while major offenders escape, or could cut short the gathering of necessary on-the-scene evidence.

1. The passage implies that most citizens

A. Will start to riot if they see an arrest being made.

B. Appreciate the work that law enforcement officers do.

C. Do not realize that making arrests is only a small part of law enforcement.

D. Never call for assistance unless they are involved in a personal argument or a husband and wife quarrel.

2. According to the passage, one way in which law enforcement officers can prevent crimes from happening is by

A. Arresting suspicious characters.

B. Letting minor offenders go free.

C. Taking action on potential violations.

D. Refusing to get involved in husband and wife fights.

14

3. According to the passage, which of the following statements is not true of situations involving emotionally disturbed persons?

   A.   It is a waste of time to call on law enforcement officers for assistance in such situations.

   B.   Such situations may not involve illegal behavior.

   C.   Such situations often do not result in arrests.

   D.   Citizens often turn to law enforcement officers for help in such situations.

4. The last sentence in the passage mentions "detention of minor offenders." Of the following, which best explains the meaning of the word "detention" as used here?

   A.   Sentencing someone.

   B.   Indicting someone.

   C.   Calling someone before a grand jury.

   D.   Arresting someone.

Answer questions 5 through 8 on the basis of the information given in the following passage.

Automobile tire tracks found at the scene of a crime constitute an important link in the chain of physical evidence. In many cases, tire tracks are the only clues available.
(5) In some areas, unpaved ground adjoins the highway or paved streets. A suspect will often park his or her car off the paved portion of the street when committing a crime, sometimes leaving excellent
(10) tire tracks. Comparison of the tire-track impressions with the tires is possible only when the vehicle has been found. However, the initial problem facing the police is the task of determining what kind of car
(15) probably made the impressions found at the scene of the crime. If the make, model, and year of the car that made the impressions can be determined, it is obvious that the task of elimination is greatly lessened.

5. The one of the following that is the most appropriate title for this passage is

   A.   "The Use of Automobiles in the Commission of Crimes"

   B.   "The Use of Tire Tracks in Police Work"

   C.   "The Capture of Criminals by Scientific Police Work"

   D.   "The Positive Identification of Criminals Through Their Cars"

6. When searching for clear signs left by the car used in the commission of a crime, the most likely place for the police to look would be on the

   A.   Highway adjoining unpaved streets.

   B.   Highway adjacent to paved streets.

   C.   Paved streets adjacent to a highway.

   D.   Unpaved ground adjacent to a highway.

7. Automobile tire tracks found at the scene of a crime are of value as evidence in that they are

A. Generally sufficient to trap and convict a suspect.

B. The most important link in the chain of physical evidence.

C. Often the only evidence at hand.

D. Circumstantial rather than direct.

8. The primary reason that the police try to determine the make, model, and year of the car involved in the commission of a crime is to

A. Compare the tire tracks left at the scene of the crime with the type of tires used on cars of that make.

B. Determine whether the mud on the tires of the suspected car matches the mud in the unpaved road near the scene of the crime.

C. Reduce, to a large extent, the amount of work involved in determining the particular car used in the commission of a crime.

D. Alert the police patrol forces to question the occupants of all automobiles of this type.

Answer questions 9 through 12 on the basis of the information given in the following passage:

When stopping vehicles on highways to check for suspects or fugitives, the police use an automobile roadblock whenever possible. This consists of three cars (5) placed in prearranged positions: Car 1 is parked across the left lane of the roadway with the front diagonally facing toward the center line. Car 2 is parked across the right lane, with the front of the vehicle also (10) toward the center line, in a position perpendicular to car 1 and approximately 20 feet to the rear. Continuing another 20 feet to the rear along the highway, car 3 is parked in an identical manner to car 1. The (15) width of the highway determines the angle or position in which the autos should be placed. In addition to the regular road-

block signs and the use of flares at night only, there is an officer located at both the (20) entrance and exit to direct and control traffic from both directions. This type of roadblock forces all approaching autos to reduce speed and zigzag around the police cars. Officers standing behind the (25) parked cars can most safely and carefully view all passing motorists. Once a suspect is inside the block, it becomes extremely difficult for him or her to crash out.

14

9. Of the following, the most appropriate title for this passage is
   A. "The Construction of an Escape-Proof Roadblock"
   B. "Regulation of Automobile Traffic Through a Police Roadblock"
   C. "Safety Precautions Necessary in Making an Automobile Roadblock"
   D. "Structure of a Roadblock to Detain Suspects or Fugitives"

10. When setting up a three-car roadblock, the relative positions of the cars should be such that
    A. The front of car 1 is placed diagonally to the center line and facing car 3.
    B. Car 3 is placed parallel to the center line and its front faces the right side of the road.
    C. Car 2 is placed about 20 feet from car 1 and its front faces the left side of the road.
    D. Car 3 is parallel to and about 20 feet away from car I.

11. Officers can observe occupants of all cars passing through the roadblock with greatest safety when
    A. Warning flares are lighted to illuminate the area sufficiently at night.
    B. Warning signs are put up at each end of the roadblock.
    C. They are stationed at both the exit and entrance of the roadblock.
    D. They take up positions behind cars in the roadblock.

12. The type of automobile roadblock described in the passage is of value in police work because
    A. A suspect is unable to escape its confines by using force.
    B. It is frequently used to capture suspects with no danger to police officers.
    C. It requires only two officers to set up and operate.
    D. Vehicular traffic within its confines is controlled as to speed and direction.

Answer questions 13 through 15 on the basis of the information given in the following passage.

When Police Officers search for a stolen car, they first check for the color of the car, then for the make, model, year, body damage, and finally for the license number.
(5) The first five checks can be made from almost any angle, while the recognition of the license number is often not immediately apparent. The serial number and motor number, although less likely to be
(10) changed than the easily substituted license number, cannot be observed in initial detection of a stolen car.

13. According to the passage, the one of the following features that is least readily observed in checking for a stolen car in moving traffic is the
    A. License number
    B. Serial number
    C. Model
    D. Make

14. The feature of the car that cannot be determined from most angles of observation is the

A. Make

B. Model

C. Year

D. License number

15. Of the following, the feature of a stolen car that is most likely to be altered by a car thief shortly after the car is stolen is the

A. License number

B. Motor number

C. Color

D. Minor body damage

Answer questions 16 and 17 on the basis of the information given in the following passage.

A survey has shown that crime-prevention work is most successful if the officers are assigned on rotating shifts to provide around-the-clock coverage. An

(5) officer may work for days at a time and then be switched to nights. The prime object of the night work is to enable the officer to spot conditions inviting burglars. Complete lack of, or faulty locations of,

(10) night lights and other conditions that may invite burglars—and that may go unnoticed during the daylight hours—can be located and corrected more readily through night work. Night work also

(15) enables the officer to check local hangouts of teenagers, such as where a teenage dance is held every Friday night. Detectives also join Patrol Officers cruising in radio patrol cars to check on teenagers

(20) loitering late at night and to spot-check local bars for teenagers.

16. The most important purpose of assigning officers to night shifts is to make it possible for them to

A. Correct conditions that may not be readily noticed during the day.

B. Discover the location of and replace missing and faulty night lights.

C. Locate criminal hangouts.

D. Notice things at night that cannot be noticed during the daytime.

17. The shifting of officers that best prevents crime has

A. Day-shift officers rotated to night work.

B. Rotating shifts that provide sufficient officers for coverage 24 hours a day.

C. An officer work around the clock on a 24-hour basis as police needs arise.

D. Rotating shifts to give officers varied experience.

14

Answer questions 18 through 20 on the basis of the information given in the following passage.

In addition to making the preliminary investigation of crimes, Police Patrol Officers should serve as eyes, ears, and legs for the detective division. The patrol division
(5) may be used for surveillance, to serve warrants and bring in suspects and witnesses, and to perform a number of routine tasks for the detectives: this approach increases the time available for tasks that require
(10) their special skills and facilities. It is to the advantage of individual detectives, as well as of the detective division, to have Patrol Officers working in this manner. More cases are cleared by arrest—
(15) and a greater proportion of stolen property is recovered—when, in addition to the detective regularly assigned, a number of Patrol Officers also work on the case. Detectives may stimulate the interest
(20) and participation of Patrol Officers by keeping them informed of the presence, identity, or description of hangouts, associates, vehicles, and methods of operation for each criminal known to be in the
(25) community.

18. According to this passage, a Patrol Officer should

A. Assist the detective in certain routine functions.

B. Be considered for assignment as a detective on the basis of patrol performance.

C. Leave the scene once a detective arrives.

D. Perform as much of the detective's duties as time permits.

19. According to this passage, Patrol Officers should aid detectives by

A. Accepting from detectives assignments that give promise of recovering stolen property.

B. Making arrests of witnesses for the detectives' interrogation.

C. Performing all special investigative work for detectives.

D. Producing for questioning individuals who may aid the detectives in the investigation.

20. According to this passage, detectives can keep Patrol Officers interested by

A. Ascertaining that Patrol Officers are doing investigative work properly.

B. Having Patrol Officers directly under their supervision during an investigation.

C. Informing Patrol Officers of the value of their efforts in crime prevention.

D. Supplying the Patrol Officers with information regarding known criminals in the community.

Answer questions 21 and 22 on the basis of the information given in the following passage.

The medical examiner may contribute valuable data to the investigator of fires that cause fatalities. By careful examination of the bodies of any victims, the *(5)* examiner not only establishes cause of death but may also furnish, in many instances, answers to questions relating to the identity of the victim and the source and origin of the fire. The medical examiner *(10)* is of greatest value to law enforcement agencies because he or she is able to determine the exact cause of death through an examination of tissue of the apparent arson victims. Thorough study of a burned *(15)* body or even of parts of a burned body will frequently yield information that can help clarify problems confronting the arson investigator and the police.

21. According to the passage, the most important task of the medical examiner in the investigation of arson is to obtain information concerning the

    A. Identity of arsonists.
    B. Cause of death.
    C. Identity of victims.
    D. Source and origin of fires.

22. The central thought of the passage is that the medical examiner aids in the solution of crimes of arson when

    A. A person is burned to death.
    B. Identity of the arsonist is unknown.
    C. The cause of the fires is unknown.
    D. Trained investigators are not available.

Answer Key

1.	C	9.	D	17.	B
2.	C	10.	C	18.	A
3.	A	11.	D	19.	D
4.	D	12.	D	20.	D
5.	B	13.	B	21.	B
6.	D	14.	D	22.	A
7.	C	15.	A		
8.	C	16.	D		

14

Answer Explanations

1. **(C)** Refer to the first sentence of the passage.

2. **(C)** Refer to the third sentence of the passage.

3. **(A)** It is stated in the fourth sentence that many of the situations in which police assistance is required involved emotionally disturbed persons.

4. **(D)** A Police Officer arrests; the courts sentence, indict, or call people before a grand jury.

5. **(B)** The passage talks exclusively about tire tracks. No mention is made of autos being used in the commission of crimes, of scientific police work, or of positive identification through cars.

6. **(D)** Refer to the third and fourth sentences of the passage.

7. **(C)** Refer to the second sentence of the passage.

8. **(C)** Refer to the last sentence of the passage.

9. **(D)** The paragraph doesn't state that the type of roadblock mentioned is escape proof, but it does state that the roadblock described will force all approaching vehicles to reduce speed and make it extremely difficult for vehicles to crash out of the roadblock.

10. **(C)** Refer to the fourth sentence of the passage. If the car is parked in the right lane with its front facing the center line, the front is necessarily facing the left side of the road.

11. **(D)** Refer to the next-to-the-last sentence of the passage.

12. **(D)** Refer to the eighth sentence of the passage.

13. **(B)** Refer to the last sentence of the passage.

14. **(D)** Refer to the second sentence of the passage.

15. **(A)** Refer to the last sentence of the passage. The changing of color or the repairing of body damage could not be accomplished in a short period of time.

16. **(D)** Certain conditions that might go unnoticed by day are visible at night, especially lighting problems. Officers notice these on the night shift; building owners thus alerted can make the corrections.

17. **(B)** Refer to the first sentence of the passage.

18. **(A)** The first sentence of the passage states that the Patrol Officer "should serve as eyes, ears, and legs for the detective division." No statement in the passage makes any mention of Police Officers being considered for assignment to the detective division, leaving the scene when detectives arrive, or performing detectives' duties.

19. **(D)** Refer to the second sentence of the passage.

20. **(D)** Refer to the last sentence of the passage.

21. **(B)** Refer to the third sentence of the passage.

22. **(A)** Refer to the first sentence of the paragraph. The medical examiner deals with dead human bodies not with trying to identify arson suspects or with determining the cause of a fire.

HOUR 15

Sample Correction Officer Observation and Memory Exam

What You'll Learn in This Hour

In this hour, you are presented with an excerpt from an actual Observation and Memory exam. To make this test as realistic as possible (or as close to the experience you are likely to have on test day), you should follow all the instructions as if you were taking a real test.

Here is a list of your goals for this hour:

- Take the sample exam
- Check your answers against the answer key
- Review the answer explanations

Answer Sheet

1. (A) (B) (C) (D)	11. (A) (B) (C) (D)	21. (A) (B) (C) (D)
2. (A) (B) (C) (D)	12. (A) (B) (C) (D)	22. (A) (B) (C) (D)
3. (A) (B) (C) (D)	13. (A) (B) (C) (D)	23. (A) (B) (C) (D)
4. (A) (B) (C) (D)	14. (A) (B) (C) (D)	24. (A) (B) (C) (D)
5. (A) (B) (C) (D)	15. (A) (B) (C) (D)	25. (A) (B) (C) (D)
6. (A) (B) (C) (D)	16. (A) (B) (C) (D)	26. (A) (B) (C) (D)
7. (A) (B) (C) (D)	17. (A) (B) (C) (D)	27. (A) (B) (C) (D)
8. (A) (B) (C) (D)	18. (A) (B) (C) (D)	28. (A) (B) (C) (D)
9. (A) (B) (C) (D)	19. (A) (B) (C) (D)	29. (A) (B) (C) (D)
10. (A) (B) (C) (D)	20. (A) (B) (C) (D)	30. (A) (B) (C) (D)

Sample Exam

> **DIRECTIONS:** You will be given 10 minutes to study the following five photographs. Concentrate on each and try to notice and remember as many details as you can. You may not take any notes.

A courtroom scene.

A portion of a cell block.

A car being ticketed.

Civilian employees in the office.

15

A staff training session.

> **DIRECTIONS:** Questions 1 to 30 are based on the five photographs you just studied. On your answer sheet, darken the letter of the multiple-choice answer you select. Answer true or false questions by darkening A for true and B for false. These questions are worth 1/2 point each.

Questions 1 to 6 are based on the photograph of a courtroom.

1. The judge is

   A. Addressing the witness.

   B. Conferring with the attorney.

   C Looking over some papers.

   D. Handing documents to a court officer.

2. The person standing is

   A. Waving papers at the judge.

   B. Curly haired.

   C. Wearing a dark suit.

   D. Looking at the witness.

3. The man in the light suit is wearing dark socks.

   A. True

   B. False

4. Two people can be seen seated in the jury box.

   A. True

   B. False

5. The stenographer is not wearing glasses.

   A. True

   B. False

6. An American flag is to the left of the judge.

   A. True

   B. False

Questions 7 to 12 are based on the photograph of a portion of a prison cell block.

7. The lighting in the cellblock is provided by

   A. Skylights.

   B. Fluorescent tubes.

   C. Spotlights that are not visible in the picture.

   D. Incandescent ceiling fixtures.

8. The cells in the two middle tiers appear to be designed for

   A. One inmate only.

   B. At least two inmates.

   C. Four inmates.

   D. There is no way to tell.

9. Hanging of laundry is a permitted use for the walkway in front of the cells.

   A. True

   B False

10. Two people are seated at a table on the floor of the cellblock.

   A. True

   B. False

15

11. This photograph was taken with many cell doors open.

A. True

B. False

12. Someone has hung a message on the grate of a cell.

A. True

B. False

Questions 13 to 18 are based on the photograph of the car being ticketed.

13. The car is best described as a

A. Four-door sedan.

B. Two-door convertible.

C. Three-door hatchback.

D. Two-door sedan.

14. The automobile is getting a ticket because it

A. Is facing the wrong way down a one-way street.

B. Is parked on the wrong side of the street.

C. Is parked beside a fire hydrant.

D. Has overstayed its meter.

15. The car has whitewall tires.

A. True

B. False

16. The person giving the ticket is wearing a tie.

A. True

B. False

17. This ticketing is occurring on a sunny day.

A. True

B. False

18. There is heavy traffic on the street.

A. True

B. False

Questions 19 to 24 are based on the photograph of civilian employees in the office.

19. The man with glasses is

A. Pointing at his paper with his finger.

B. Reading a magazine.

C. Taking notes.

D. Studying a graph.

20. Behind the man and woman can be seen

A. A row of notebooks.

B. An open box.

C. A telephone.

D. A window.

21. The man who is wearing a tie is wearing glasses.

A. True

B. False

22. There is an empty chair in the room.

A. True

B. False

23. There is a Styrofoam cup on one desk.

A. True

B. False

24. The woman is wearing boots.

A. True

B. False

Questions 25 to 30 are based on the photograph of the staff training session.

25. The person wearing a white jacket is
   A. Looking at the instructor.
   B. Wearing glasses.
   C. Holding a pen.
   D. Sitting in a wooden chair.

26. The man with the mustache is
   A. Left-handed.
   B. African American.
   C. Wearing a turtleneck shirt.
   D. Taking notes.

27. The instructor is pointing to the figures on a chart.
   A. True
   B. False

28. The person to the right of the instructor is speaking or is about to speak.
   A. True
   B. False

29. There are two open books on the table.
   A. True
   B. False

30. The person in the plaid jacket is wearing earrings.
   A. True
   B. False

Answer Key

1.	C	11.	B	21.	B
2.	C	12.	A	22.	B
3.	A	13.	D	23.	A
4.	B	14.	C	24.	B
5.	A	15.	A	25.	C
6.	B	16.	A	26.	D
7.	D	17.	A	27.	B
8.	B	18.	B	28.	A
9.	A	19.	D	29.	A
10.	B	20.	A	30.	B

Answer Explanations

1. **(C)** The judge is studying some papers before him.

2. **(C)** The person standing, presumably an attorney, is wearing a dark suit. He has straight hair and seems to be waiting to proceed.

3. **(A)** The stenographer, who is wearing a light suit. is wearing dark socks.

4. **(B)** Only one person, a woman, can be seen in a corner of the jury box (to the left of the attorney's head).

5. **(A)** The stenographer is not wearing glasses. The judge is wearing glasses, and the witness is wearing dark glasses.

6. **(B)** Whether or not a flag is in the courtroom cannot be determined.

7. **(D)** Incandescent ceiling fixtures can be seen above the walkways.

8. **(B)** A careful look into the cells indicates that they contain bunk beds. There is no way to tell whether there is more than one bunk bed per cell.

9. **(A)** Clothes are hanging along the walkway of the lowest tier.

10. **(B)** There is only one person seated at a table on the floor level.

11. **(B)** The doors to a few cells in the lowest tier appear to be open but most are closed.

12. **(A)** Some message is hanging on the outside of a third-tier cell.

13. **(D)** The car is a full-size two-door hardtop.

14. **(C)** The car is parked beside a fire hydrant.

15. **(A)** The left rear tire has a narrow whitewall strip.

16. **(A)** The ticketing officer is wearing a tie.

17. **(A)** Bright sunshine is reflecting from the car's rear window, and objects are casting heavy shadows.

18. **(B)** There is no traffic at all.

19. **(D)** The man at the right is wearing glasses and is studying a graph.

20. **(A)** There is a row of loose-leaf notebooks on the shelf behind the man and woman seated at the same desk. The open box is behind the other man.

21. **(B)** The man in the suit and tie is not wearing glasses.

22. **(B)** There are no empty chairs in the room.

23. **(A)** The Styrofoam cup is next to the pen in a pen-stand in front of the man in the suit.

24. **(B)** The woman is wearing white low-heeled shoes.

25. **(C)** The woman in the white jacket, with pen in hand, is looking at someone across the table. She is seated in an upholstered chair and is not wearing glasses.

26. **(D)** The man with the mustache is taking notes with his right hand. He is wearing a shirt and tie and is not African American.

27. **(B)** The instructor has her back to the class writing on the chart or board.

28. **(A)** The instructor is intently waiting to hear what he has to say.

29. **(A)** Each of the women seated at the table has a large book open before her.

30. **(B)** If the woman in the plaid suit is wearing earrings, we cannot see them because her hair covers her ears. The other women are wearing earrings.

HOUR 16

Sample Correction Officer Reading Comprehension Exam

What You'll Learn in This Hour

This hour focuses on an excerpt from a Correction Officer Exam, with emphasis on the reading comprehension section. To make this test as realistic as possible (or as close to the experience you are likely to have on test day), you should follow all instructions as if you were taking a real test.

Here's a list of your goals for this hour:

- Take the sample exam
- Review the answers and explanations

Answer Sheet

1. Ⓐ Ⓑ Ⓒ Ⓓ   11. Ⓐ Ⓑ Ⓒ Ⓓ   21. Ⓐ Ⓑ Ⓒ Ⓓ

2. Ⓐ Ⓑ Ⓒ Ⓓ   12. Ⓐ Ⓑ Ⓒ Ⓓ   22. Ⓐ Ⓑ Ⓒ Ⓓ

3. Ⓐ Ⓑ Ⓒ Ⓓ   13. Ⓐ Ⓑ Ⓒ Ⓓ   23. Ⓐ Ⓑ Ⓒ Ⓓ

4. Ⓐ Ⓑ Ⓒ Ⓓ   14. Ⓐ Ⓑ Ⓒ Ⓓ   24. Ⓐ Ⓑ Ⓒ Ⓓ

5. Ⓐ Ⓑ Ⓒ Ⓓ   15. Ⓐ Ⓑ Ⓒ Ⓓ   25. Ⓐ Ⓑ Ⓒ Ⓓ

6. Ⓐ Ⓑ Ⓒ Ⓓ   16. Ⓐ Ⓑ Ⓒ Ⓓ

7. Ⓐ Ⓑ Ⓒ Ⓓ   17. Ⓐ Ⓑ Ⓒ Ⓓ

8. Ⓐ Ⓑ Ⓒ Ⓓ   18. Ⓐ Ⓑ Ⓒ Ⓓ

9. Ⓐ Ⓑ Ⓒ Ⓓ   19. Ⓐ Ⓑ Ⓒ Ⓓ

10. Ⓐ Ⓑ Ⓒ Ⓓ   20. Ⓐ Ⓑ Ⓒ Ⓓ

Sample Exam

DIRECTIONS: Each question has four suggested answers, lettered A, B, C, and D. Decide which one is the best answer. On the sample answer sheet, locate the question number and darken the area corresponding to your answer choice. Allow yourself 40 minutes to answer these questions.

16

Questions 1 through 25 describe situations that might occur in a correctional institution. The institution houses its inmates in cells divided into groups called cell blocks. In answering these questions, assume that you are a Correction Officer.

1. Correction Officers are often required to search inmates and the various areas of the correctional institution for any items that may be considered dangerous or that are not permitted. In making a routine search, officers should not neglect to examine an item just because it is usually regarded as a permitted item. For instance, some innocent-looking object can be converted into a weapon by sharpening one of its parts or by replacing a part with a sharpened or pointed blade. Which of the following objects could most easily be converted into a weapon in this way?

   A. A ball-point pen

   B. A pad of paper

   C. A crayon

   D. A handkerchief

2. "Only authorized employees are permitted to handle keys. Under no circumstances should an inmate be permitted to use door keys. When not in use, all keys are to be deposited with the Security Officer." Which one of the following actions does not violate these regulations?

   A. A Correction Officer has given a trusted inmate the key to a supply room and sent the inmate to bring back a specific item from that room.

   B. A priest comes to make authorized visits to inmates. The Correction Officer is very busy, so he or she gives the priest the keys needed to reach certain groups of cells.

   C. An inmate has a pass to go to the library. A cellblock officer examines the pass and then unlocks the door to let the inmate through.

   D. At the end of the day, a Correction Officer puts the keys in the pocket of his or her street clothes and takes them home.

3. Decisions about handcuffing or restraining inmates are often up to the Correction Officers involved. An officer is legally responsible for exercising good judgment and for taking necessary precautions to prevent harm both to the inmate involved and to others. In which one of the following situations is handcuffing or other physical restraint most likely to be needed?

A. An inmate seems to have lost control of his senses and is banging his fists repeatedly against the bars of his cell.

B. During the past two weeks, an inmate has deliberately tried to start three fights with other inmates.

C. An inmate claims to be sick and refuses to leave his cell for a scheduled meal.

D. During the night, an inmate begins to shout and sing, disturbing the sleep of other inmates.

4. "Some utensils that are ordinarily used in a kitchen can also serve as dangerous weapons—for instance, vegetable parers, meat saws, skewers, and ice picks. These should be classified as extremely hazardous." The most sensible way of solving the problem caused by the use of these utensils in a correctional institution is to

A. Try to run the kitchen without using any of these utensils.

B. Provide careful supervision of inmates using such utensils in the kitchen.

C. Assign only trusted inmates to kitchen duty and let them use the tools without regular supervision.

D. Take no special precautions because inmates are not likely to think of using these commonplace utensils as weapons.

5. "Inmates may try to conceal objects that can be used as weapons or as escape devices. Therefore, routine searches of cells or dormitories are necessary for safety and security." Of the following, it would probably be most effective to schedule routine searches to take place

A. On regular days and always at the same time of day.

B. On regular days but at different times of the day.

C. At frequent but irregular intervals, always at the same time of day.

D. At frequent but irregular intervals and at different times of day.

6. "One of the purposes of conducting routine searches for forbidden items is to discourage inmates from acquiring such items in the first place. Inmates should soon come to realize that only possessors of these items have reason to fear or resent such searches." Inmates are most likely to come to this realization if

A. The searching officer leaves every inmate's possessions in a mess to make it clear that a search has taken place.

B. The searching officer confiscates something from every cell, although he may later return most of the items.

C. Other inmates are not told when a forbidden item is found in an inmate's possession.

D. All inmates know that possession of a forbidden item will result in punishment.

7. Suppose that you are a Correction Officer supervising a work detail of 22 inmates. All 22 checked in at the start of the work period. Making an informal count an hour later, you count only 21 inmates. What is the first action to take?

A. Count again to make absolutely sure how many inmates are present.

B. Report immediately that an inmate has escaped.

C. Try to figure out where the missing inmate could be.

D. Wait until the end of the work period and then make a formal roll call.

8. "The officer who is making a count at night when inmates are in bed must make sure that he sees each man. The rule 'See living breathing flesh' must be followed in making accurate counts." Of the following, which is the most likely reason for this rule?

A. An inmate may be concealing a weapon in a bed.

B. A bed may be arranged to give the appearance of being occupied even when the inmate is not there.

C. Waking inmates for the count is a good disciplinary measure because it shows them that they are under constant guard.

D. It is important for officers on duty at night to have something to keep them busy.

9. "When counting a group of inmates on a work assignment, great care should be taken to ensure accuracy. The count method should be adapted to the number of inmates and to the type of location." Suppose that you are supervising 15 inmates working in a kitchen. Most of them are moving about constantly, carrying dishes and equipment from one place to another. To make an accurate count, which of the following methods would be most suitable under these circumstances?

A. Have the inmates "freeze" where they are whenever you call for a count, even though some of them may be carrying hot pans or heavy stacks of dishes.

B. Have the inmates stop their work and gather in one place whenever it is necessary to make a count.

C. Circulate among the inmates and make an approximate count while they are working.

D. Divide the group into sections according to type of work and assign one inmate in each group to give you the number in his or her section.

16

10. "Officers on duty at entrances must exercise the greatest care to prevent movement of unauthorized persons. At vehicle entrances, all vehicles must be inspected and a record kept of their arrival and departure." Assume that, as a Correction Officer, you have been assigned to duty at a vehicle entrance. Which of the following is probably the best method of preventing the movement of unauthorized persons in vehicles?

A. If passenger identifications are checked when the vehicle enters, no check is necessary when the vehicle leaves.

B. Passenger identification should be checked for all vehicles when the vehicle enters and when it leaves.

C. Passenger identifications need not be checked when the vehicle enters, but should always be checked when the vehicle leaves.

D. Except for official vehicles, passenger identifications should be checked when the vehicle enters and when it leaves.

11. In making a routine search of an inmate's cell, an officer finds various items. Although there is no immediate danger, he is not sure whether the inmate is permitted to have one of the items. Of the following, the best action for the officer to take is to

A. Confiscate the item immediately.

B. Give the inmate the benefit of the doubt and let him keep the item.

C. Consult the rule book or a supervising officer to find out whether the inmate is permitted to have the item.

D. Leave the item in the inmate's cell but plan to report the inmate for an infraction of the rules.

12. It is almost certain that there will be occasional escape attempts or an occasional riot or disturbance that requires immediate emergency action. A well-developed emergency plan for dealing with these events includes not only planning for prevention and control and planning for action during the disturbance, but also planning for steps to be taken when the disturbance is over. When a disturbance is ended, which of the following steps should be taken first?

A. Punish the ringleaders.

B. Give first aid to inmates or other persons who were injured.

C. Make an institutional count of all inmates.

D. Adopt further security rules to make sure that such an incident does not occur again.

13. It is often necessary to make notes about an occurrence that will require a written report or personal testimony. Assume that a Correction Officer has made the following notes for the warden of the institution about a certain occurrence: "10:45 A.M. March 16, 1999. Cellblock A. Robert Brown was attacked by another inmate and knocked to the floor. Brown's head hit the floor hard. He was knocked out. I reported a medical emergency. Dr. Thomas Nunez came and examined Brown. The doctor recommended that Brown be transferred to the infirmary for observation. Brown was taken to the infirmary at 11:15 A.M." Which of the following important items of information is missing or is incomplete in these notes?

A. The time at which the incident occurred.

B. The place where the incident occurred.

C. The names of both inmates involved in the fight.

D. The name of the doctor who makes the medical recommendation.

14. A Correction Officer has made the following notes for the warden about an incident involving an infraction of the rules: "March 29, 1998. Cellblock B-4. Inmates involved were A. Whitman, T. Brach, M. Prulin, M. Verey. Whitman and Brach started the trouble about 7:30. I called for assistance. Officer Haley and Officer Blair responded. Officer Blair got cut, and blood started running down his face. The bleeding looked very bad. He was taken to the hospital and needed 8 stitches." Which of the following items of information is missing or incomplete in these notes?

A. The time and date of the incident.

B. The place of the incident.

C. Which inmates took part in the incident.

D. What the inmates did that broke the rules.

15. Your supervising officer has instructed you to follow a new system for handling inmates' requests. It seems to you that the new system is not going to work very well and that inmates may resent it. What should you do?

A. Continue handling requests the old way, but do not let your supervising officer know that you are doing this.

B. Continue using the old system until you have a chance to discuss the matter with your supervising officer.

C. Begin using the new system, but plan to discuss the matter with your supervising officer if the system really does not work well.

D. Begin using the new system, but make sure that the inmates know that it is not your idea and that you do not approve of it.

16. Inmates who are prison-wise may know a good many tricks for putting something over. For instance, it is an officer's duty to stop fights among inmates. Therefore, inmates who want to distract the officer's attention from something that is going on in one place may arrange for a phony fight to take place some distance away. To avoid being taken in by a trick like this, a Correction Officer should

A. Ignore any fights that break out among inmates.

B. Always make an inspection tour to see what is going on elsewhere before breaking up a fight.

C. Be alert for other suspicious activity when there is any disturbance.

D. Refuse to report inmates involved in a fight if the fight seems to have been phony.

16

17. Copies of the regulations are posted at various locations in the cellblock so that inmates can refer to them. Suppose that one of the regulations is changed, and the Correction Officers receive revised copies to post in their cellblocks. Of the following, the most effective way of informing the inmates about the revision is to

A. Let the inmates know that you are taking down the old copies and putting up new ones in their place.

B. Post the new copies next to the old ones, so that inmates can compare them and learn about the change for themselves.

C. Leave the old copies until you have had a chance to explain the change to each inmate.

D. Post the new copies in place of the old ones and also explain the change orally to the inmates.

18. A *fracture* is a broken bone. In a *simple fracture*, the skin is not broken. In a *compound fracture*, a broken end of the bone pierces the skin. Whenever a fracture is feared, the first thing to do is to prevent motion of the broken part. Suppose that an inmate has just tripped on a stairway and twisted his ankle. He says it hurts badly, but you cannot tell what is wrong merely by looking at it. Of the following, the best action to take is to

A. Tell the inmate to stand up and see whether he can walk.

B. Move the ankle gently to see whether you can feel any broken ends of bones.

C. Tell the inmate to rest a few minutes and promise to return to see whether his condition has improved.

D. Tell the inmate not to move his foot and put in a call for medical assistance.

19. "It is part of institutional procedure that, at specified times during each 24-hour period, all inmates in the institution are counted simultaneously. Each inmate must be counted at a specific time. All movement of inmates ceases from the time the count starts until it is finished and cleared as correct." Assume that, as a Correction Officer, you are making such a count when an inmate in your area suddenly remembers he has an important 9 A.M. clinic appointment. You check his clinic pass and find that it is true. What should you do?

A. Let him go to the clinic even though he may be counted again there.

B. Take him off your count and tell him to be sure that he is included in the count being made at the clinic.

C. Keep him in your count and tell him to inform the officer at the clinic that he has already been counted.

D. Ask him to wait a few minutes until the counting period is over and then let him go to the clinic.

20. "Except in the case of a serious illness or injury (when a doctor should see the inmate immediately), emergency sick calls should be kept to a minimum, and inmates should be encouraged to wait for regular sick-call hours." In which of the following cases is an emergency sick call most likely to be justified?

A. An inmate has had very severe stomach pain for several hours.

B. An inmate has cut his hand and the bleeding has now stopped.

C. An inmate's glasses have been broken, and he is nearly blind without them.

D. A normally healthy inmate has lost his appetite and does not want to eat.

21. "People who have lost their freedom are likely to go through periods of depression, or to become extremely resentful or unpleasant. A Correction Officer can help inmates who are undergoing such periods of depression by respecting their feelings and treating them in a reasonable and tactful manner." Suppose that an inmate reacts violently to a simple request made in a normal, routine manner by a Correction Officer. Of the following, which is likely to be the most effective way of handling the situation?

A. Point out to the inmate that it is his own fault that he is in jail and that he has nobody to blame for his troubles but himself.

B. Tell the inmate that he is acting childishly and that he had better straighten out.

C. Tell the inmate in a friendly way that you can see he is feeling down but that he should comply with your request.

D. Let the inmate know that you are going to report his behavior unless he changes.

22. An inmate tells you. a Correction Officer, of his concern about the ability of his wife and children to pay for rent and food while he is in an institution. Of the following, which is the best action to take?

A. Assure him that his wife and children are getting along fine, although you do not actually know this to be true.

B. Put him in touch with the social worker or the correction employee who handles such problems.

C. Offer to lend him money yourself if his family is really in need.

D. Advise him to forget about his family and start concentrating on his own problems.

23. "It is particularly important to notice changes in the general pattern of an inmate's behavior. When an inmate who has been generally unpleasant and who has not spoken to an officer unless absolutely necessary becomes very friendly and cooperative, something has happened, and the officer should take steps to determine what." Of the following possible explanations, which one is the least likely to be the cause of the change in behavior?

A. The inmate may be planning some kind of disturbance or escape attempt and is trying to fool the officer.

B. The inmate may be trying to get on the officer's good side for some reason of his own.

C. The inmate's friendliness and cooperation may indicate a developing mental illness.

D. The inmate may be overcoming his hostile reactions to his imprisonment.

16

24. As a Correction Officer, you have an idea about a new way of handling a certain procedure. Your method could require a minor change in the regulations, but you are sure that it would be a real improvement. The best thing for you to do is

A. Discuss the idea with your supervisor, explaining why it would work better than the present method.

B. Try your idea on your own cellblock, telling inmates that it is just an experiment and not official.

C. Attempt to get officers on other cellblocks to use your method on a strictly unofficial basis.

D. Forget the whole thing because it might be too difficult to change the regulations.

25. "Correction Officers assigned to visiting areas have a dual supervisory function because their responsibilities include receiving persons other than inmates as well as handling inmates. Here, of all places, it is important for an officer to realize that he is acting as a representative of his institution and that what he is doing is very much like public relations work." Assume that you are a Correction Officer assigned to duty in a visiting area. Which of the following ways of carrying out this assignment is most likely to result in good public relations?

A. You should treat inmates and visitors sternly, because this will let them know that the institution does not put up with nonsense.

B. You should be friendly to inmates, but suspicious of visitors.

C. You should be stern with inmates, but polite and tactful with visitors.

D. You should treat both inmates and visitors in a polite and tactful way.

Answer Key

1.	A	11.	C	21.	C
2.	C	12.	B	22.	B
3.	A	13.	C	23.	C
4.	B	14.	D	24.	A
5.	D	15.	C	25.	D
6.	D	16.	C		
7.	A	17.	D		
8.	B	18.	D		
9.	B	19.	D		
10.	B	20.	A		

Answer Explanations

1. **(A)** Although the corner of a pad of paper might serve as a blunt instrument, actual conversion into a weapon is most feasible with a ball-point pen.

2. **(C)** In choice A, an inmate is handed a key, clearly a violation. In choice B, the priest, although not an inmate, is not an authorized employee, so his being handed a key is a violation. The Correction Officer who takes home the keys in choice D is violating the regulation that keys must be deposited with the Security Officer when not in use.

3. **(A)** The inmate who repeatedly bangs his fists against the bars of his cell is in danger of causing himself bodily harm. This inmate must be restrained.

4. **(B)** A kitchen cannot be operated without certain utensils that can potentially be used as dangerous weapons. The sensible cautionary procedure is to maintain careful supervision in the kitchen.

5. **(D)** The element of surprise is necessary for effective searches. Any pattern to the searches would serve as a warning to inmates to temporarily stash weapons or escape devices in an area not subject to search.

6. **(D)** Choices A and B would have the reverse effect: Inmates would come for fear searches even if they are not guilty. Choice C doesn't serve the purpose at all because inmates would not learn of the punishment that follows possession of a forbidden item.

7. **(A)** Don't jump the gun and sound the alarm on the basis of an informal count, but do make the formal count right away. Then you can act on the basis of the fact if an inmate really is missing.

8. **(B)** Cover of darkness is best for escape, so the officer must be certain that the blanketed heap in the bed is really the inmate.

9. **(B)** To ensure accuracy, you must count inmates yourself, and you must count them when they are not in motion. Endangering their safety is not necessary; you can let the inmates put things down before you count.

10. **(B)** Accomplices may be smuggled into the prison, so vehicles must be checked at entry as well as at exit. Escapees can hide in official vehicles, too, so those vehicles must also be searched.

11. **(C)** A Correction Officer shouldn't act rashly but should always follow through with research and consultations whenever there is a doubt.

12. **(B)** Health and safety always come first. Tend to the injured.

13. **(C)** The reporting officer has forgotten to name the inmate who attacked Brown.

14. **(D)** The officer has neglected to state the nature of the trouble and what rules were broken.

15. **(C)** You must follow your supervisor's instructions. If you have an opportunity to discuss the new methods before they are to go into effect, by all means raise your questions with your supervisor. If you don't have that opportunity, you must start using the new procedures. If they don't work well, speak to your supervisor about the problems you've noted. Professional behavior dictates that you **never** discuss your misgivings with the inmates.

16. **(C)** The rule is that you must act to stop the fight, but you must be aware that the fight might be a diversionary tactic and so must keep alert.

17. **(D)** Never assume literacy. Always explain changes along with your posting.

18. **(D)** Because there is the possibility of a fracture, and a fracture must not be moved, the best policy is to have the inmate sit still and to send for medical assistance.

19. **(D)** This prison rule is stated very clearly. The clinic can wait. Count the prisoner in the proper place at the proper time.

20. **(A)** Severe stomach pains may indicate appendicitis or some other true medical emergency. The other three choices describe problems that can wait until morning.

21. **(C)** Within prison limits, try tact and kindness first.

22. **(B)** The well-being of dependents is a very real concern. The inmate should be introduced to professionals who can contact the family members and take necessary steps to assist them.

23. **(C)** Sudden cooperativeness is not a common sign of impending mental illness. Look for other causes.

24. **(A)** Innovation and initiative are fine qualities, but get permission from your supervisor before making changes.

25. **(D)** You should treat everyone in a polite and tactful way.

Hour **17**

Sample Police Officer Reading Exam

What You'll Learn in This Hour

This hour focuses on an excerpt from a Police Officer exam, with emphasis on the reading comprehension section. To make this test as realistic as possible (or as close to the experience you are likely to have on test day), you should follow all instructions as if you were taking a real test.

Give yourself 50 minutes to answer the questions. If you finish before the time is up, go back and check the answers you marked on the supplied answer sheet.

Here's a list of your goals for this hour:

- Take the sample exam
- Check your answers against the answer key
- Review the answer explanations

Answer Sheet

1. (A) (B) (C) (D)	10. (A) (B) (C) (D)	19. (A) (B) (C) (D)	28. (A) (B) (C) (D)
2. (A) (B) (C) (D)	11. (A) (B) (C) (D)	20. (A) (B) (C) (D)	29. (A) (B) (C) (D)
3. (A) (B) (C) (D)	12. (A) (B) (C) (D)	21. (A) (B) (C) (D)	30. (A) (B) (C) (D)
4. (A) (B) (C) (D)	13. (A) (B) (C) (D)	22. (A) (B) (C) (D)	31. (A) (B) (C) (D)
5. (A) (B) (C) (D)	14. (A) (B) (C) (D)	23. (A) (B) (C) (D)	32. (A) (B) (C) (D)
6. (A) (B) (C) (D)	15. (A) (B) (C) (D)	24. (A) (B) (C) (D)	33. (A) (B) (C) (D)
7. (A) (B) (C) (D)	16. (A) (B) (C) (D)	25. (A) (B) (C) (D)	34. (A) (B) (C) (D)
8. (A) (B) (C) (D)	17. (A) (B) (C) (D)	26. (A) (B) (C) (D)	
9. (A) (B) (C) (D)	18. (A) (B) (C) (D)	27. (A) (B) (C) (D)	

Sample Exam

DIRECTIONS: This part of the test consists of several reading passages, each followed by a number of statements. Analyze each statement on the basis of the material given. Then mark your answer sheet A, B, C, or D.

Mark it A if the statement is entirely true.
Mark it B if the statement is entirely false.
Mark it C if the statement is partially true and partially false.
Mark it D if the statement cannot be judged on the basis of the facts given in the excerpt.

Allow yourself 50 minutes to answer all 34 questions in this exam.

Questions 1 through 5 are to be answered on the basis of the following paragraph.

17

A Sheriff, or other officer or person, who allows a prisoner, lawfully in his custody, in any action or proceedings, civil or criminal, or in any prison under his charge or
(5)   control, to escape or go at large, except as permitted by law, or connives at or assists such escape, or omits an act or duty whereby such escape is occasioned, or contributed to, or assisted is 1. If he
(10) corruptly and willfully allows, connives at, or assists the escape, guilty of a felony; 2. In any other case, guilty of a misdemeanor. Any officer who is convicted of the offense specified forfeits his office and
(15) is forever disqualified to hold any office, or place of trust, honor, or profit, under the constitution or laws of this state.

1. If a prisoner escapes from a guard through no fault of the latter, the guard is not liable to any action.

2. A prison guard assisting the escape of a felon is himself open to a charge constituting felony.

3. A person having legal custody over a prisoner, who unlawfully permits his freedom, is liable to forfeiture of his office if the charge against the prisoner is criminal but is not so liable if the charge is civil.

4. A guard who, through negligence in his duty, permits a prisoner to escape is not open to a criminal charge.

5. A Sheriff illegally permitting a prisoner in a civil action, not under a charge of felony, to go at large may be punished as a misdemeanant.

Questions 6 through 10 are to be answered on the basis of the following paragraph.

A person who gives or offers a bribe to any executive officer, or to a person elected or appointed to become an executive officer, of this state with intent to influence
(5) that person in respect to any act, decision, vote, opinion, or other proceedings as such officer, is punishable by imprisonment in a state prison not exceeding ten years or by a fine not exceeding five thousand dollars,
(10) or by both.

6. An elected executive officer may not generally be punished for accepting a small bribe.

7. An appointed executive officer convicted of accepting a bribe may be punished by either fine or imprisonment.

8. Bribing an executive officer with intent to influence the officer's vote is deemed a criminal act and, in certain instances, may be punishable by life imprisonment.

9. The length of a sentence to which a person is liable after conviction for offering a bribe to an executive officer is limited to ten years.

10. An executive officer accepting a bribe is equally guilty as the person offering the bribe, although the punishment is not as severe.

Questions 11 through 15 are to be answered on the basis of the following paragraph.

A Commissioner of Correction, warden, or other officer or prison guard, employed at any of the prisons who 1. Shall be directly or indirectly interested in any
(5) contract, purchase, or sale, for, by, or on account of such prison; or 2. Accepts a present from a contractor or contractor's agent, directly or indirectly, or employs the labor of a convict or another person
(10) employed in such prison on any work for the private benefit of such commissioner, warden, or guard, is guilty of a misdemeanor, except that the warden shall be entitled to employ prisoners for necessary
(15) household services.

11. A guard who employs the labor of prisoners in his or her own interests is guilty of a misdemeanor, except that such labor may be so employed indirectly.

12. Only a Commissioner of Correction may accept a small present from a contractor, and then only indirectly.

13. In no case may a prison guard be directly interested in a contract in which the prison is a party.

14. It is illegal to employ the labor of a convict in any case.

15. A warden may only indirectly be interested in the sale of merchandise on account of the prison at which he or she is employed.

DIRECTIONS: For this part of the test, each question has four suggested answers, lettered A, B, C, and D. Decide which one is the best answer. On the answer sheet, locate the question number and darken the area corresponding to your answer choice.

Questions 16 through 23 are based on the following excerpt from an annual report of a police department. This material should be read first and then referred to in answering these questions, which are to be answered solely on the basis of the material herein contained.

Legal Bureau

One of the more important functions of this bureau is to analyze and furnish the department with pertinent information concerning federal and state statutes and
(5)   local laws which affect the department, law enforcement, or crime prevention. In addition, all measures introduced in the state legislature and the city council, which may affect this department, are carefully
(10) reviewed by members of the Legal Bureau and, where necessary, opinions and recommendations thereon are prepared. Another important function of this office is the prosecution of cases in the
(15) Criminal Court. This is accomplished by assignment of attorneys who are members of the Legal Bureau to appear in those cases which are deemed to raise issues of importance to the department or questions
(20) of law that require technical presentation to facilitate proper determination; and also in the cases where request is made for such appearances by a magistrate, some other official of the city, or a member of the
(25) force. Attorneys are regularly assigned to prosecute all cases in the Supreme Court. Proposed legislation was prepared and sponsored for introduction in the state legislature and, at this writing, one of these

(30) proposals has already been enacted into law and five others are presently on the governor's desk awaiting executive action. The new law prohibits the sale or possession of a hypodermic syringe or
(35) needle by an unauthorized person. The bureau's proposals awaiting executive action pertain to: an amendment to the Code of Criminal Procedure prohibiting desk officers from taking bail in gambling cases
(40) or in cases mentioned in Section 552, Code of Criminal Procedure; including confidence men and swindlers as jostlers in the Penal Law; prohibiting the sale of switchblade knives of any size to children
(45) under 16; and bills extending the licensing period of gunsmiths.

17

Following is a report of the activities of the bureau during Year 2 as compared with Year 1:

	YEAR 2	YEAR 1
Memoranda of law prepared	83	68
Legal matters forwarded to Corporation Counsel	122	144
Letters requesting legal information	756	807
Letters requesting departmental records	139	111
Matters for publication	26	17
Court appearances of members of bureau	4,678	4,621
Conferences	94	103
Lectures at Police Academy	30	33
Reports on proposed legislation	255	194
Deciphering of codes	79	27
Expert testimony	31	16
Notices to court witnesses	81	55
Briefs prepared	22	18
Court papers prepared	258	

16. One of the functions of the Legal Bureau is to

A. Review and make recommendations on proposed federal laws affecting law enforcement.

B. Prepare opinions on all measures introduced in the state legislature and the city council.

C. Furnish the department with pertinent information concerning all new federal and state laws.

D. Analyze all laws affecting the work of the department.

17. The one of the following that is not a function of the Legal Bureau is

A. Law enforcement and crime prevention.

B. Prosecution of all cases in Supreme Court.

C. Prosecution of cases in Criminal Court.

D. Lecturing at the Police Academy.

18. Members of the Legal Bureau frequently appear in Criminal Court for the purpose of

A. Defending members of the department.

B. Raising issues of importance to the department.

C. Prosecuting all offenders arrested by the members of the department.

D. Facilitating proper determination of questions of law requiring technical presentation.

19. The Legal Bureau sponsored a bill that would

A. Extend the licenses of gunmen.

B. Prohibit the sale of switchblade knives to children of any size.

C. Place confidence men and swindlers in the same category as jostlers in the Penal Law.

D. Prohibit desk officers from admitting gamblers, confidence men, and swindlers to bail.

20. From the report, it is not reasonable to infer that

A. Fewer briefs were prepared in Year 1.

B. The preparation of court papers was a new activity assumed in Year 2.

C. The Code of Criminal Procedure authorizes desk officers to accept bail in certain cases.

D. The penalty for jostling and swindling is the same.

21. According to the report, the activity showing the greatest increase in Year 2 as compared with Year 1 was

A. Matters for publication.

B. Reports on proposed legislation.

C. Notices to court witnesses.

D. Memoranda of law prepared.

22. According to the report, the activity showing the greatest percentage of increase in Year 2 as compared with Year 1 was

A. Court appearances of members of the bureau.

B. Giving expert testimony.

C. Deciphering of codes.

D. Letters requesting departmental records.

23. According to the report, the percentage of bills prepared and sponsored by the Legal Bureau which were passed by the State Legislature and sent to the governor for approval was

A. Approximately 3.1 percent.

B. Approximately 2.6 percent.

C. Approximately 0.5 percent.

D. Not capable of determination from the data given.

17

Answer questions 24 through 27 on the basis of the following statement.

Disorderly conduct, in the abstract, does not constitute any crime known to law; it is only when it tends to a breach of the peace, under the circumstances detailed in section 1458 of the Consolidation Act, that it constitutes a minor offense cognizable by the judge, and when it in fact threatens to disturb the peace, it is a misdemeanor as well under section 675 of the Penal Code as at common law, and not within the jurisdiction of the judge, but of the Criminal Court.

24. Of the following, the most accurate statement on the basis of the preceding paragraph is that

A. An act that merely threatens to disturb the peace is not a crime.

B. Disorderly conduct, by itself, is not a crime.

C. Some types of disorderly conduct are indictable.

D. A minor offense may or may not be cognizable.

25. Of the following, the least accurate statement on the basis of the preceding paragraph is that

A. Disorderly conduct that threatens to disturb the peace is within the jurisdiction of the judge.

B. Disorderly conduct that "tends to a breach of the peace" may constitute a minor offense.

C. Section 1458 of the Consolidation Act discusses a "breach of the peace."

D. Disorderly conduct that "tends to a breach of the peace" is not the same as that which threatens to disturb the peace.

26. The preceding paragraph does not clarify the difference between

A. Jurisdiction of a judge and jurisdiction of the Criminal Court.

B. Disorderly conduct as a crime and disorderly conduct not as a crime.

C. What "tends to a breach of the peace" and what threatens to disturb the peace.

D. A minor offense and a misdemeanor.

27. Of the following generalizations, the one that is best illustrated by the preceding paragraph is that

A. Acts that in themselves are not criminal may become criminal as a result of their effect.

B. Abstract conduct may, in and of itself, be criminal.

C. Criminal acts are determined by results rather than by intent.

D. An act that is criminal to begin with may not be criminal if it fails to have the desired effect.

Questions 28 and 29 pertain to the following section of the Penal Code.

Section 1942. A person who, after having been three times convicted within this state of felonies or attempts to commit felonies, or under the law of any other state, government, or country of crimes which if committed within this state would become felonious, commits a felony, other than murder, first or second degree, or treason, within this state, shall be sentenced upon conviction of such fourth, or subsequent, offense to imprisonment in a state prison for an indeterminate term, the maximum term provided for first offenders for the crime for which the individual has been convicted, but, in any event, the minimum term upon conviction for a felony as the fourth or subsequent offense, shall not be less than fifteen years, and the maximum thereof shall be his natural life.

28. Under the terms of the quoted portion of section 1942 of the Penal Code, a person must receive the increased punishment therein provided if

   A. He or she is convicted of a felony and has been three times previously convicted of felonies.

   B. He or she has been three times previously convicted of felonies, regardless of the nature of his or her present conviction.

   C. His or her fourth conviction is for murder, first or second degree, or treason.

   D. He or she has previously been convicted three times of murder, first or second degree, or treason.

29. Under the terms of the quoted portion of section 1942 of the Penal Code, a person convicted of a felony for which the penalty is imprisonment for a term not to exceed ten years, and who has been three times previously convicted of felonies in this state, shall be sentenced to a term the minimum of which shall be

   A. Ten years

   B. Fifteen years

   C. Indeterminate

   D. His or her natural life

17

In answering questions 30 through 34, the following definitions of crimes should be applied, bearing in mind that all elements contained in the definitions must be present in order to charge a person with that crime.

BURGLARY is the breaking and entering of a building with intent to commit some crime therein.

EXTORTION is the obtaining of property from another, with his or her consent, induced by a wrongful use of force or fear, or under color of official right.

LARCENY is the taking and carrying away of the personal property of another with intent to deprive or defraud the owner of the use and benefit of such property.

ROBBERY is the unlawful taking of the personal property of another from his or her person or in his or her presence, by force or violence or by putting that person in fear of injury, immediate or future, to his or her person or property.

30. If A entered B's store during business hours, tied B to a chair, and then helped himself to the contents of B's cash register, A should, after arrest, be charged with
   A. Burglary
   B. Extortion
   C. Larceny
   D. Robbery

31. If A broke the pane of glass in the window of B's store, stepped in and removed some merchandise from the window, A should, after arrest, be charged with
   A. Burglary
   B. Extortion
   C. Larceny
   D. Robbery

32. If A, after B had left for the day, found the door of B's store open, walked in, took some merchandise, and then left through the same door, he should, after arrest, be charged with

   A. Burglary
   B. Extortion
   C. Larceny
   D. Robbery

33. If A, by threatening to report B for failure to pay to the city the full amount of sales tax he had collected from various customers, induced B to give him the contents of his cash register, A should, after arrest, be charged with
   A. Burglary
   B. Extortion
   C. Larceny
   D. Robbery

34. If A, on a crowded train, put his hand into B's pocket and removed B's wallet without B's knowledge, A should, after arrest, be charged with
   A. Burglary
   B. Extortion
   C. Larceny
   D. Robbery

Answer Key

1.	D	13.	A	25.	A
2.	A	14.	B	26.	D
3.	C	15.	B	27.	A
4.	B	16.	D	28.	A
5.	A	17.	A	29.	B
6.	D	18.	D	30.	D
7.	D	19.	C	31.	A
8.	B	20.	D	32.	C
9.	A	21.	B	33.	B
10.	D	22.	C	34.	C
11.	C	23.	D		
12.	B	24.	B		

17

Answer Explanations

1.   **(D)** (Cannot be judged.) This condition is not referred to in the paragraph at all.

2.   **(A)** (True.) Refer to the fourth line of the paragraph.

3.   **(C)** (Partially true, partially false.) It is true if the charge against the prisoner is of a criminal nature. It is also true if the action is civil. Therefore the statement is partially true and partially false.

4.   **(B)** (False.) Refer to lines 7-8 of the paragraph that reads, "or omits an act of duty...".

5.   **(A)** (True.) Refer to the sixth line of the paragraph (the sentence numbered 2).

6.   **(D)** (Cannot be judged.) There is no reference in the paragraph to the *acceptance* of a bribe.

7.   **(D)** (Cannot be judged.) Again, there is no reference in the paragraph to the acceptance of a bribe. The paragraph refers only to the offering of a bribe.

8.   **(B)** (False.) The maximum time one may be sentenced to prison for the bribing of an executive officer is ten years.

9.   **(A)** (True.) This is stated at the end of the paragraph.

10.   **(D)** (Cannot be judged.) There is no information in the paragraph concerning the punishment of an executive officer who accepts a bribe.

11.   **(C)** (Partially true, partially false.) The first half of the statement is true. The second part, which refers to indirect employment of prisoners, is false.

12.   **(B)** (False.) No employee of the Department of Correction may accept a small present from a contractor. The paragraph does not differentiate one level of employment from the other. Top to bottom, all employees are prohibited from accepting gifts from contractors.

13. **(A)** (True.) This is the implication contained in the regulation.

14. **(B)** (False.) The regulation states that it is illegal to use the labor of a convict for private benefit only.

15. **(B)** (False.) A warden may not have an interest in the sale of merchandise produced or used in the prison directly or indirectly.

16. **(D)** This is stated in the last sentence of the first paragraph.

17. **(A)** There is no implication in the reading that the Legal Bureau has any responsibility in law enforcement or crime prevention.

18. **(D)** This is stated in the second sentence of the second paragraph.

19. **(C)** Refer to the last part of the third paragraph.

20. **(D)** There is nothing in the question in support of this contention.

21. **(B)** The chart provides the following information about the increase in activity in Year 2 as compared with Year 1:

Matters for publication: 9

Reports on proposed legislation: 61

Notices to court witnesses: 26

Memoranda of law prepared: 15

22. **(C)** The chart provides the following information about the percentage of increase in activity in Year 2 as compared with Year 1:

Court appearances of members: 1.2%

Giving expert testimony: 9.4%

Deciphering codes: 19.3%

Letters requesting departmental records: 2.5%

23. **(D)** This information is not contained anywhere in the report.

24. **(B)** Refer to the beginning of the paragraph.

25. **(A)** Disorderly conduct that threatens to disturb the peace is a misdemeanor and is within the jurisdiction of the Criminal Court, not of the judge.

26. **(D)** The paragraph gives examples of minor offense and misdemeanor but does not define either one.

27. **(A)** This inference is supported in the very beginning of the paragraph.

28. **(A)** This is true according to the paragraph, even though the convictions had taken place for crimes committed in other states.

29. **(B)** Refer to the last part of the paragraph.

30. **(D)** A took B's property in B's presence by force using violence (tying B to a chair).

31. **(A)** A broke into B's store taking B's property when B was not present.

32. **(C)** The act of "breaking and entering" was not involved.

33. **(B)** A obtained B's property with B's consent. However, the consent was forthcoming only because A instilled appropriate fear in B's mind.

34. **(C)** A took B's property without B's consent. A's intention was to deprive B of the use of B's property. A's plan for the use of the property is not an element in the crime.

HOUR **18**

Sample State Trooper Arithmetic and General Procedural Skills Exam

What You'll Learn in This Hour

This chapter tests your arithmetic and general procedural skills. Follow all directions closely, marking the best answer to each question. An answer key and detailed answer explanations follow the exam questions.

Here's a list of your goals for this hour:

- Take the sample exam
- Review the answers and explanations

Answer Sheet

1. Ⓐ Ⓑ Ⓒ Ⓓ   21. Ⓐ Ⓑ Ⓒ Ⓓ   41. Ⓐ Ⓑ Ⓒ Ⓓ

2. Ⓐ Ⓑ Ⓒ Ⓓ   22. Ⓐ Ⓑ Ⓒ Ⓓ   42. Ⓐ Ⓑ Ⓒ Ⓓ

3. Ⓐ Ⓑ Ⓒ Ⓓ   23. Ⓐ Ⓑ Ⓒ Ⓓ   43. Ⓐ Ⓑ Ⓒ Ⓓ

4. Ⓐ Ⓑ Ⓒ Ⓓ   24. Ⓐ Ⓑ Ⓒ Ⓓ   44. Ⓐ Ⓑ Ⓒ Ⓓ

5. Ⓐ Ⓑ Ⓒ Ⓓ   25. Ⓐ Ⓑ Ⓒ Ⓓ   45. Ⓐ Ⓑ Ⓒ Ⓓ

6. Ⓐ Ⓑ Ⓒ Ⓓ   26. Ⓐ Ⓑ Ⓒ Ⓓ   46. Ⓐ Ⓑ Ⓒ Ⓓ

7. Ⓐ Ⓑ Ⓒ Ⓓ   27. Ⓐ Ⓑ Ⓒ Ⓓ   47. Ⓐ Ⓑ Ⓒ Ⓓ

8. Ⓐ Ⓑ Ⓒ Ⓓ   28. Ⓐ Ⓑ Ⓒ Ⓓ   48. Ⓐ Ⓑ Ⓒ Ⓓ

9. Ⓐ Ⓑ Ⓒ Ⓓ   29. Ⓐ Ⓑ Ⓒ Ⓓ   49. Ⓐ Ⓑ Ⓒ Ⓓ

10. Ⓐ Ⓑ Ⓒ Ⓓ   30. Ⓐ Ⓑ Ⓒ Ⓓ   50. Ⓐ Ⓑ Ⓒ Ⓓ

11. Ⓐ Ⓑ Ⓒ Ⓓ   31. Ⓐ Ⓑ Ⓒ Ⓓ

12. Ⓐ Ⓑ Ⓒ Ⓓ   32. Ⓐ Ⓑ Ⓒ Ⓓ

13. Ⓐ Ⓑ Ⓒ Ⓓ   33. Ⓐ Ⓑ Ⓒ Ⓓ

14. Ⓐ Ⓑ Ⓒ Ⓓ   34. Ⓐ Ⓑ Ⓒ Ⓓ

15. Ⓐ Ⓑ Ⓒ Ⓓ   35. Ⓐ Ⓑ Ⓒ Ⓓ

16. Ⓐ Ⓑ Ⓒ Ⓓ   36. Ⓐ Ⓑ Ⓒ Ⓓ

17. Ⓐ Ⓑ Ⓒ Ⓓ   37. Ⓐ Ⓑ Ⓒ Ⓓ

18. Ⓐ Ⓑ Ⓒ Ⓓ   38. Ⓐ Ⓑ Ⓒ Ⓓ

19. Ⓐ Ⓑ Ⓒ Ⓓ   39. Ⓐ Ⓑ Ⓒ Ⓓ

20. Ⓐ Ⓑ Ⓒ Ⓓ   40. Ⓐ Ⓑ Ⓒ Ⓓ

Sample Exam

Although the questions in this hour here are actual exam questions, they represent only a partial exam. (Yes, there will be more questions on the real thing!) However, if you can do well on these practice questions, you should be well prepared for the types of questions you will see on test day.

To best simulate test day, give yourself a limited amount of time to answer these questions (50 minutes is a good time frame) and mark your answers on the answer sheet. Then, when you're done, carefully check your answers against those provided in the answer key. Make sure that you read all the answer explanations, even the ones you got right. You may find strategies included in the explanations that can help you on other questions you missed.

Administrative Procedures: Forms

DIRECTIONS: Questions 1 through 5 test your ability to fill out forms correctly. An incident is described requiring that a police form be filled out. Read the questions that apply to the form. For each question, choose the one best answer (A, B, C, or D) and darken the area corresponding to your answer choice on the separate answer sheet.

Answer questions 1 through 5 on the basis of the following passage and the Report of Aid Given form shown on page 239.

Troopers Margaret Firestone and Harry Davis are partners on patrol. They see a man lying on his back on the southwest corner of Capital Highway. Trooper Firestone leaves the patrol car to look at him more closely. The man is dressed in clean clothes and seems to have stopped breathing. Trooper Firestone bends over him, makes a quick inspection, and tells Trooper Davis to send for an ambulance. She begins to administer mouth-to-mouth resuscitation. At this point, the man becomes fully conscious and states that this has happened before. He insists that all he needs is a glass of water. He does not want to go to the hospital, nor does he want to be driven home. Trooper Davis gets a glass of water for the man from a nearby store. The man refuses to give his name and will not wait for the ambulance. He drinks the water, thanks the officers for their help, and walks north on Second, where he disappears from view.

1. Under *Identification*, the correct entry for Place is

   A. Capital Highway

   B. Second and Seventh

   C. Corner of Sixth Avenue and Second Street

   D. Second Avenue North, East Sixth Street

2. Because the man refused to give his name, Trooper Firestone should check the box for

   A. Other, under *Aid Given*

   B. Unknown, under *Identification*

   C. Other, under *Disposition of Case*

   D. Unknown, under *Nature of Illness or Injury*

3. Under *Nature of Problem*, the correct box to check is

   A. Injured

   B. Ill

   C. Neglected

   D. Destitute

4. The correct boxes to check under *Aid Given* are

   A. Food or Water, and Other

   B. Food or Water, and Clothing or Blankets

   C. Artificial Respiration, and Food or Water

   D. Artificial Respiration, and Other

5. Under *Disposition of Case*, Officer Firestone should check the box for

   A. Removed to Hospital

   B. Left in Custody of Friend or Relative

   C. Other

   D. Left at Place of Occurrence

REPORT OF AID GIVEN

Identification

Date _____   Time _____   Place _____

Name of Person Aided _____   [ ] Unknown

Nature of Problem

[ ] Abandoned   [ ] Destitute   [ ] Ill

[ ] Neglected   [ ] Lost   [ ] Injured

Nature of Illness or Injury

[ ] Mental   [ ] Physical   [ ] Unknown

Aid Given

[ ] Artificial Respiration   [ ] Food or Water

[ ] Control of Bleeding   [ ] Clothing or Blankes

[ ] Temporary Splint   [ ] Other

Disposition of Case

[ ] Taken Home   [ ] Left in Custody of Friend or Relative

[ ] Removed to Hospital   [ ] Taken to Morgue

[ ] Left at Place of Occurrence [ ] Other

Name of Officer Report_____

18

Assume that you are a State Trooper. A duty roster (shown here) has been posted in the barracks. Answer questions 6 through 15 on the basis of only this duty roster.

TROOPER'S NAME	MON.	TUES.	WED.	THURS.	FRI.	SAT.	SUN.
T. Adams	A	D	A	A	A	A	A
R. Brown	D	B	A	C	B	B	B
B. Carlos	C	C	C	C	C	C	D
R. Donaldson	A	C	D	A	C	C	C
A. Edwards	B	B	D	A	A	A	A
C. Frederickson	B	D	S	S	C	C	C
H. Galway	A	A	C	C	D	A	A
L. Isaacson	B	B	B	B	D	B	B
D. Jackson	A	A	A	D	C	A	A
R. Karlsen	C	C	D	A	A	A	A
M. Latimer	B	B	B	B	D	B	B
P. Goldberg	C	C	D	B	B	B	B
L. Mulvaney	A	D	A	A	A	A	A

CODE:

A = 8:30 A.M. to 4:30 P.M.

B = 4:30 P.M. to 12:30 A.M.

C = 12:30 A.M. to 8:30 A.M.

D = Day Off

6. The Troopers who have only one tour during the week are

   A. Adams and Carlos

   B. Karlsen and Mulvaney

   C. Galway and Latimer

   D. Edwards and Galway

7. The one of the following Troopers who shifts from Tour A to Tour C is

   A. Isaacson

   B. Jackson

   C. Karlsen

   D. Goldberg

8. The Troopers assigned exclusively to Tour B are

   A. Isaacson and Latimer

   B. Brown and Edwards

   C. Goldberg and Brown

   D. Edwards and Frederickson

9. The one of the following Troopers who shifts only from Tour C to Tour B is

   A. Latimer

   B. Brown

   C. Galway

   D. Goldberg

10. The one of the following Troopers who is assigned on all three tours during the week is

A. Donaldson

B. Brown

C. Karlsen

D. Galway

11. The one of the following Troopers who is assigned exclusively to Tour A is

A. Galway

B. Frederickson

C. Mulvaney

D. Latimer

12. The following pairs of Troopers who could be assigned as partners on highway patrol each day of the week are

A. Galway and Jackson

B. Edwards and Frederickson

C. Latimer and Goldberg

D. Adams and Mulvaney

13. The following pairs of Troopers who could be assigned as partners on highway patrol each day of the week are

A. Carlos and Galway

B. Isaacson and Latimer

C. Donaldson and Jackson

D. Latimer and Mulvaney

14. The one of the following Troopers who is assigned exclusively to Tour C is

A. Donaldson

B. Carlos

C. Goldberg

D. Galway

15. The one of the following who could have the least regular sleeping hours is

A. Karlsen

B. Goldberg

C. Brown

D. Edwards

Arithmetic Questions Based on Mileage

16. On a certain map, a distance of 10 miles is represented by $\frac{1}{2}$ inch. If two towns are $3\frac{1}{2}$ inches apart on this map, the actual distance in miles between the two towns is

A. 35 miles

B. 65 miles

C. 70 miles

D. 80 miles

17. If a highway patrol car averages 18 miles to a gallon of gasoline, how many gallons of gasoline will be needed on a trip of 369 miles?

A. $20\frac{1}{2}$ gallons

B. 28 gallons

C. 15 gallons

D. 12 gallons

18. A distance of 25 miles is represented by $2\frac{1}{2}$ inches. On the map, 1 inch is therefore

A. 5 miles

B. 10 miles

C. 15 miles

D. 20 miles

19. On a road map, $\frac{1}{4}$ inch represents 8 miles of actual road distance. How many miles apart are two towns that are represented by points $2\frac{1}{8}$ inches apart on the map?

A. 32 miles

B. 64 miles

C. 68 miles

D. 72 miles

20. A family is planning a trip of 4,000 miles. Later, they increase the estimated mileage by 25 percent. They plan to average 250 miles per day. How many days will the trip take?

A. 20 days

B. 40 days

C. 60 days

D. None of these

Calendar-Based Calculations

21. A State Trooper, while completing his report of a multicar accident, should know that during a year in which the 1st of November falls on a Saturday, an accident that occurred on October 13th happened on

A. Monday

B. Tuesday

C. Wednesday

D. Thursday

22. If the last day of June occurs on a Sunday, June 1st will have fallen on

A. Monday

B. Tuesday

C. Saturday

D. Thursday

23. If, during a given year, Christmas is celebrated on a Thursday, the first of that month of December falls on

A. Monday

B. Tuesday

C. Wednesday

D. Thursday

24. A State Trooper, before testifying in court, notes from his memorandum book that he had made an arrest on November 6th. If he were asked to testify in court about the day of the week on which the arrest took place, he could do so by

A. Determining the number of days from election day.

B. Determining the number of days from the third Thursday in the month.

C. Counting back from his last payday.

D. Determining the day on which that month began.

25. During the year 1985, one month contained all the days of the week, each only four times. The month was

A. March

B. September

C. February

D. October

General Practices and Procedures: Patrol

26. A highway has two lanes, one in each direction. The lanes are separated by a yellow line. Cars are permitted to pass when the yellow line is dotted. When the yellow line is solid or double, passing is forbidden. Further on, the solid line occurs as the highway climbs a hill. The solid line is necessary to prevent

   A. Cars passing each other in the face of oncoming traffic that cannot be seen.

   B. Motorists attempting to pass slow-moving vehicles.

   C. Truck drivers crawling up a hill and blocking traffic.

   D. Cars in the right lane being unable to drive onto the shoulder of the road in an emergency.

27. Many states have laws to control and penalize motorists who drive while intoxicated (DWI). Such laws are most effective in instances where

   A. Troopers stop and check all vehicles.

   B. All DWI operators are given jail sentences.

   C. Traffic restrictions are enforced strictly.

   D. Enforcement is combined with publicity about the dangers of DWI.

28. A State Trooper is patrolling a busy highway and passes a small pickup truck driven by a person who appears to be a young girl. The trooper is concerned because

   A. The girl could get in trouble.

   B. Motor vehicles should not be driven by underage persons who may not be licensed operators.

   C. Drivers of other vehicles may be distracted by this pickup truck.

   D. The truck could be involved in an accident.

29. Large. slow-moving vehicles, such as garbage-collection or building-material trucks, often cause passenger-car drivers to become impatient and irritable. The best one of the following practices that a trooper should enforce to avoid trouble in these situations is

   A. Keep slow-moving vehicles in one right lane.

   B. Order all slow-moving vehicles off the highway onto side roads.

   C. Give operators of slow-moving vehicles court summonses.

   D. All of the above.

18

30. Posted symbols used as highway signs are placed not only for the convenience of motorists but also for safety precautions. A double zigzag line near the top of a hill indicates

A. A steep, straight incline on descent from the top.

B. A curve on descent from the hill with an obstructed view of oncoming traffic.

C. An intersecting road at the top of the hill.

D. An intersection at the bottom of the hill with an obstructed view of oncoming traffic.

31. At a certain highway intersection, left and right turns are permitted in any direction at all hours on the green signal light. Right-turns-only are permitted on the red signal light. In patrolling this intersection, the Highway Patrol Trooper should mainly be concerned with

A. Left turns against the red signal light.

B. Right turns on the green signal light.

C. Traffic volume during the night hours.

D. Traffic volume during daylight hours.

32. State Troopers on highway patrol must stop to assist motorists involved in accidents that may have resulted in personal injury. The major concern of the highway patrol is to

A. Keep traffic moving as efficiently as possible.

B. Call for emergency medical assistance.

C. See that motorists involved have each other's license number and insurance company's name.

D. All of the above.

33. A State Trooper assigned to highway patrol passes two motorists who appear to be arguing over some body damage to their vehicles. Traffic is restricted to one lane moving slowly past the scene. The most important action for the trooper to take is to

A. Stop the argument.

B. Direct traffic so that motorists do not stop to observe the scene.

C. Call for assistance to direct traffic and move the vehicles.

D. Arrest the motorists.

34. Automobile accidents unfortunately often result in serious injury. The one of the following that is the primary duty of the State Trooper is to

A. Render first aid.

B. Call for emergency medical service assistance immediately.

C. Contact relatives of the injured.

D. Direct traffic at the site of the accident.

35. A State Trooper is on highway patrol on a median-barrier-divided highway and observes two cars that appear to be in a high-speed chase but are in the lanes going in the opposite direction. The Trooper should

A. Jump the barrier to follow the two cars.

B. Speed in the same direction he has been following until he finds a legal crossing through the median barrier.

C. Radio for other police vehicles to investigate.

D. Ignore the situation.

Answer questions 36 through 45 on the basis of the diagram shown below.

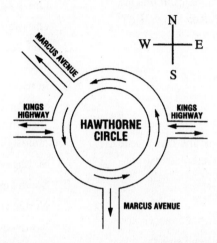

36. In the traffic circle shown above, vehicles traveling from east to west must

    A. Drive north around the circle.

    B. Drive south around the circle.

    C. Cross Marcus Avenue south and proceed thereon.

    D. Drive completely around the circle.

37. In the traffic circle shown above, Marcus Avenue

    A. Flows from east to west.

    B. Flows from north to south.

    C. Flows south to northwest.

    D. Is a dead-end road.

38. The traffic circle shown above provides a safe passage for vehicles chiefly because

    A. The circle separates traffic going in different directions, thus avoiding left and right turns.

    B. It provides a means of exit from Kings Highway.

    C. It can allow for maximum traffic speed.

    D. Highway patrols can observe traffic from various stationary positions.

39. A disadvantage of the traffic circle shown above is that

    A. Distance traveled is modified by time saved.

    B. Traffic flow within the circle is one-way.

    C. To get to Marcus Avenue south from Kings Highway going west, a vehicle would have to drive almost $\frac{3}{4}$ of the way around the circle.

    D. Traffic volume can modify traffic patterns.

40. To go east along Kings Highway, vehicles coming from the west travel around the circle

    A. South and east

    B. North and west

    C. North and east

    D. South and west

18

41. In examining the preceding map, a vehicle driver could consider traveling around the circle to reverse direction on Kings Highway by driving

A. Clockwise

B. Counterclockwise

C. Either direction

D. None of the above

42. In examining the map of the Hawthorne Traffic Circle, it is most reasonable to conclude that

A. U-turns are forbidden.

B. U-turns are feasible but unnecessary.

C. There are two dead-end streets.

D. None of the above.

43. Marcus Avenue vehicles can travel

A. One-way northwest

B. One-way south

C. Both northwest and south from the circle

D. In two-way traffic in either direction

44. A vehicle driving east on Kings Highway and desiring to enter Marcus Avenue South must drive in the traffic circle

A. Southeast

B. Southwest

C. Northeast

D. Northwest

45. Reversing traffic around the traffic circle would necessitate reversal of the direction on

A. Marcus Avenue

B. Kings Highway

C. Marcus Avenue north only

D. None of the above

For questions 46 through 50, refer to the following direction indicator:

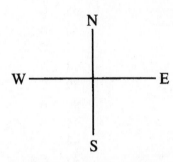

46. A vehicle proceeding north and veering diagonally right is said to be traveling

  A. Northeast

  B. Northwest

  C. Southeast

  D. None of the above

47. A vehicle proceeding diagonally northwest and veering right is said to be traveling

  A. Northwest

  B. North by northwest

  C. North by northeast

  D. North

48. A vehicle proceeding east and veering right diagonally toward the southeast is said to be traveling

  A. East by northeast

  B. East by southeast

  C. South by southeast

  D. North by northeast

49. In describing a location as south and west of a right-angle intersection, a Trooper would be required to indicate a

  A. Southbound road with a right turn at the closest intersection to the destination.

  B. Southbound road with a left turn at the closest intersection to the destination.

  C. Westbound road with a left turn at the closest intersection to the destination.

  D. Southwest path that is available only to pedestrians.

50. In describing a location as north and west of a right-angle intersection, a trooper would be required to indicate a

  A. Northbound road with a right turn at the closest intersection to the destination.

  B. Northbound road with a left turn at the closest intersection to the destination.

  C. Westbound road with a right turn at the closest intersection to the destination.

  D. Westbound road with an alternate northbound road in an easterly diagonal direction.

18

Answer Key

1.	A	18.	B	35.	C
2.	B	19.	C	36.	A
3.	B	20.	A	37.	C
4.	C	21.	A	38.	A
5.	C	22.	C	39.	C
6.	A	23.	A	40.	A
7.	B	24.	D	41.	B
8.	A	25.	C	42.	A
9.	D	26.	A	43.	C
10.	B	27.	D	44.	A
11.	C	28.	B	45.	D
12.	D	29.	A	46.	A
13.	B	30.	B	47.	B
14.	B	31.	A	48.	B
15.	C	32.	B	49.	A
16.	C	33.	C	50.	B
17.	A	34.	B		

Answer Explanations

For answers 1 through 5, no explanations are necessary.

6. **(A)** Troopers Adams and Carlos are the only ones who have one tour listed next to their names. Therefore, A is the only answer. Karlsen, Galway, and Edwards each have two tours. Mulvaney and Latimer have one tour but are partners with others who have two tours; therefore, the other options are not correct.

7. **(B)** Jackson shifts from Tour A to Tour C on Friday. Isaacson is entirely on Tour B. Karlsen goes from Tour C to Tour A, and Goldberg goes from Tour C to Tour B.

8. **(A)** An inspection of the table shows that only Isaacson and Latimer are on Tour B during the entire week. Goldberg goes from Tour C to Tour B on Thursday. Brown shifts from Tour B to Tour A, to Tour C, and then to Tour B. Edwards shifts from Tour B to Tour A on Thursday, and Frederickson shifts from Tour B to Tour A and Tour C.

9. **(D)** Goldberg is the only Trooper of those listed who shifts from Tour C to Tour B. Latimer is only on Tour B, Brown is on all three tours, and Galway goes from Tour A to Tour C.

10. **(B)** As noted in the explanation for question 8, Brown is assigned to all three tours. Donaldson, Karlsen, and Galway have two tours each.

11. **(C)** Of the choices given, Mulvaney is the only one assigned to Tour A during the entire week. Galway is on Tours A and C. Frederickson is on all three tours, and Latimer is on Tour B for the entire week.

12. **(D)** Adams and Mulvaney are assigned to Tour A each day of the week and therefore could be assigned as partners for the week. Galway, Jackson, Goldberg, Edwards, and Frederickson change tours. Latimer is on Tour B.

13. **(B)** Isaacson and Latimer are both assigned to Tour B each day of the week. Mulvaney and Latimer are on different tours, as are Carlos and Galway. Donaldson and Jackson shift tours during the week.

14. **(B)** Of the choices given, Carlos is the only one assigned to Tour C. Donaldson, Goldberg, and Galway shift tours during the week.

15. **(C)** Trooper Brown has all three tours during the week, therefore Brown's sleeping hours change Tuesday, Wednesday, and Friday. Karlsen has only two duty tours with a day off between; the same applies to Goldberg and Edwards.

16. **(C)** 10 miles= $\frac{1}{2}$ inch

20 miles = 1 inch

60 miles = 3 inches

Therefore, $3\frac{1}{2}$ inches = 70 miles

17. **(A)** Divide 369 by 18. The answer is 20 $\frac{1}{2}$ gallons.

18. **(B)** 25 divided by $2\frac{1}{2}$ = 25 divided by $\frac{5}{2}$ = 25 x $\frac{2}{5}$ = $\frac{50}{5}$ = 10

19. **(C)** $\frac{1}{4}$ inch = 8 miles

1 inch=8 x 4 = 32 miles

2 inches=32 x 2 = 64 miles

$\frac{1}{8}$ inch = $\frac{1}{2}$ of $\frac{1}{4}$ inch

Therefore, $\frac{1}{8}$ inch = 4 miles

Total for $2\frac{1}{8}$ inches = 68 miles

20. **(A)** 25 percent of 4,000 = 1,000

Total mileage is 5,000

5,000 divided by 250 = 20 days

21. **(A)** Monday.

OCTOBER

S	M	T	W	Th	F	S
12	13					
19	20	21	22	23	24	25
26	27	28	29	30	31	1

22. **(C)** Saturday.

JUNE

S	M	T	W	Th	F	S
						1
2						
9						
16						
23	24	25	26	27	28	29
30						

18

23.   (A) Monday.

DECEMBER

S	M	T	W	Th	F	S
	1	2	3	4		
				11		
				18		
				25		

24.   **(D)** The date of the election day varies (it is the first Tuesday after the first Monday in November, regardless of the date); so answer A is incorrect. The third Thursday is far ahead of the 6th of November, so answer B is incorrect. Counting back from the last payday would be indeterminate depending on the day of the court testimony. so answer C is incorrect. Answer D is the correct and logical calculation. If November 1st falls on a Sunday, the sixth day would be Thursday, 6 days after.

25.   **(C)** February has 28 days. Each week contains 7 days. 28 is evenly divisible by 4.

26.   **(A)** The use of a solid line dividing a highway with traffic in both directions prevents cars from passing each other by driving in the lane for traffic going in the opposite direction. This avoids head-on collisions. Answers B and C are not relevant, and answer D is not affected by the lines.

27.   **(D)** Publicity as a form of education is often used to aid law enforcement; this answer specifically cites public awareness efforts, and thus provides the best response. Answer A is incorrect because of the word *all*. Answers B and C may be part of the law enforcement plan but aren't necessarily obvious to the public at large.

28.   **(B)** All states have a minimum age for driving vehicles. Answers A, C, and D are speculative.

29.   **(A)** This is the most common practice. Answer B would be impossible to enforce. There is no stated law against slow-moving vehicles, so answer C is incorrect. For these reasons, answer D is inoperative.

30.   **(B)** A zigzag line logically means a curve or curves. There is no need for a zigzag line if the road is straight.

31.   **(A)** Of the four options given, answer A is the only one that is forbidden by the terms of the question and is a general prohibition to motorists.

32.   **(B)** No explanation necessary.

33.   **(C)** Two conditions are stated in the question: The motorists are arguing and the traffic is moving slowly. Because the Trooper cannot handle both situations, he would be wise to call for assistance.

34.   **(B)** The primary duty of the Trooper is to ensure that victims get medical treatment as soon as possible. All the other choices, although important, are secondary considerations.

35.   **(C)** The Trooper cannot jump his vehicle over a median barrier without considerable risk to himself, his vehicle, and others. If he continues in the same direction, even at high speed, he would still lose time. Because he cannot ignore such an obviously suspicious occurrence, his best action is to use his radio.

36.   **(A)** Note the arrows in the circle. If you enter the circle from the right of the map, you will be going from east to west. See now that the arrow goes northerly to get around the circle.

37. **(C)** This answer can be determined by looking at the map. Marcus Avenue leaves the circle at the bottom of the map going south; it leaves the top of the map going northwest.

38. **(A)** Answer A is clearly correct as shown on the map by the arrows within the circle.

39. **(C)** Note that the question asks for a *disadvantage*. If you look at the right side of the map, you will see the arrow going from east to west. After entering the circle, the arrow goes only north, then west, and then southeast. Thus a vehicle would have to drive $\frac{3}{4}$ of the way around the circle.

40. **(A)** This question is the opposite of question 39. If you look at the left side of the map and at the cross compass, you see Kings Highway going east. After entering the circle, a vehicle must "turn down south" and then "go up east."

41. **(B)** This question is self-explanatory. If you imagine this map placed on a clock face, the arrows go opposite to the direction of the minute hand.

42. **(A)** Answer A is clearly the answer because traffic in the circle is going only one way. Because a dead-end street has no means of exit (and all the roads in the diagram clearly empty into the circle and continue beyond the borders of the diagram), answer C is false. Answer B is false because the traffic goes in one direction around the circle.

43. **(C)** This question can be explained by referring to question 37 and its explanation.

44. **(A)** Looking at the left side of the map, you will see the arrow going east. The vehicle would enter the traffic circle in a southerly direction and go around for a short distance in an easterly direction to exit at Marcus Avenue South.

45. **(D)** This question is understandable if you place the map on a clock; "reversal of traffic" would mean a clockwise direction. Because all the streets are either two-way or exit from the circle, there is no need to change direction for any accessible street.

18

Explanation for Compass Direction Questions

In answering questions on compass directions, the reader should imagine that facing forward is north, the right hand is east, the left hand is west, and the rear is south. In a circular view, the compass may be depicted as shown here:

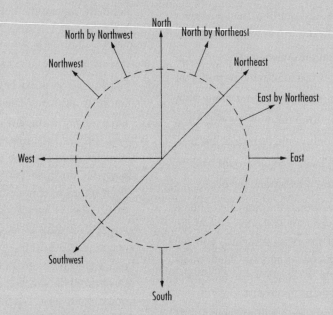

The directions between the four points are stated in terms of the nearest quarter direction. Thus, going from north to east, the compass runs like this: north by northeast, northeast, east by northeast, east.

Diagonally opposite northeast is southwest.

46. **(A)** Note the introduction: veering right moves toward the east.

47. **(B)** See the preceding diagram: To the right of northwest is north by northwest.

48. **(B)** If the reader faces north and then turns right, he or she will be facing east. If the reader continues to veer right, the direction is east by southeast.

49. **(A)** Following the circular diagram above, the vehicle would go south and then make a right turn to go west.

50. **(B)** Northwest is shown on the preceding diagram as a leftward direction from north of the center of the circle.

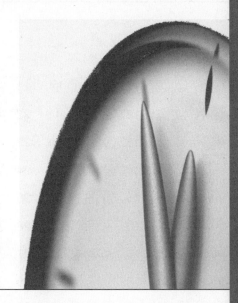

HOUR 19

Sample State Trooper Investigative Judgment Exam

What You'll Learn in This Hour

This hour focuses on an excerpt from a State Trooper exam, with emphasis on the Investigative Judgment section. To make this test as realistic as possible (or as close to the experience you are likely to have on test day), you should follow all the instructions as if you were taking a real test. Where you're instructed to answer questions about material without referring back to that material, don't cheat. Stick with the times given by the instructions. Use this sample section to practice the questions *and* the test-taking process itself.

Here are your goals for this hour:

- Take the sample exam
- Review the answers and explanations

Answer Sheet

1. Ⓐ Ⓑ Ⓒ Ⓓ   11. Ⓐ Ⓑ Ⓒ Ⓓ   21. Ⓐ Ⓑ Ⓒ Ⓓ

2. Ⓐ Ⓑ Ⓒ Ⓓ   12. Ⓐ Ⓑ Ⓒ Ⓓ   22. Ⓐ Ⓑ Ⓒ Ⓓ

3. Ⓐ Ⓑ Ⓒ Ⓓ   13. Ⓐ Ⓑ Ⓒ Ⓓ   23. Ⓐ Ⓑ Ⓒ Ⓓ

4. Ⓐ Ⓑ Ⓒ Ⓓ   14. Ⓐ Ⓑ Ⓒ Ⓓ   24. Ⓐ Ⓑ Ⓒ Ⓓ

5. Ⓐ Ⓑ Ⓒ Ⓓ   15. Ⓐ Ⓑ Ⓒ Ⓓ   25. Ⓐ Ⓑ Ⓒ Ⓓ

6. Ⓐ Ⓑ Ⓒ Ⓓ   16. Ⓐ Ⓑ Ⓒ Ⓓ   26. Ⓐ Ⓑ Ⓒ Ⓓ

7. Ⓐ Ⓑ Ⓒ Ⓓ   17. Ⓐ Ⓑ Ⓒ Ⓓ   27. Ⓐ Ⓑ Ⓒ Ⓓ

8. Ⓐ Ⓑ Ⓒ Ⓓ   18. Ⓐ Ⓑ Ⓒ Ⓓ   28. Ⓐ Ⓑ Ⓒ Ⓓ

9. Ⓐ Ⓑ Ⓒ Ⓓ   19. Ⓐ Ⓑ Ⓒ Ⓓ   29. Ⓐ Ⓑ Ⓒ Ⓓ

10. Ⓐ Ⓑ Ⓒ Ⓓ   20. Ⓐ Ⓑ Ⓒ Ⓓ   30. Ⓐ Ⓑ Ⓒ Ⓓ

Sample Exam

DIRECTIONS: For each question, choose the one best answer (A, B, C, or D) and darken the area corresponding to your answer choice on the separate answer sheet. You should allow yourself 40 minutes to answer these 30 sample questions.

Questions 1 through 15 are to be answered on the basis of the description of the police action that follows. You will have 10 minutes to read and study the description. Then you must answer the 15 questions about the incident without referring back to the description of the incident.

State Police Officers Smith and Jones were working a midnight-to-8-A.M. tour of duty. It was a Saturday morning in the month of July, and the weather was clear. At about 4:30 A.M., they received a radio call reporting a burglary in progress at 777 Seventh Street, the address of an appliance store.

After their arrival at the scene, the Troopers could not find any evidence of a break-in. However, as they continued their investigation, they heard noises coming from the rear of the building. As they raced to the rear of the building, they saw four people alighting from the roof, by way of a ladder, and climbing over a fence that led to the rear of a warehouse. The Troopers climbed over the fence and observed two people running into an alleyway on the west side of the warehouse, and the other two people running into a parking lot on the east side of the warehouse.

Smith, using a walkie-talkie, called for assistance and proceeded to give chase after the two persons who had entered the alley. The description of these two individuals was as follows: One was a white male with long blond hair, wearing light pants, a blue shirt, and white sneakers; he was carrying what appeared to be a portable TV set. The other was also a white male, this one with short dark hair, wearing dungarees, a white T-shirt,

and cowboy boots, and carrying what appeared to be a portable cassette-stereo-radio.

Jones gave chase to the two individuals who had entered the parking lot. The description of these two individuals was as follows: One was an Hispanic male with long dark hair, wearing dark pants, a yellow shirt, and dark shoes, and carrying what appeared to be a video recorder. The other was a black male with a bald head, wearing dungarees, a white T-shirt, and white sneakers and carrying what appeared to be a baseball bat and a portable TV set.

As Smith emerged from the alley onto the sidewalk, the Trooper again observed the two individuals he had been chasing. They were entering a dark blue Chevrolet with a license plate beginning with the letters *AKG*. The vehicle drove west on Seventh Street. The male with the long blond hair appeared to be driving.

As Jones reached the parking lot, he observed the two individuals he was pursuing speed off in a white station wagon, heading west on Seventh Street. The license plate could not be discerned. Officer Jones found a broken portable TV set in the parking lot.

Smith broadcast this additional information, and both officers then quickly returned to their radio car to conduct a search of the area.

Do NOT refer back to the preceding description while answering questions 1 through 15.

1. Officers Smith and Jones responded to a "burglary in progress" call at approximately

    A. Midnight

    B. 8:00 A.M.

    C. 4:30 P.M.

    D. 4:30 A.M.

2. The suspects in the burglary gained entrance to the store by

    A. Breaking a front window.

    B. Breaking a rear window.

    C. Breaking in from an adjoining warehouse.

    D. Using a ladder to get to the roof.

3. The suspects, when fleeing from the burglary,

    A. All ran into an alleyway.

    B. All ran into a parking lot.

    C. All ran into a warehouse.

    D. Went in different directions.

4. The white male with the long blond hair was carrying what appeared to be a

    A. Portable TV set

    B. Portable cassette-stereo-radio

    C. Video recorder

    D. Portable cassette player

5. The Hispanic male was carrying what appeared to be a

    A. Video recorder

    B. Portable cassette-stereo-radio

    C. Portable TV set

    D. Portable cassette player

6. The white male with the short hair was carrying what appeared to be a

    A. Portable TV set

    B. Portable cassette-stereo-radio

    C. Video recorder

    D. Portable cassette player

7. The suspect wearing cowboy boots was the

    A. White male with long blond hair

    B. Black male

    C. Hispanic male

    D. White male with short hair

8. The suspect wearing light pants and a blue shirt was the

    A. Black male

    B. White male with long blond hair

    C. Hispanic male

    D. White male with short hair

9. The suspect wearing dark pants and a yellow shirt was the

    A. White male with long blond hair

    B. Black male

    C. White male with short hair

    D. Hispanic male

10. When the suspects were fleeing, the two white males entered a

    A. Blue station wagon with unknown license plates.

    B. White station wagon with license plates beginning with *AKG*.

    C. Blue Chevrolet with license plate beginning with the letters *AKG*.

    D. White Chevrolet with unknown license plates.

11. From reading the description of the incident, one could assume

    A. That Seventh Street is one-way westbound.

    B. That Seventh Street is a two-way street.

    C. That Seventh Street is one-way eastbound.

    D. None of the above.

12. After entering the parking lot, Jones found a broken portable TV set that had apparently been dropped by the

    A. White male with blond hair

    B. White male with dark hair

    C. Black male

    D. Hispanic male

13. The black male was

    A. Bald and wearing dark pants, a yellow shirt, and dark shoes.

    B. Bald and wearing dungarees, a white T-shirt, and white sneakers.

    C. Wearing dungarees, a white T-shirt, and cowboy boots and had dark hair.

    D. Bald and wearing light pants and a blue shirt.

14. The suspect who was carrying the baseball bat was also carrying what appeared to be a

    A. Portable TV set

    B. Video recorder

    C. Portable cassette-stereo-radio

    D. Portable cassette player

15. A description of the suspects was broadcast to other police units so that they could assist in searching the area. This was done by

    A. Both Jones and Smith because they both had walkie-talkies.

    B. Trooper Jones because he had a walkie-talkie.

    C. Trooper Smith because he had a walkie-talkie.

    D. Both troopers after returning to their radio car.

16. In the investigation of a homicide, it is desirable to have photos taken of the body in its original condition and position. Of the following, the best reason for this practice is that the photos

    A. Show the motive for the homicide and thus indicate likely suspects.

    B. Indicate whether the corpse has been moved in any way.

    C. Form a permanent record of the body and the scene of the crime.

    D. Reveal the specific method used in committing the homicide.

19

17. A State Trooper hears two shots fired and proceeds in the direction of the shots. The Trooper comes upon an intoxicated man who is angrily screaming at a woman. The Trooper notices that the handle of a pistol is protruding from the man's pocket and orders him to surrender the pistol. The man apparently ignores the order and continues screaming at the woman. If the Trooper now fired a warning shot over man's head, that would be

   A. Bad. It is quite possible that the man is so intoxicated that he did not clearly hear or understand the Trooper's order.

   B. Bad. The Trooper should realize that an intoxicated man is not entirely responsible for his actions.

   C. Good. The warning shot will impress the man with the seriousness of the situation.

   D. Good. Because the man had already fired twice, the Trooper should take no further chances.

18. The practice of writing down confessions while a suspect is being questioned is

   A. Bad. Chiefly because the time taken to put a confession into written form may prove to be a waste of time— the confession may later be declared inadmissible as evidence in court.

   B. Bad. Chiefly because this may cause the suspect to withhold information when he or she knows that the confession is being recorded.

   C. Good. Chiefly because the suspect cannot claim at a later date that the information was obtained by force.

   D. Good. Chiefly because the suspect is thereby given more time to gather his or her thoughts and give the information wanted by the police.

19. An escaped prisoner has been wounded and is lying flat on his stomach with his head turned to one side. The one of the following directions from which a State Trooper should approach the prisoner to make it most difficult for the prisoner to fire quickly and accurately at the police officer is from the side

   A. Directly behind the prisoner's head.

   B. Facing the top of the prisoner's head.

   C. Facing the prisoner's face.

   D. Facing the prisoner's heels.

20. A gas-main explosion has caused some property damage. Examination by an emergency crew clearly indicates that no further explosions will occur. Nevertheless, rumors are circulating that more explosions are going to occur. The situation has resulted in a high degree of fear among local residents. The best of the following actions for a State Trooper on duty at the scene to take first would be to

   A. Ignore the rumors because they are false and no real danger exists.

   B. Inform the people of the true circumstances of the emergency.

   C. Question several people at the scene in an attempt to determine the source of the rumors.

   D. Order everyone to leave the area quickly and in an orderly fashion.

21. A State Trooper finds a young child wandering around a residential area. After unsuccessfully questioning the child about the location of her home, the Trooper phones police headquarters and is informed that no child meeting the description given by the officer has been reported missing. The officer decides to make inquiries about the child in the immediate area before taking any other action. The action is advisable chiefly because

A. The child's parents probably know of her whereabouts because headquarters has received no report of the missing child.

B. The child has probably been away from home only a short time because no report of a missing child has been received.

C. The child is less likely to become emotionally disturbed if she remains in her own neighborhood.

D. Young children, when lost, never wander more than a short distance from home.

22. While a Trooper in plain clothes is following and watching a suspect in a homicide case, the Trooper becomes convinced that the suspect realizes he is being watched. The suspect's identity is known to the police, but he is also known to have changed his place of residence frequently during the past few months. The Trooper does not have sufficient evidence to arrest the suspect at this time. Of the following, the best actions for the Trooper to take are to

A. Approach the suspect, inform him that he is being followed, and demand an explanation of his suspicious past conduct.

B. Continue to follow the suspect until an opportunity is presented for the officer to telephone for a replacement.

C. Continue to follow the suspect because he will probably commit an illegal act eventually.

D. Discontinue following the suspect and attempt to gain evidence by other means.

23. Probationary State Police Officers A and B are given a special assignment by the Sergeant. Officer B does not fully understand some of the instructions given by the Sergeant concerning how to carry out the assignment. Of the following, it would be best for Officer B to

A. Proceed with those parts of the assignment that he understands and ask for an explanation from the Sergeant when he can go no further.

B. Observe Officer A's work carefully to determine how the assignment is to be carried out.

C. Ask the Sergeant to explain the portion of the instructions that he does not fully understand before starting the assignment.

D. Suggest to Officer A that Officer A supervise the operation because he or she probably understands the instructions better.

19

24. A State Police Officer responds at night to a telephone complaint that a prowler has been observed at a particular location. The officer arrives at the location and notices someone who appears to fit the description of the prowler previously given by the complaint. In approaching this individual, it would be best for the officer to

A. Consider this individual to be a potentially dangerous criminal.

B. Avoid taking any precautionary measures because there is no way of knowing whether any offense has been committed.

C. Consider that this individual is probably harmless and is only a "Peeping Tom."

D. Fire a warning shot over the man's head.

25. A State Police Officer has been asked by a merchant on his post to recommend the best make of burglar alarm for his store. The chief reason that the Police Officer should not make a specific recommendation is that

A. The officer does not have enough technical knowledge of the operation of burglar alarms.

B. The merchant may interpret the officer's recommendation as an official police department endorsement.

C. Such a recommendation would imply that the police are incapable of protecting the merchant's property.

D. The officer is not likely to know the prices of various makes and models available.

26. Two State Police Officers in a radio patrol car stop a car that they recognize as having been reported stolen. The Police Officers immediately separate the two occupants of the car and proceed to question them apart from each other. Of the following, the most important reason for questioning them separately is to

A. Give each suspect the opportunity to admit guilt out of the presence of the other suspect.

B. Prevent the suspects from agreeing on an explanation of their presence in the car.

C. Prevent the errors that may arise when attempting to record in a notebook two separate statements being made at the same time.

D. Determine which of the two suspects actually planned the theft of the car.

27. The manager of a supermarket informs a State Trooper that an object that appears to be a homemade bomb has been discovered in his market. The Trooper's first action should be to

A. Go to the market and make sure that everyone leaves it immediately.

B. Go to the market, examine the bomb, and then decide what action should be taken.

C. Question the manager in detail in an effort to determine whether there really is a bomb.

D. Telephone the bomb squad for instructions on how the bomb should be rendered harmless.

28. The most reasonable advice a State Police Officer can give to a merchant who asks what he should do if he receives a telephone call from a person he doesn't recognize regarding an alleged emergency at his store after ordinary business hours is that the merchant should go to the store, and, if officers are not on the scene, the merchant should

A. Continue past the store and call the police for assistance.

B. Continue past the store, and return and enter if there doesn't seem to be an emergency.

C. Enter the store and ascertain whether the alleged emergency exists.

D. Enter the story only if no one is apparently loitering in the vicinity.

29. Whenever a crime has been committed, the criminal has disturbed the surroundings in one way or another by his or her presence. The least valid deduction for the police to make from this statement is

A. Clues are thus present at all crime scenes.

B. Even the slightest search at crime scenes will turn up conclusive evidence.

C. The greater the number of criminals involved in a crime, the greater the number of clues likely to be available.

D. The completely clueless crime is rarely encountered in police work.

30. An off-duty State Police Officer was seated in a restaurant when two men entered, drew guns, and robbed the cashier. The officer made no attempt to prevent the robbery or to apprehend the criminals. Later, he justified his conduct by stating that an officer, when off duty, is a private citizen with the same duties and rights of all private citizens. The officer's conduct was

A. Wrong. A Police Officer must act to prevent crimes and apprehend criminals at all times.

B. Right. The Police Officer was out of uniform at the time of the robbery.

C. Wrong. The officer should have obtained necessary information and descriptions after the robbers left.

D. Right. It would have been foolhardy for the officer to intervene when outnumbered by armed robbers.

19

Answer Key

1.	D	11.	D	21.	B
2.	D	12.	C	22.	B
3.	D	13.	B	23.	C
4.	A	14.	A	24.	A
5.	A	15.	C	25.	B
6.	B	16.	C	26.	B
7.	D	17.	A	27.	A
8.	B	18.	B	28.	A
9.	D	19.	A	29.	B
10.	C	20.	B	30.	A

Answer Explanations

1.   **(D)** Refer to the third sentence of the description.

2.   **(D)** The officers observed the suspects alighting from the roof by way of ladder.

3.   **(D)** The two white males ran into an alleyway, and the black male and Hispanic male ran into a parking lot.

4.   **(A)** This information is included in the description of the white male with long blond hair.

5.   **(A)** This information is included in the description of the Hispanic male.

6.   **(B)** This information is included in the description of the white male with short hair.

7.   **(D)** This information is included in the description of the white male with short hair.

8.   **(B)** This information is included in the description of the white male with long blond hair.

9.   **(D)** This information is included in the description of the Hispanic male.

10.   **(C)** This is the description of the vehicle in which the two white males fled.

11.   **(D)** The description states only that the escape vehicles fled west on Seventh Street. There is no information about what type of street Seventh Street is.

12.   **(C)** Both the black male and the Hispanic male entered the parking lot. However, it was the black male who was carrying what appeared to be a portable TV set.

13.   **(B)** This information is included in the description of the black male.

14.   **(A)** This information is included in the description of the black male.

15.   **(C)** The description refers only to Officer Smith using a walkie-talkie to broadcast information.

16. **(C)** Photographs form a permanent record of how the crime scene appeared when the police arrived. These pictures can be introduced as evidence at a criminal trial.

17. **(A)** There is no immediate danger to the officer or to the woman because the gun is in the man's pocket. Therefore, it is not necessary or proper for the officer to fire a warning shot. The officer should repeat the order before taking any further action.

18. **(B)** If the suspect observes that notes are being taken, he or she may freeze up or not talk as freely because the suspect knows that what he or she is saying will become part of the permanent record.

19. **(A)** The prisoner would either have to roll over or turn his head completely around to see the officer if he were to shoot accurately. The time required for this type of movement would allow the officer to take cover or to fire the first shot.

20. **(B)** Ignoring the rumors or not supplying the true circumstances of the emergency as soon as they are available only increases the fear people may have and may result in a possible panic situation.

21. **(B)** If a child has been missing for an extended period of time, police headquarters usually would have received information concerning the child.

22. **(B)** If the plainclothes officer were to stop following the suspect now, the suspect would be difficult to locate again because he is known to have changed residences.

23. **(C)** If a Police Officer doesn't fully understand the instructions given by a supervisor, the officer should immediately ask the supervisor for clarification so that he or she can carry out the assignment properly.

24. **(A)** A Police Officer should always be alert and on guard until the nature of the situation in which he or she is involved is made completely clear.

25. **(B)** Police Officers and police departments should never recommend a specific product or business. Endorsements tend to indicate favoritism; Police Officers should always be impartial.

26. **(B)** Suspects and witnesses should always be questioned separately so that the description that one person gives does not influence the description given by any other persons at the scene.

27. **(A)** If there is the slightest chance that the object could be a bomb, all persons should be removed from the location for safety reasons.

28. **(A)** The call could be a set-up for robbing both the owner and his store. If there were a real emergency, the police would most likely be on the scene.

29. **(B)** In most cases, it takes a thorough search of the crime scene to uncover the clues left by the criminal. Most clues in and of themselves are not conclusive. However, when used collectively, they form the foundation for proving the guilt or innocence of the suspect.

30. **(A)** The officer was wrong. The principle here is that a Police Officer has a responsibility to protect the public at all times, even when off duty.

19

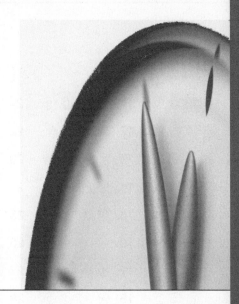

Hour **20**

Sample Arithmetic Reasoning Exam, Part I

What You'll Learn in This Hour

This hour presents sample exam questions covering ratio and proportion problems, work problems, and distance problems. You'll have a chance to practice other types of arithmetic reasoning questions in Hour 21, "Sample Arithmetic Reasoning Exam, Part II."

Here's a list of your goals for this hour:

- Take the sample arithmetic reasoning exam
- Check your answers against the answer key
- Review the answer explanations

> **Tip**
> Be sure to review Hour 13, "Teach Yourself Math Strategies," for strategies and tips concerning arithmetic reasoning questions.

Answer Sheet

1. Ⓐ Ⓑ Ⓒ Ⓓ   11. Ⓐ Ⓑ Ⓒ Ⓓ   21. Ⓐ Ⓑ Ⓒ Ⓓ

2. Ⓐ Ⓑ Ⓒ Ⓓ   12. Ⓐ Ⓑ Ⓒ Ⓓ   22. Ⓐ Ⓑ Ⓒ Ⓓ

3. Ⓐ Ⓑ Ⓒ Ⓓ   13. Ⓐ Ⓑ Ⓒ Ⓓ   23. Ⓐ Ⓑ Ⓒ Ⓓ

4. Ⓐ Ⓑ Ⓒ Ⓓ   14. Ⓐ Ⓑ Ⓒ Ⓓ   24. Ⓐ Ⓑ Ⓒ Ⓓ

5. Ⓐ Ⓑ Ⓒ Ⓓ   15. Ⓐ Ⓑ Ⓒ Ⓓ   25. Ⓐ Ⓑ Ⓒ Ⓓ

6. Ⓐ Ⓑ Ⓒ Ⓓ   16. Ⓐ Ⓑ Ⓒ Ⓓ   26. Ⓐ Ⓑ Ⓒ Ⓓ

7. Ⓐ Ⓑ Ⓒ Ⓓ   17. Ⓐ Ⓑ Ⓒ Ⓓ   27. Ⓐ Ⓑ Ⓒ Ⓓ

8. Ⓐ Ⓑ Ⓒ Ⓓ   18. Ⓐ Ⓑ Ⓒ Ⓓ   28. Ⓐ Ⓑ Ⓒ Ⓓ

9. Ⓐ Ⓑ Ⓒ Ⓓ   19. Ⓐ Ⓑ Ⓒ Ⓓ   29. Ⓐ Ⓑ Ⓒ Ⓓ

10. Ⓐ Ⓑ Ⓒ Ⓓ   20. Ⓐ Ⓑ Ⓒ Ⓓ   30. Ⓐ Ⓑ Ⓒ Ⓓ

Sample Exam

> **DIRECTIONS:** Select the correct answer to each question and fill in the corresponding circle on the answer sheet. Work as quickly as possible. If you have time, go back and double-check your answers. You should allow yourself 50 minutes to answer the following 30 questions.

1. The ratio of 24 to 64 is
   A. 8:3
   B. 24:100
   C. 3:8
   D. 64:100

2. The Indianapolis Colts won 8 games and lost 3. The ratio of games won to games played is
   A. 8:11
   B. 3:11
   C. 8:3
   D. 3:8

3. The ratio of $\frac{1}{4}$ to $\frac{3}{5}$ is
   A. 1 to 3
   B. 3 to 20
   C. 5 to 12
   D. 3 to 4

4. If there are 16 boys and 12 girls in a class, the ratio of the number of girls to the number of children in the class is
   A. 3 to 4
   B. 3 to 7
   C. 4 to 7
   D. 4 to 3

5. 259 is to 37 as
   A. 5 is to 1
   B. 63 is to 441
   C. 84 is to 12
   D. 130 is to 19

6. 2 dozen cans of dog food at the rate of 3 cans for $1.45 would cost
   A. $10.05
   B. $11.20
   C. $11.60
   D. $11.75

7. A snapshot measures $2\frac{1}{2}$ inches by $1\frac{7}{8}$ inches. It is to be enlarged so that the longer dimension will be 4 inches. The length of the enlarged shorter dimension will be
   A. $2\frac{1}{2}$ inches
   B. 3 inches
   C. $3\frac{3}{8}$ inches
   D. None of these

8. Men's white handkerchiefs cost $2.29 for 3. The cost per dozen handkerchiefs is
   A. $27.48
   B. $13.74
   C. $9.16
   D. $6.87

20

9. A certain pole casts a shadow 24 feet long. At the same time, another pole 3 feet high casts a shadow 4 feet long. How high is the first pole if the heights and shadows are in proportion?

A. 18 feet

B. 19 feet

C. 20 feet

D. 21 feet

10. The actual length represented by $3\frac{1}{2}$ inches on a drawing having a scale of $\frac{1}{8}$ inch to the foot is

A. 3.75 feet

B. 28 feet

C. 360 feet

D. 120 feet

11. If 314 clerks filed 6,595 papers in 10 minutes, what is the number filed per minute by the average clerk?

A. 2

B. 2.4

C. 2.1

D. 2.5

12. Four men, working together, can dig a ditch in 42 days. They begin, but one man works only half-days. How long will it take to complete the job?

A. 48 days

B. 45 days

C. 43 days

D. 44 days

13. A clerk is requested to file 800 cards. If the clerk can file cards at the rate of 80 cards an hour, the number of cards remaining to be filed after 7 hours of work is

A. 140

B. 240

C. 260

D. 560

14. If it takes 4 days for 3 machines to do a certain job, it will take two machines

A. 6 days

B. $5\frac{1}{2}$ days

C. 5 days

D. $4\frac{1}{2}$ days

15. A stenographer has been assigned to place entries on 500 forms. She places entries on 25 forms by the end of half an hour, when she is joined by another stenographer. The second stenographer places entries at the rate of 45 an hour. Assuming that both stenographers continue to work at their respective rates of speed, the total number of hours required to carry out the entire assignment is

A. 5

B. $5\frac{1}{2}$

C. $6\frac{1}{2}$

D. 7

16. If, in 5 days, a clerk can copy 125 pages, 36 lines each, 11 words to the line, how many pages of 30 lines each and 12 words to the line can the clerk copy in 6 days?

A. 145

B. 155

C. 160

D. 165

17. A and B can do a job together in 2 hours. Working alone, A does the job in 5 hours. How long will it take B to do the job alone?

A. $3\frac{1}{3}$ hours

B. $2\frac{1}{4}$ hours

C. 3 hours

D. 2 hours

18. A stenographer transcribes notes at the rate of one line typed in 10 seconds. At this rate, how long (in minutes and seconds) will it take to transcribe notes, which will require seven pages of typing, 25 lines to the page?

A. 29 minutes, 10 seconds

B. 17 minutes, 50 seconds

C. 40 minutes, 10 seconds

D. 20 minutes, 30 seconds

19. A group of five clerks has been assigned to insert 24,000 letters into envelopes. The clerks perform this work at the following rates of speed: Clerk A, 1,100 letters an hour; Clerk B, 1,450 letters an hour; Clerk C, 1,200 letters an hour; Clerk D, 1,300 letters an hour; Clerk E, 1,250 letters an hour. At the end of two hours of work, Clerks C and D are assigned to another task. From the time that Clerks C and D were taken off the assignment, the number of hours required for the remaining clerks to complete this assignment is

A. Less than 3 hours

B. 3 hours

C. More than 3 hours, but less than 4 hours

D. More than 4 hours

20. If a certain job can be performed by 18 workers in 26 days, the number of workers needed to perform the job in 12 days is

A. 24

B. 30

C. 39

D. 52

21. A 10-car train took 6 minutes to travel between two stations that are 3 miles apart. The average speed of the train was

A. 20 mph

B. 25 mph

C. 30 mph

D. 35 mph

22. A police car is ordered to report to the scene of a crime 5 miles away. If the car travels at an average rate of 40 miles per hour, the time it will take to reach its destination is

A. 3 minutes

B. 7.5 minutes

C. 10 minutes

D. 13.5 minutes

23. If the average speed of a train between two stations is 30 miles per hour, and the two stations are $\frac{1}{2}$ mile apart, the time it takes the train to travel from one station to the other is

A. 1 minute

B. 2 minutes

C. 3 minutes

D. 4 minutes

20

24. A car completes a 10-mile trip in 20 minutes. If it does one-half the distance at a speed of 20 mph, its speed for the remainder of the distance must be
   A. 30 mph
   B. 40 mph
   C. 50 mph
   D. 60 mph

25. An express train leaves one station at 9:02 and arrives at the next station at 9:08. If the distance traveled is $2\frac{1}{2}$ miles, the average speed of the train (in mph) is
   A. 15 mph
   B. 20 mph
   C. 25 mph
   D. 30 mph

26. A motorist averaged 60 miles per hour going a distance of 240 miles. He made the return trip over the same distance in 6 hours. What was his average speed for the entire trip?
   A. 40 mph
   B. 48 mph
   C. 50 mph
   D. 60 mph

27. A city has been testing various types of gasoline for economy and efficiency. It has been found that a police radio patrol car can travel 18 miles on a gallon of Brand A gasoline, costing $1.30 a gallon; the car can go 15 miles on a gallon of Brand B gasoline, costing $1.25 a gallon. For a distance of 900 miles, Brand B will cost
   A. $10 more than Brand A
   B. $10 less than Brand A
   C. $100 more than Brand A
   D. $100 less than Brand A

28. The Mayflower sailed from Plymouth, England, to Plymouth Rock, a distance of approximately 2,800 miles, in 63 days. The average speed was closest to which one of the following?
   A. $\frac{1}{2}$ mph
   B. 1 mph
   C. 2 mph
   D. 3 mph

29. If a vehicle is to complete a 20-mile trip at an average rate of 30 miles per hour, it must complete the trip in
   A. 20 minutes
   B. 30 minutes
   C. 40 minutes
   D. 50 minutes

30. A car began a trip with 12 gallons of gasoline in the tank and ended with $7\frac{1}{2}$ gallons. The car traveled 17.3 miles for each gallon of gasoline. During the trip, gasoline was bought for $100.00, at a cost of $1.25 a gallon. The total number of miles traveled during this trip was most nearly
   A. 79
   B. 196
   C. 216
   D. 229

Answer Key

1.	C	11.	C	21.	C
2.	A	12.	A	22.	B
3.	C	13.	B	23.	A
4.	B	14.	A	24.	D
5.	C	15.	B	25.	C
6.	C	16.	D	26.	B
7.	B	17.	A	27.	A
8.	C	18.	A	28.	C
9.	A	19.	B	29.	C
10.	B	20.	C	30.	C

Answer Explanations

1. **(C)** The ratio 24 to 64 can be written 24:64 or $\frac{24}{64}$. In fraction form, the ratio can be reduced as follows:

$$\frac{24}{64} = \frac{3}{8}, \text{ or } 3{:}8$$

2. **(A)** The number of games played was 3 + 8 = 11. The ratio of games won to games played is 8:11.

3. **(C)** We know the following facts about this problem:

$$\frac{1}{4} : \frac{3}{5} = \frac{1}{4} \div \frac{3}{5}$$

$$= \frac{1}{4} \times \frac{5}{3}$$

$$= \frac{5}{12}$$

$$= 5{:}12, \text{ or } 5 \text{ to } 12$$

4. **(B)** There are 16 + 12 = 28 children in the class. The ratio of number of girls to number of children is 12:28:

$$\frac{12}{28} = \frac{3}{7}, \text{ or } 3 \text{ to } 7$$

5. **(C)** The ratio $\frac{259}{37}$ reduces by 37 to $\frac{7}{1}$. The ratio $\frac{84}{12}$ also reduces to $\frac{7}{1}$. Therefore, $\frac{259}{37} = \frac{84}{12}$ is a proportion, reading "84 is to 12."

6. **(C)** The number of cans is proportional to the price. Let p represent the unknown price:

$$\frac{3}{24} = \frac{1.45}{p}$$

$$p = \frac{1.45 \times 24}{3}$$

$$p = \frac{34.80}{3}$$

$$p = \$11.60$$

20

7.   **(B)** Let s represent the unknown shorter dimension:

$$\frac{2\frac{1}{2}}{4} = \frac{1\frac{7}{8}}{s}$$

$$s = \frac{4 \times 1\frac{7}{8}}{2\frac{1}{2}}$$

$$s = \frac{4 \times \frac{15}{8}}{2\frac{1}{2}}$$

$$s = \frac{15}{2} \div 2\frac{1}{2}$$

$$s = \frac{15}{2} \div \frac{5}{2}$$

$$s = \frac{15}{2} \times \frac{2}{5}$$

$$s = 3 \text{ inches}$$

8.   **(C)** Let p represent the cost per dozen (12):

$$\frac{3}{12} = \frac{2.29}{p}$$

$$p = \frac{12 \times 2.29}{3}$$

$$p = 9.16$$

9.   **(A)** If f is the height of the first pole, then the proportion is

$$\frac{f}{24} = \frac{3}{4}$$

$$f = \frac{24 \times 3}{4}$$

$$f = 18 \text{ feet}$$

10. **(B)** Let y represent the unknown length:

$$3\frac{1}{2} \div \frac{1}{8} = \frac{y}{1}$$

$$y = 3\frac{1}{2} \times 1 \div \frac{1}{8}$$

$$y = 3\frac{1}{2} \div \frac{1}{8}$$

$$y = \frac{7}{2} \times \frac{8}{1}$$

$$y = 28 \text{ feet}$$

11. **(C)** We know the following about this problem: 6,595 papers ÷ 314 clerks = 21 papers per clerk in 10 minutes. 21 papers ÷ 10 minutes = 2.1 papers per minute filed by the average clerk.

12. **(A)** It would take 1 man 42 x 4 = 168 days to complete the job, working alone. If $3\frac{1}{2}$ men are working (one man works half-days, the other 3 work full days), the job would take $168 \div 3\frac{1}{2} = 48$ days.

13. **(B)** In 7 hours, the clerk files 7 x 80 = 560 cards. Because 800 cards must be filed, there are 800 - 560 = 240 remaining cards.

14. **(A)** It would take 1 machine 3 x 4 = 12 days to do the job. Two machines could do the job in 12 ÷ 2 = 6 days.

15. **(B)** At the end of the first half-hour, there are 500 - 25 = 475 forms remaining. If the first stenographer completed 25 forms in half an hour, her rate is 25 x 2 = 50 forms per hour. The combined rate of the two stenographers is 50 + 45 = 95 forms per hour. The remaining forms can be completed in 465 ÷ 95 = 5 hours. Adding the first half hour, the entire job requires $5\frac{1}{2}$ hours.

16. **(D)** 36 lines x 11 words = 396 words per page. 125 pages x 396 words = 49,500 words in 5 days. 49,500 ÷ 5 = 9,900 words in 1 day. 12 words x 30 lines = 360 words on each page. 9,900 ÷ 360 = $27\frac{1}{2}$ pages in one day. $27\frac{1}{2}$ x 6 = 165 pages in 6 days.

17.   **(A)** If A can do the job alone in 5 hours, A can do $\frac{1}{5}$ of the job in 1 hour. Working together, A and B can do the job in 2 hours; therefore, in 1 hour, they do $\frac{1}{2}$ the job.

In 1 hour, B does

$\frac{1}{2} - \frac{1}{5} = \frac{5}{10} - \frac{2}{10} = \frac{3}{10}$ of the job. It would take B $\frac{10}{3}$ hours = $3\frac{1}{3}$ hours to do the whole job alone.

18.   **(A)** The stenographer must type 7 x 25 = 175 lines. At the rate of 1 line per 10 seconds, it will take 175 x 10 = 1,750 seconds. 1,750 seconds ÷ 60 = $29\frac{1}{6}$ minutes, or 29 minutes and 10 seconds.

19.   **(B)** The following chart shows us what we know about the problem:

Clerk	Number of Letters per Hour
A	1,100
B	1,450
C	1,200
D	1,300
E	1,250
	Total = 6,300

All 5 clerks working together process a total of 6,300 letters per hour. After 2 hours, they have processed 6,300 x 2 = 12,600 letters. Of the original 24,000 letters, there are 24,000 - 12,600 = 11,400 letters remaining.

Clerks A, B, and E working together process a total of 3,800 letters per hour. It will take them 11,400 ÷ 3,800 = 3 hours to process the remaining letters.

20.   **(C)** The job could be performed by 1 worker in 18 x 26 days = 468 days. To perform the job in 12 days would require 468 ÷ 12 = 39 workers.

21.   **(C)** We know the following facts about the problem:

6 min = $\frac{6}{60}$ hr = .1 hr

Speed (rate) = distance ÷ time

Speed = 3 ÷ .1 = 30 mph

22.   **(B)** We know the following facts about the problem:

Time = distance ÷ rate

Time = 5 ÷ 40 = .125 hr

Time = .125 hr = .125 x 60 min

Time = 7.5 minutes

23.   **(A)** We know the following facts about the problem:

Time = distance ÷ rate

Time = $\frac{1}{2}$ mi ÷ 30 mph

Time = $\frac{1}{60}$ hr

Time = $\frac{1}{60}$ hr = 1 min

24.   **(D)** The first part of trip = $\frac{1}{2}$ of 10 miles.

Time for first part = 5 ÷ 20

Time = $\frac{1}{4}$ hour

Time = 15 minutes

The second part of trip was 5 miles, completed in 20 - 15 minutes, or 5 minutes:

5 minutes = $\frac{1}{12}$ hour

Rate = 5 mi ÷ $\frac{1}{12}$ hr

Rate = 60 mph

20

25. **(C)** The time is 6 minutes, or .1 hour.

Speed = distance ÷ time

Speed = $2\frac{1}{2}$ ÷ .1

Speed = 2.5 ÷ .1

Speed = 25 mph

26. **(B)** The time for the first 240 miles = 240 ÷ 60 = 4 hours. The time for the return trip = 6 hours. The total time for the round trip = 10 hours. The total distance for the round trip = 480 mi.

Average rate = 480 mi ÷ 10 hr = 48 mph

27. **(A)** Brand A requires 900 ÷ 18 = 50 gal

50 gal x $1.30/gal = $65

Brand B requires 900 ÷ 15 = 60 gal

60 gal x $1.25/gal = $75

$75 - $65 = $10 more than Brand A

28. **(C)** 63 days = 63 x 24 hours = 1,512 hours

Speed = 2,800 mi ÷ 1,512 hrs

Speed = 1.85 mph

29. **(C)** Time = 20 mi ÷ 30 mph

Time = $\frac{2}{3}$ hr

$\frac{2}{3}$ hr = $\frac{2}{3}$ x 60 min = 40 min

30. **(C)** The car used this much gas:

12 - $7\frac{1}{2}$ = $4\frac{1}{2}$ gal, *plus*

$10.00 ÷ $1.25/gal = 8 gal

for a total of $12\frac{1}{2}$ gal or 12.5 gal

Now calculate the number of miles traveled with that much gas:

12.5 gal x 17.3 mpg = 216.25 miles for the trip

Hour **21**

Sample Arithmetic Reasoning Exam, Part II

What You'll Learn in This Hour

In this hour, you'll have the chance to practice sample exam questions covering arithmetic reasoning. The problems include taxation problems, profit-and-loss problems, and formula problems.

Here's what you'll do in this hour:

- Answer some sample arithmetic reasoning questions taken from a portion of a law enforcement exam

- Review the answers and answer explanations

Follow the directions for the test, and don't go beyond the allotted time. Mark your answers on the answer sheet. When you've finished (or when the test time is up), check your answers against the answer key and then review the answer explanations. Don't panic! The good news is that the correct answer is given to you for each question—you just have to identify it!

Answer Sheet

1. Ⓐ Ⓑ Ⓒ Ⓓ   11. Ⓐ Ⓑ Ⓒ Ⓓ   21. Ⓐ Ⓑ Ⓒ Ⓓ

2. Ⓐ Ⓑ Ⓒ Ⓓ   12. Ⓐ Ⓑ Ⓒ Ⓓ   22. Ⓐ Ⓑ Ⓒ Ⓓ

3. Ⓐ Ⓑ Ⓒ Ⓓ   13. Ⓐ Ⓑ Ⓒ Ⓓ   23. Ⓐ Ⓑ Ⓒ Ⓓ

4. Ⓐ Ⓑ Ⓒ Ⓓ   14. Ⓐ Ⓑ Ⓒ Ⓓ   24. Ⓐ Ⓑ Ⓒ Ⓓ

5. Ⓐ Ⓑ Ⓒ Ⓓ   15. Ⓐ Ⓑ Ⓒ Ⓓ   25. Ⓐ Ⓑ Ⓒ Ⓓ

6. Ⓐ Ⓑ Ⓒ Ⓓ   16. Ⓐ Ⓑ Ⓒ Ⓓ   26. Ⓐ Ⓑ Ⓒ Ⓓ

7. Ⓐ Ⓑ Ⓒ Ⓓ   17. Ⓐ Ⓑ Ⓒ Ⓓ   27. Ⓐ Ⓑ Ⓒ Ⓓ

8. Ⓐ Ⓑ Ⓒ Ⓓ   18. Ⓐ Ⓑ Ⓒ Ⓓ   28. Ⓐ Ⓑ Ⓒ Ⓓ

9. Ⓐ Ⓑ Ⓒ Ⓓ   19. Ⓐ Ⓑ Ⓒ Ⓓ   29. Ⓐ Ⓑ Ⓒ Ⓓ

10. Ⓐ Ⓑ Ⓒ Ⓓ   20. Ⓐ Ⓑ Ⓒ Ⓓ

Arithmetic Reasoning Questions

1. Mr. Jones's income for a year is $15,000. He pays $2,250 for income taxes. The percent of his income that he pays for income taxes is

   A. 9

   B. 12

   C. 15

   D. 22

2. If the tax rate is $3\frac{1}{2}$% and the amount to be raised is $64.40. what is the base?

   A. $1,800

   B. $1,840

   C. $1,850

   D. $1,860

3. What is the tax rate per $1,000 if a base of $338,500 would yield $616.07?

   A. $1.80

   B. $1.90

   C. $1.95

   D. $1.82

4. A person buys an electric light bulb for 54 cents, which includes a 20% tax. What is the cost of the bulb without the tax?

   A. 43 cents

   B. 44 cents

   C. 45 cents

   D. 46 cents

5. What tax rate on a base of $3,650 would raise $164.25?

   A. 4%

   B. 5%

   C. $4\frac{1}{2}$%

   D. $5\frac{1}{2}$%

6. A piece of property is assessed at $22,850 and the tax rate is $4.80 per thousand. What is the amount of tax that must be paid on the property?

   A. $109

   B. $112

   C. $109.68

   D. $112.68

7. $30,000 worth of land is assessed at 120% of its value. If the tax rate is $5.12 per $1,000 assessed valuation, the amount of tax to be paid is

   A. $180.29

   B. $184.32

   C. $190.10

   D. $192.29

8. Of the following real estate tax rates, which is the largest?

   A. $31.25 per $1,000

   B. $3.45 per $100

   C. 32 cents per $10

   D. 3 cents per $1

21

9. A certain community needs $185,090.62 to cover its expenses. If its tax rate is $1.43 per $100 of assessed valuation, what must be the assessed value of its property?

A. $12,900,005

B. $12,943,400

C. $12,940,000

D. $12,840,535

10. A man's taxable income is $14,280. The state tax instructions tell him to pay 2% on the first $3,000 of his taxable income, 3% on each of the second and third $3,000, and 4% on the remainder. What is the total amount of tax he must pay?

A. $265.40

B. $309.32

C. $451.20

D. $454.62

11. Dresses are sold at $65 each. The dresses cost $50 each. The percentage of increase of the selling price over the cost is

A. 40

B. $33\frac{1}{3}$

C. $33\frac{1}{2}$

D. 30

12. A dealer bought a ladder for $27.00. What must it be sold for if the dealer wants to make a profit of 40% on the selling price?

A. $38.80

B. $43.20

C. $45.00

D. $67.50

13. A typewriter was listed at $120 and was bought for $96. What was the rate of discount?

A. $16\frac{2}{3}\%$

B. 20%

C. 24%

D. 25%

14. A dealer sells an article at a loss of 50% of the cost. Based on the selling price, the loss is

A. 25%

B. 50%

C. 100%

D. None of these

15. What would be the marked price of an article if the cost was $12.60 and the gain was 10% of the cost price?

A. $11.34

B. $12.72

C. $13.86

D. $14.28

16. A stationer buys note pads at $.75 per dozen and sells them at 25 cents apiece. The profit based on the cost is

A. 50%

B. 300%

C. 200%

D. 100%

17. An article costing $18 is to be sold at a profit of 10% of the selling price. The selling price will be

A. $19.80

B. $36

C. $18.18

D. $20

18. A calculating machine company offered to sell a city agency four machines at a discount of 15% from the list price, and to allow the agency $85 for each of two old machines being traded in. The list price of the new machines is $625 per machine. If the city agency accepts this offer, the amount of money it will have to provide for the purchase of these four machines is

A. $1,785

B. $2,295

C. $1,955

D. $1,836

19. Pencils are purchased at $9 per gross and sold at 6 for 75 cents. The rate of profit based on the selling price is

A. 100%

B. 67%

C. 50%

D. 25%

20. The single equivalent discount of 20% and 10% is

A. 15%

B. 28%

C. 18%

D. 30%

21. If a train travels M miles in H hours, how many hours will it take the train to travel the next N miles at the same rate?

A. $\frac{H}{MN}$

B. $\frac{HM}{N}$

C. $\frac{HN}{M}$

D. $\frac{M}{HN}$

22. If the average of A and B is Q, and the average of C, D, and E is R, what is the average of A, B, C, D, and E in terms of Q and R?

A. $\frac{Q+R}{2}$

B. $\frac{2Q+3R}{5}$

C. $\frac{2Q+R}{5}$

D. $\frac{Q+3R}{5}$

23. A certain truck can travel M miles on G gallons of gasoline. How many gallons of gasoline are needed for 7 of these trucks if each one must travel 300 miles?

A. $\frac{2,100G}{M}$

B. $\frac{2,100M}{G}$

C. $\frac{MG}{2,100}$

D. $\frac{GM}{2,100}$

24. If a taxi driver charges C cents for the first quarter-mile, and $\frac{C}{4}$ cents for each additional quarter-mile, how much does it cost, in cents, for a trip of M miles?

A. $C\left(M+\frac{1}{4}\right)$

B. $\frac{C}{4}\left(M+\frac{4}{15}\right)$

C. $C\left(M+\frac{3}{4}\right)$

D. $C\left(M-\frac{1}{4}\right)$

21

25. An item that normally sells for X dollars is marked down to Y dollars. What is the percent of markdown?

A. $(\frac{X-Y}{Y})100$

B. $(\frac{Y-X}{Y})100$

C. $(X - Y)100$

D. $(\frac{X-Y}{X})100$

26. In a certain company, 5 employees earn $16,000 a year, 3 employees earn $20,000 a year, and 2 employees earn $24,000 a year. What is the average annual salary for these employees?

A. $\dfrac{(\$16,000 + \$20,000 + \$24,000)}{(5 + 3 + 2)}$

B. $(5 + 3 + 2)\left(\dfrac{\$16,000}{5} + \dfrac{\$20,000}{3} + \dfrac{\$24,000}{2}\right)$

C. $\dfrac{5(\$16,000)+3(\$20,000)+2(\$24,000)}{5+3+2}$

D. $\dfrac{(5+3+2)(\$16,000+\$20,000+\$24,000)}{5+3+2}$

27. A Deputy U.S. Marshall is 24 years older than her son. In eight years, the Deputy Marshall will be twice as old as her son will be then. How old is her son now?

A. $N + 24 = 2N + 8$

B. $N + 24 + 8 = 2(N + 8)$

C. $N + 24 = 2(N + 8)$

D. $\frac{8N+24}{2} = 2N + (24 - 8)$

28. In a foreign language school, 64% of the students are studying Spanish, 52% are studying French, and 28% are studying some language other than Spanish or French. What percent of the students at the school is studying both Spanish and French?

A. $(100 - 28) - [(72 - 64) + (72 - 52)]$

B. $100 - (64 + 52)$

C. $(100 - 28) + 64 + 72$

D. $(64 + 52 + 28) - [(100) - (100 - 72)]$

29. What is the average of a student who received a 90 in English, 84 in Algebra, 75 in French, and 76 in Music if the subjects have the following weights: English 4, Algebra 3, French 3, and Music 1?

A. $\dfrac{4(90+84+75+76)}{4+3+3+1}$

B. $\dfrac{4(90)+6(84+75)+76}{4\times3\times3\times1}$

C. $\dfrac{\frac{90+84+75+76}{4}}{4+3+3+1}$

D. $\dfrac{(90\times4)+(84\times3)+(75\times3)+(76\times1)}{4+3+3+1}$

Answer Key

1.	C	11.	D	21.	C
2.	B	12.	C	22.	B
3.	D	13.	B	23.	A
4.	C	14.	C	24.	C
5.	C	15.	C	25.	D
6.	C	16.	B	26.	C
7.	B	17.	D	27.	B
8.	B	18.	C	28.	A
9.	B	19.	C	29.	D
10.	C	20.	B		

Answer Explanations

1. **(C)** For this problem, we know the following:

Tax = $2,250

Base = $15,000

Tax rate = Tax ÷ Base

Tax rate = $2,250 ÷ $15,000 = .15

Tax rate = .15 or 15%

2. **(B)** For this problem, we know the following:

Tax rate = $3\frac{1}{2}\% = .035$

Tax = $64.40

Base = Tax ÷ tax rate

Base = $64.40 ÷ .035

Base = $1,840

3. **(D)** For this problem, we know the following:

Base = $338,500

Tax = $616.07

Denomination = $1,000

$\frac{\$338,500}{\$1,000} = 338.50$

$\frac{\$616.07}{338.50} = \$1.82$ per $1,000

4. **(C)** For this problem, we know the following:

54 cents is 120% of the base (the cost without tax)

Base = 54 ÷ 120%

Base = 54 ÷ 1.20

Base = 45 cents

21

5. **(C)** For this problem, we know the following:

    Base = $3,650

    Tax = $164.25

    Tax rate = Tax ÷ Base

    Tax rate = $164.25 ÷ $3,650

    Tax rate = .045

    Tax rate = $4\frac{1}{2}\%$

6. **(C)** For this problem, we know the following:

    Base = $22,850

    Denomination = $1,000

    Tax rate = $4.80 per thousand

    $\frac{\$22,850}{\$1,000} = 22.85$

    22.85 x $4.80 = $109.68

7. **(B)** For this problem, we know the following:

    Base = Assessed valuation

    Base = 120% of $30,000

    Base = 1.20 x $30,000

    Base = $36,000

    Denomination = $1,000

    Tax rate = $5.12 per thousand

    $\frac{\$36,000}{\$1,000} = 36$

    36 x $5.12 = $184.32

8. **(B)** Express each tax rate as a decimal:

    $31.25 per $1,000 = $\frac{31.25}{1,000} = .03124$

    $3.45 per $100 = $\frac{3.45}{100} = .0345$

    32 cents per $10 = $\frac{.32}{10} = .0320$

    3 cents per $1 = $\frac{.03}{1} = .0300$

    The largest decimal is .0345

9. **(B)** For this problem, we know the following:

    Tax rate = $1.43 per $100

    Tax rate = $\frac{1.43}{100} = .0143$

    Tax rate = 1.43%

    Tax = $185,090.62

    Base = $\dfrac{\text{Tax}}{\text{Tax rate}}$

    Base = $\frac{185,090.62}{.0143}$

    Base = $12,943,400

10. **(C)** For this problem, we know the following:

    First $3,000: .02 x $3,000 = $60.00

    Second $3,000: .03 x $3,000 = $90.00

    Third $3,000: .03 x 3,000 = $90.00

    Remainder ($14,280 - $9,000) = $5,280

    .04 x $5,280 = $211.20

    Total tax = $451.20

11. **(D)** The increase is the selling price - cost:

    $65 - $50 = $15

    Now we express that increase as a percentage of the selling price over the cost, like this:

    $\frac{\$15}{\$50} = .30 = 30\%$

12. **(C)** Cost price = 60% of selling price, because the profit is 40% of the selling price, and the whole selling price is 100%.

    $27 = 60% of selling price

    Selling price = $27 ÷ 60%

    Selling price = $27 ÷ .6

    Selling price = $45.00

13.   **(B)** The discount was $120 - $96 = $24

Rate of discount = $\frac{\$24}{\$120}$ = .20, or 20%

14.   **(C)** Loss = cost - selling price

Considering the cost to be 100% of itself, if the loss is 50% of the cost, the selling price is also 50% of the cost (50% = 100% - 50%). Because the loss and the selling price are therefore the same, the loss is 100% of the selling price.

15.   **(C)** For this problem, we know the following:

Gain (profit) = 10% of $12.60

Profit = .10 x $12.60

Profit = $1.26

Selling price = cost + profit

Selling price = $12.60 + $1.26

Selling price = $13.86

16.   **(B)** Each dozen note pads costs 75 cents and is sold for 12 x .$25 = $3.00.

The profit is $3.00 - $.75 = $2.25

Profit based on cost = $\frac{\$2.25}{\$.75}$ = 3, or 300%

17.   **(D)** If profit = 10% of selling price, then cost = 90% of selling price.

$18 = 90% of selling price

Selling price = $18 ÷ 90%

Selling price = $18 ÷ .90

Selling price = $20

18.   **(C)** The discount for each new machine is calculated this way:

15% of $625 = .15 x $625, or $93.75

Each new machine will cost

$625 - $93.75 = $531.25

Four new machines will cost

$531.25 x 4 = $2,125

But there is an allowance of $85 each for 2 old machines:

$85 x 2 = $170

Final cost to city:

$2,125 - $170 = $1,955

19.   **(C)** We define 1 gross as 144 units.

Selling price for 6 pencils = 75 cents

Selling price for 1 pencil = $\frac{75 \text{ cents}}{6}$

Selling price for 1 gross of pencils = $\frac{75 \text{ cents}}{6}$ x 144, or $18

Cost for 1 gross of pencils = $9

Profit for 1 gross of pencils = $18 - $9, or $9

$\frac{\text{Profit}}{\text{Selling Price}} = \frac{\$9}{\$18}$ = .5, or 50%

20.   **(B)** For this problem, we know the following:

100% - 20% = 80%

10% of 80% = 8%

80% - 8% = 72%

100% - 72% = 28% single equivalent discount

21.   **(C)** Let X = the number of hours it will take the train to travel the next N miles.

$\frac{\text{miles}}{\text{hours}} = \frac{M}{H} = \frac{N}{X}$ (cross multiply here)

$MX = HN$

$X = \frac{HN}{M}$

22.   **(B)** For this problem, we know the following:

$\frac{A+B}{2} = Q$

$A + B = 2Q$

$\frac{C+D+E}{3} = R$

$C + D + E = 3R$

Thus, the average of

A, B, C, D, and $E = \frac{A+B+C+D+E}{5} = \frac{2Q+3R}{5}$

23.   **(A)** Because 7 trucks must each travel 300 miles, the total distance traveled will be 2,100 miles. Let X = the number of gallons of gasoline needed to travel 2,100 miles:

$\frac{\text{miles}}{\text{gallons}} = \frac{M}{G} = \frac{2,100}{X}$ (cross multiply here)

$MX = 2,100G$

$X = \frac{2,100G}{M}$

24.   **(C)** After the first quarter-mile, the number of miles remaining in the trip = $M - \frac{1}{4}$

This is equivalent to $4(M - \frac{1}{4}) = 4M - 1$ quarter-miles.

Total cost = Cost of first quarter-mile + cost of remaining part

Total cost = $C + \frac{C}{4}(4M - 1)$

Total cost = $C + CM - \frac{C}{4}$

Total cost = $C(1 + M - \frac{1}{4})$

Total cost = $C(M + \frac{3}{4})$

25.   **(D)** Let N = the percent of markdown:

$\frac{\text{Amount of markdown}}{\text{Original value}} = \frac{\text{Percent of markdown}}{100}$

$(\frac{X-Y}{X})100 = N$

26.   **(C)** The combined average =

$\frac{5(\$16,000)+3(\$20,000)+2(\$24,000)}{5+3+2}$

27.   **(B)** Let N = the son's age now and let $N + 24$ = the Deputy Marshall's age now. In 8 years, the son's age will be $N + 8$ and the Deputy Marshall's age will be $N + 24 + 8$, which will be twice the son's age, or $2(N + 8)$. So, $N + 24 + 8 = 2(N + 8)$.

28.   **A** First, you must define your universe:

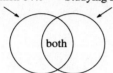

Studying Spanish 64% ⟶ Studying French 52%

⟶ Studying neither 28%

The population with which you are concerned excludes the 28%, so 100% - 28% = 72%

With this awareness, you can flesh out the formula:

$(100 - 28) - [(72 - 64) + (72 - 52)]$

29.   **D** Let's set up this chart:

Subject	Grade	Weight
English	90	4
Algebra	84	3
French	75	3
Music	76	1

$$\frac{\text{Sum of weighed grades}}{\text{sum of weights}} =$$

$$\frac{(90 \times 4)+(84 \times 3)+(75 \times 3)+(76 \times 1)}{4+3+3+1}$$

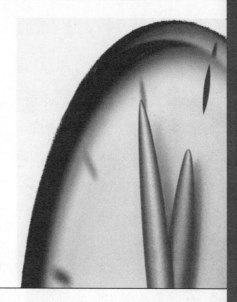

Hour **22**

Sample TEA Problems for Investigation Exam

What You'll Learn in This Hour

In this hour, we'll focus on some sample Treasury Enforcement Agent (TEA) problems for investigation. Read each question carefully, choosing the best answer from the list of choices that follow.

Here are your goals for this hour:

- Take the sample exam
- Review the answers and the answer explanations

Sample Investigative Judgment Exam

Study each paragraph and the statements that follow, making sure that you choose the statement that is best supported by the paragraph. Mark your answer on the answer sheet. Allow yourself 50 minutes to answer all the questions presented here.

Answer Sheet

1. Ⓐ Ⓑ Ⓒ Ⓓ	11. Ⓐ Ⓑ Ⓒ Ⓓ	21. Ⓐ Ⓑ Ⓒ Ⓓ
2. Ⓐ Ⓑ Ⓒ Ⓓ	12. Ⓐ Ⓑ Ⓒ Ⓓ	22. Ⓐ Ⓑ Ⓒ Ⓓ
3. Ⓐ Ⓑ Ⓒ Ⓓ	13. Ⓐ Ⓑ Ⓒ Ⓓ	23. Ⓐ Ⓑ Ⓒ Ⓓ
4. Ⓐ Ⓑ Ⓒ Ⓓ	14. Ⓐ Ⓑ Ⓒ Ⓓ	24. Ⓐ Ⓑ Ⓒ Ⓓ
5. Ⓐ Ⓑ Ⓒ Ⓓ	15. Ⓐ Ⓑ Ⓒ Ⓓ	25. Ⓐ Ⓑ Ⓒ Ⓓ
6. Ⓐ Ⓑ Ⓒ Ⓓ	16. Ⓐ Ⓑ Ⓒ Ⓓ	26. Ⓐ Ⓑ Ⓒ Ⓓ
7. Ⓐ Ⓑ Ⓒ Ⓓ	17. Ⓐ Ⓑ Ⓒ Ⓓ	27. Ⓐ Ⓑ Ⓒ Ⓓ
8. Ⓐ Ⓑ Ⓒ Ⓓ	18. Ⓐ Ⓑ Ⓒ Ⓓ	28. Ⓐ Ⓑ Ⓒ Ⓓ
9. Ⓐ Ⓑ Ⓒ Ⓓ	19. Ⓐ Ⓑ Ⓒ Ⓓ	29. Ⓐ Ⓑ Ⓒ Ⓓ
10. Ⓐ Ⓑ Ⓒ Ⓓ	20. Ⓐ Ⓑ Ⓒ Ⓓ	30. Ⓐ Ⓑ Ⓒ Ⓓ

Questions 1 through 7 are based on the following paragraph and statements.

Ellen Bascomb, an Internal Security Inspector with the IRS, received a letter from a citizen, John Riley, alleging misconduct by an IRS agent in the downtown Phoenix, Arizona, office. Riley alleged that his next door neighbor. Ronald Strachan, had "gotten off the hook" after an IRS audit by bribing the agent assigned to the case. Riley did not give the name of the agent.

During the course of the investigation, the following statements were made:

1. Ronald Strachan said that his 1983 Federal Income Tax return, which was in perfect order, had been routinely audited by agent Martin Galuski in October 1984.

2. John Riley said that Ronald Strachan had purchased an expensive stereo outfit in November and played it loudly at all hours.

3. Agent Martin Galuski said that he had audited Ronald Strachan's return and that he had interviewed Strachan in the company of his accountant during the afternoon of October 23, 1984.

4. Ronald Strachan's accountant, Barbara Cabrini, said that she had accompanied Strachan to his hearing on the afternoon of October 23, 1984, and that she had not heard Strachan offer a bribe nor Galuski imply that he might accept one.

5. Warren Cheung, the IRS agent who occupies the desk next to Galuski's, said that he neither saw nor heard anything out of the ordinary on the afternoon of October 23, 1984.

6. Ronald Strachan said that John Riley was an unpleasant neighbor whose house needed painting and that he seldom even said "hello" to him.

7. Martin Galuski told Ellen Bascomb that the final disposition of Strachan's case had not yet been made.

8. Security guard Harold Henshaw said that he had seen Galuski and Strachan enter the men's room together.

9. Bank teller Jesus Ramos said that Warren Cheung had deposited $500 in his savings account on October 24, 1984.

10. Mrs. Strachan said that her husband, Ronald, is an honest person who does not lie. cheat, or manipulate.

1. Which of the following statements is most damaging to the accused agent?

   A. Statement 3

   B. Statement 5

   C. Statement 7

   D. Statement 8

   E. Statement 9

2. Which of the following statements along with statement 5 indicates that a bribe was not offered during the hearing?

   A. Statement 3

   B. Statement 4

   C. Statement 7

   D. Statement 8

   E. Statement 10

3. To which of the following statements are the authorities likely to pay **least** attention in determining guilt or innocence in this case?

   A. Statement 4

   B. Statement 7

   C. Statement 8

   D. Statement 9

   E. Statement 10

4. Which two of the following statements are likely to make Ellen Bascomb suspicious of the reliability of Riley's information?

   A. Statements 2 and 6

   B. Statements 1 and 10

   C. Statements 3 and 4

   D. Statements 4 and 6

   E. Statements 5 and 9

5. Which two of the following statements totally corroborate each other?

   A. Statements 1 and 3

   B. Statements 2 and 6

   C. Statements 3 and 7

   D. Statements 4 and 10

   E. Statements 5 and 10

6. Which of the following statements implies the possibility of collusion?

   A. Statement 4

   B. Statement 5

   C. Statement 8

   D. Statement 9

   E. Statement 10

7. Which of the following statements presents purely circumstantial evidence?

   A. Statement 1

   B. Statement 6

   C. Statement 7

   D. Statement 9

   E. Statement 10

Questions 8 through 15 are based on the following paragraph and statements.

ATF Special Agent Minna Tharp received an anonymous tip that whiskey was being illegally distilled at 995 $\frac{1}{2}$ Canal Street and was being sold at the Goodlife Drugstore at 83 Bommel Street. Based on the tip and the strong distillery smell in the neighborhood of 995 $\frac{1}{2}$ Canal Street, Minna Tharp got a search warrant and discovered a distillery in operation in the ground floor apartment A. Sam Mong was found in the apartment where the distillery was operating. Three other apartments of the six in the building were occupied; the rest were vacant. Special Agent Zack Titus purchased a bottle of whiskey that did not have a federal tax seal at the Goodlife Drugstore.

During the course of the investigation, the following statements were made:

1. Fred Rank, owner and manager of the Goodlife Drugstore, stated that he knew nothing about sales of whiskey at his drugstore.

2. Alex Skoll, who sold the whiskey to Zack Titus, stated that he did not know that the tax on the whiskey had not been paid and that the whiskey he sold Mr. Titus was the same as the whiskey he had been selling for a long time.

3. Sam Mong stated that he had just been passing by and had entered the apartment in order to get out of the cold. He said he knew nothing about the whiskey.

4. Natalie Norton, who lives in apartment B directly above apartment A, stated that she had been frightened and knew nothing. However, she knew that the owner of the building, Karl Fitz, was guilty because he had been trying to make her move out.

5. Jack Sweet, who lives in apartment C, above Natalie Norton, stated that he frequently saw Sam Mong coming in or going out of the building.

6. Susan Hubble, who lives with her husband and one child in apartment E, stated that she had complained months ago to the janitor, Harvey Stone, about the smell and the activity in apartment A, which was supposed to be empty, but that he hadn't done anything about it.

7. Harvey Stone stated that he was not paid enough to do anything more than clean and supply heat.

8. Karl Fitz, owner of the building, stated that he had no knowledge of the use of apartment A. He tried to persuade the remaining tenants to move each month when he collected rent so that he could tear the building down and build a hi-rise modern building.

8. Which one of the following statements best indicates that the illegal still had been operating at 995 1/2 Canal Street for months?

A. Statement 1
B. Statement 2
C. Statement 5
D. Statement 6
E. Statement 7

9. Which of the following statements along with statement 3 connects Sam Mong with the distillery?

A. Statement 4
B. Statement 5
C. Statement 6
D. Statement 7
E. Statement 8

10. Which of the following statements along with statement 8 connects Karl Fitz with knowledge of the distillery?

A. Statement 2
B. Statement 3
C. Statement 4
D. Statement 5
E. Statement 6

11. Which one of the following statements is **least** likely to be used in proving a case?

A. Statement 4
B. Statement 5
C. Statement 6
D. Statement 7
E. Statement 8

12. Which of the following statements best indicates that the illegal sale of whiskey had been going on for months?

A. Statement 1
B. Statement 2
C. Statement 3
D. Statement 4
E. Statement 5

13. Which of the following statements along with statement 1 connects Fred Rank with the sale of whiskey without legal tax stamps?

A. Statement 2
B. Statement 3
C. Statement 5
D. Statement 6
E. Statement 8

14. Of the following, the two statements that appear to provide the most helpful information toward solving this case are

A. Statements 1 and 3
B. Statements 2 and 5
C. Statements 2 and 3
D. Statements 3 and 7
E. Statements 7 and 8

15. Which single statement presents the most damaging evidence concerning the illegal production of whiskey?

A. Statement 2
B. Statement 5
C. Statement 6
D. Statement 7
E. Statement 8

22

Questions 16 through 22 are based on the following paragraph and statements.

The president's entourage was turning the corner from Hoover Street onto Main Street where the president was to make an address from the courthouse steps. Secret Service Special Agent Myrna Meyers was among the Special Agents mingling with the crowd lining the route. Agent Meyers was standing in front of a condemned tenement inhabited by down-and-out squatters. Suddenly the air was peppered with short sharp blasts. Agent Meyers wheeled about and, with Secret Service Special Agent Juan Mendoza at her side, searched for the source of the shot-like sounds. The source was not immediately apparent, and the president continued on his way unharmed.

During the course of the investigation that followed this incident, the following statements were made:

1. John Doe, a regular police informer, said that Harvey Laveille, an unemployed typesetter residing at 1183 North Hoover Street, was the owner of a shotgun.
2. Lorraine Brooks, a salesperson at Gregory's Department Store at the corner of Hoover and Main, said that Bill Butlein, a stock boy, often muttered obscenities about the president.
3. Takeshi Matsuoka, an artist living at 381 Walnut Street which runs parallel to Main, said that in the past few days a total stranger—a tall, thin, balding man— had been walking about on the roof of 386 Walnut Street with what appeared to be surveyor's instruments.
4. Evelyn Bass said that Martina Meadows of 420 Walnut Street had threatened to kill the president if her son Willy were not accepted into the program at the Northside Day Care Center.
5. George Laveille, brother of Harvey Laveille, said that, as the new superintendent of 386 Walnut Street, he intended to clear the building of drug dealers and trespassers.
6. Ricardo Mancini, owner of the Parkway Diner, said that Bill Butlein and his girlfriend, Jody White, often talked of their disappointment with the president and of how they would do things differently.
7. Bill Butlein said that he held the president directly responsible for the addicts loitering at 1099 North Hoover, but that they were harmless.
8. Georgia Delaney of the sporting goods department at Gregory's Department Store said that she had sold rifle ammunition to a tall, thin, balding man whom she did not know.
9. Carmella DeAngelis said that she wished the police would stop the group of young boys who often tossed firecrackers at passing cars on High Street behind the diner.
10. Sarah Stern, a social worker, said that domestic violence is epidemic among the unemployed.
11. Ali Muhamed, who was watching the president from a third-floor window at Gregory's Department Store, said that he did not see anyone running on Hoover or Main.

16. Which of the following statements places an informant in the vicinity of the president at the time of the sounds?

A. Statement 1

B. Statement 3

C. Statement 5

D. Statement 6

E. Statement 11

17. Which of the following statements most likely represents an idle threat?

A. Statement 1

B. Statement 2

C. Statement 4

D. Statement 5

E. Statement 7

18. Which of the following statements along with statement 9 might lead Agent Meyers to assume that shots were not aimed at the president?

A. Statement 3

B. Statement 4

C. Statement 5

D. Statement 10

E. Statement 11

19. Which of the following statements along with statement 8 offers a real lead?

A. Statement 1

B. Statement 3

C. Statement 4

D. Statement 5

E. Statement 10

20. Which two of the following statements offer another useful lead for Agent Meyers?

A. Statements 1 and 5

B. Statements 2 and 6

C. Statements 6 and 7

D. Statements 7 and 10

E. Statements 9 and 11

21. Which of the following statements represents social commentary?

A. Statement 1

B. Statement 6

C. Statement 7

D. Statement 8

E. Statement 9

22. Which of the following statements illustrates cooperation between the local police and Secret Service Special Agents?

A. Statement 1

B. Statement 4

C. Statement 5

D. Statement 10

E. Statement 11

Questions 23 through 30 are based on the following paragraph and statements.

There was a crash on the turnpike between two trucks, one of which overturned. The other truck sustained rear-end damage. Cartons of cigarettes, some burst open, were found spilled onto the highway. One of the Police Officers, Ella Twain, who reported to the scene, noted that federal tax stamps on some of the cigarette packages were counterfeit. Steven Christian, the driver of the truck that overturned, was injured and had to be taken to the hospital without being questioned. The driver of the other truck, William Cook, stated that he was not carrying cigarettes and knew nothing about the ones on the highway.

During the course of the investigation, the following statements were made:

1.   Another Police Officer who reported to the scene, John Stewart, stated that he had checked the contents of both trucks. He found a quantity of unopened cases marked "cigarettes" in the overturned truck but did not open them.

2.   Sgt. Brian Schwartz, who investigated the accident, stated that there were 100 boxes of 12 cartons of cigarettes each in the overturned truck and that he had opened three of them at random and found them to contain packages of cigarettes with counterfeit tax stamps.

3.   Alex Tobin, owner of the overturned truck, stated that the truck contained a full shipment when it left the warehouse, all consigned to L&T Stationery Co. It contained no cigarettes, he stated.

4.   Mr. Tobin stated that Steven Christian was a liar and that you couldn't trust anything he said.

5.   Susan Smith, manager of L&T Stationery Co., stated that she was expecting the shipment but did not remember whether she had ordered any cigarettes.

6.   Tom Dunn, salesman for L&T Stationery Co., stated that the stationery store sold a lot of cigarettes because their price was so low.

7.   William Cook stated that he knew that Steven Christian was a crook from the poor way he drove a truck.

8.   When Dr. Simon Tate allowed his patient, Steven Christian, to be interviewed, Mr. Christian stated that he was only a truck driver and did not pay any attention to the cargo.

9.   Dr. Tate stated that Mr. Christian had been badly injured but would recover.

10.   Packages of cigarettes with counterfeit stamps were found in the L&T Stationery store by local Police Officer John Temple.

23. Which one of the following statements *best* indicates that there were cigarettes in the overturned truck?

A. Statement 1

B. Statement 2

C. Statement 3

D. Statement 4

E. Statement 6

24. Which of the following statements, along with statements 2 and 3, throws the greatest suspicion on Alex Tobin as the source of cigarettes with counterfeit stamps?

A. Statement 1

B. Statement 4

C. Statement 6

D. Statement 7

E. Statement 10

25. Which of the following statements would be *least* likely to be used proving the case?

A. Statement 1

B. Statement 5

C. Statement 6

D. Statement 7

E. Statement 10

26. Which of the following statements is the best indication that William Cook was not involved in using counterfeit cigarette stamps?

A. Statement 1

B. Statement 4

C. Statement 7

D. Statement 8

E. Statement 10

27. Which of the following statements best indicates that L&T Stationery was selling cigarettes with counterfeit stamps?

A. Statement 1

B. Statement 2

C. Statement 5

D. Statement 6

E. Statement 10

28. Which of the following two statements are the *best* indication that cigarettes with counterfeit stamps were being transported by truck for sale by L&T Stationery?

A. Statements 1 and 4

B. Statements 1 and 6

C. Statements 2 and 10

D. Statements 4 and 6

E. Statements 7 and 8

29. Which of the following two statements throws the greatest suspicion on Steven Christian as being involved in the sale of cigarettes with counterfeit stamps?

A. Statements 1 and 4

B. Statements 2 and 3

C. Statements 2 and 5

D. Statements 3 and 7

E. Statements 4 and 6

30. Which of the following statements along with statement 6 implies that L&T Stationery was knowingly stocking cigarettes with counterfeit stamps?

A. Statement 1

B. Statement 3

C. Statement 5

D. Statement 8

E. Statement 10

Answer Key

1.	D	11.	A	21.	C
2.	B	12.	B	22.	A
3.	E	13.	A	23.	B
4.	A	14.	B	24.	E
5.	A	15.	C	25.	D
6.	D	16.	E	26.	A
7.	D	17.	C	27.	E
8.	D	18.	D	28.	C
9.	B	19.	B	29.	B
10.	C	20.	A	30.	C

Answer Explanations

1. **(D)** The fact that the agent, Galuski, was seen entering the men's room with the individual whose return he was inspecting offers circumstantial evidence against him. Although no one can prove that Galuski asked for a bribe nor that Strachan offered one, this statement suggests that there was an opportunity for this to happen.

2. **(B)** Strachan's accountant, Barbara Cabrini, stated that a bribe was not offered in her presence. This statement corroborates that of Warren Cheung, who stated that he did not hear a bribe being offered.

3. **(E)** Character reference by a spouse is inadmissible in court except under very special specified conditions.

4. **(A)** The fact that Strachan and Riley evidently do not like each other must make the agent suspect that Riley is just trying to make trouble for his neighbor. Furthermore, if the two men do not speak to each other, Riley must either have fabricated the information or have gotten it from an unnamed third party.

5. **(A)** The information about the time of the inspection and the inspecting agent given by Strachan is confirmed by the agent.

6. **(D)** The implication of statement 9 is that Cheung did indeed overhear a bribe offer and that he was given money to keep him quiet.

7. **(D)** The fact that Cheung happened to make a deposit into his savings account the day after Galuski interviewed Strachan is purely circumstantial evidence.

8. **(D)** If Susan Hubble had complained months ago to the janitor about the smell, chances are pretty good that the still had been operating for some months.

9. **(B)** Because a resident of the building saw Sam Mong coming in and out frequently, it is reasonable to assume that Mong had something to do with the distillery.

10. **(C)** No proof is offered, but if Karl Fitz was trying to get tenants out, it is entirely possible that he was aware of the distillery and did not want tenants who might become aware of the activity and mention it to the authorities.

11. **(A)** The fact that a building owner asks a tenant to move out is, in itself, no indication that the owner of the building is involved in illegal activity.

12. **(B)** Alex Skoll said that he had been selling the same whiskey for a long time.

13. **(A)** The untaxed whiskey had been sold at Goodlife Drugstore for quite some time. It is most unlikely that Rank, owner and manager of the drugstore—who ordered, stocked, and inventoried—would be unaware of the illegal source of whiskey sold in his store.

14. **(B)** There may be other, more useful, statements, but of the choices offered, statement 2. which indicates the extended nature of the sale of illegal whiskey, and statement 5, which implicates Sam Mong, are the most useful.

15. **(C)** Statement 6, in which activity and smell are cited, presents the clearest evidence of the existence of the illegal distillery in apartment A.

16. **(E)** Ali Muhamed stated that he was on the third floor of Gregory's Department Store when the president passed.

17. **(C)** Martina Meadows may have been concerned about her son's placement for the following year, but her statement has the ring of complaint rather than of true threat.

18. **(D)** Sarah Stern's statement suggests that the shots may have been fired by and at residents in one of the condemned tenements. Statement 9 implies that there were no shots at all, that the noise was the sound of firecrackers.

19. **(B)** In statement 8, Georgia Delaney tells of selling rifle ammunition to a tall, thin, balding stranger. In statement 3, Takeshi Matsuoka tells of seeing a tall, thin, balding stranger on the roof of a building along the parade route.

20. **(A)** Statement 1 tells of an unhappy man who happens to be a gun owner. Statement 5 tells us that the brother of the gun owner lives in a building with convenient sight lines and within shotgun range of the parade route.

21. **(C)** The comment about the policies of the president being responsible for drug addiction is nothing more than social commentary.

22. **(A)** The services of a regular local police informer were offered to assist the Secret Service.

23. **(B)** Sergeant Schwartz opened boxes on the truck and found them to contain cigarettes with counterfeit tax stamps. Statement 1 implies that there were cigarettes on the truck because the cases were so marked, but the opening of the boxes in statement 2 offers more certain proof.

24. **(E)** Statement 3 establishes Alex Tobin as the owner of the truck and the truck's destination as L&T Stationery. Statement 2 establishes that cigarettes with counterfeit stamps were carried on Alex Tobin's truck. Statement 10 establishes that cigarettes with counterfeit tax stamps were sold in L&T Stationery, which was supplied by Alex Tobin.

25. **(D)** Driving ability has nothing to do with honesty.

22

26.   **(A)** The Police Officer makes no mention of cigarettes on William Cook's truck.

27.   **(E)** This is straightforward. Packages of cigarettes with counterfeit tax stamps were found in the L&T Stationery store.

28.   **(C)** Cigarettes with counterfeit tax stamps were found on a truck bound for the L&T Stationery store, and cigarettes with counterfeit tax stamps were found in the L&T Stationery store.

29.   **(B)** Steven Christian was the driver of a truck carrying cigarettes with counterfeit tax stamps. As such, he was involved in the sale of cigarettes with counterfeit tax stamps, knowingly or unwittingly.

30.   **(C)** It does seem unlikely that the manager of the store did not remember whether or not she had ordered cigarettes. Surely she kept records, so her "not remembering" was by nature an attempted cover-up. The price of cigarettes at L&T Stationery store was probably so low because nonpayment of tax kept the cost low.

HOUR 23

Sample TEA Verbal Reasoning Exam

What You'll Learn in This Hour

This hour presents you with a sample verbal reasoning portion of the Treasury Enforcement Agent (TEA) Exam. As you do when answering reading comprehension questions, be sure to carefully (but as quickly as possible) study each paragraph and the statements that follow. Follow the test directions carefully. To make the test more authentic, don't exceed the allotted time. When you've finished the test—or when the time is up—check your answers against the answer key. Finally, review the answer explanations at the end of this hour.

Here are your goals for this hour:

- Take the sample exam
- Review the answers and answer explanations

Answer Sheet

1. Ⓐ Ⓑ Ⓒ Ⓓ   11. Ⓐ Ⓑ Ⓒ Ⓓ   21. Ⓐ Ⓑ Ⓒ Ⓓ

2. Ⓐ Ⓑ Ⓒ Ⓓ   12. Ⓐ Ⓑ Ⓒ Ⓓ   22. Ⓐ Ⓑ Ⓒ Ⓓ

3. Ⓐ Ⓑ Ⓒ Ⓓ   13. Ⓐ Ⓑ Ⓒ Ⓓ   23. Ⓐ Ⓑ Ⓒ Ⓓ

4. Ⓐ Ⓑ Ⓒ Ⓓ   14. Ⓐ Ⓑ Ⓒ Ⓓ   24. Ⓐ Ⓑ Ⓒ Ⓓ

5. Ⓐ Ⓑ Ⓒ Ⓓ   15. Ⓐ Ⓑ Ⓒ Ⓓ   25. Ⓐ Ⓑ Ⓒ Ⓓ

6. Ⓐ Ⓑ Ⓒ Ⓓ   16. Ⓐ Ⓑ Ⓒ Ⓓ

7. Ⓐ Ⓑ Ⓒ Ⓓ   17. Ⓐ Ⓑ Ⓒ Ⓓ

8. Ⓐ Ⓑ Ⓒ Ⓓ   18. Ⓐ Ⓑ Ⓒ Ⓓ

9. Ⓐ Ⓑ Ⓒ Ⓓ   19. Ⓐ Ⓑ Ⓒ Ⓓ

10. Ⓐ Ⓑ Ⓒ Ⓓ   20. Ⓐ Ⓑ Ⓒ Ⓓ

Sample Verbal Reasoning Exam

> **DIRECTIONS:** For each verbal reasoning question, you will be given a paragraph that contains all the information necessary to infer the correct answer. Use only the information provided in the paragraph. Do not speculate or make assumptions that go beyond this information. Also, assume that all information given in the paragraph is true, even if it conflicts with some fact known to you. Only one correct answer can be validly inferred from the information contained in the paragraph. Mark its letter on your answer sheet. You should allow yourself 50 minutes to answer the following 25 questions.

23

1. A member of the department shall not indulge in liquor while in uniform. A member of the department not required to wear a uniform and a uniformed member while out of uniform shall not indulge in intoxicants to an extent unfitting the member for duty.

   The paragraph best supports the statement that

   A. An off-duty member, not in uniform, may drink liquor to the extent that it does not unfit the member for duty.

   B. A member not on duty, but in uniform and not unfit for duty, may drink liquor.

   C. An on-duty member, unfit for duty in uniform, may drink intoxicants.

   D. A uniformed member in civilian clothes may not drink intoxicants unless unfit for duty.

   E. A civilian member of the department, in uniform, may drink liquor if fit for duty.

2. Tax law specialists may authorize their assistants to sign their names to reports, letters, and papers that are not specially required to be signed personally by the tax law specialist. The signature should be: "Jane Doe, tax law specialist, by Richard Roe, tax technician." The name of the tax law specialist may be written or stamped, but the signature of the tax technician shall be in ink.

   The paragraph best supports the statement that

   A. If a tax law specialist's assistant signs official papers both by rubber stamp and in ink, the assistant has authority to sign.

   B. If a tax technician does not neglect to include his or her title in ink along with his or her signature following the word "by," the technician may sign papers that are not specially required to be signed personally by the tax law specialist.

   C. No signatory authority delegated to the tax technician by the tax law specialist may be redelegated by the tax technician to an assistant unless so authorized in ink by the tax law specialist.

   D. If a tax law specialist personally signs written requisitions in ink, the technician is not required to identify the source of the order with a rubber stamp.

   E. When a tax technician signs authorized papers for a tax law specialist, the tax technician must write out the tax law specialist's signature in full with pen and ink.

3. After retirement from service, a member shall receive a retirement allowance consisting of an annuity that shall be the actuarial equivalent of his accumulated deductions at the time of retirement; a pension in addition to his annuity that shall be one service-fraction of his final compensation multiplied by the number of years of government service since he last became a member; and a pension that is the actuarial equivalent of the reserve-for-increased-take-home-pay to which he may then be entitled, if any.

The paragraph best supports the statement that

A. A retirement allowance shall consist of an annuity plus a pension plus an actuarial equivalent of a service-fraction.

B. After retirement from service, a member shall receive an annuity plus a pension plus an actuarial equivalent of reserve-for-increased-take-home-pay if he is entitled.

C. A retiring member shall receive an annuity plus reserve-for-increased-take-home-pay, if any, plus final compensation.

D. A retirement allowance shall consist of a pension plus reserve-for-increased-take-home-pay, if any, plus accumulated deductions.

E. A retirement allowance shall consist of an annuity that is equal to one service-fraction of final compensation, a pension multiplied by the number of years of government service, and the actuarial equivalent of accumulated deductions from increased take-home-pay.

4. If you are in doubt about whether any matter is legally mailable, you should ask the postmaster. Even though the Postal Service has not expressly declared any matter to be nonmailable, the sender of such matter may be held fully liable for violation of law if he or she does actually send nonmailable matter through the mail.

The paragraph best supports the statement that

A. If the postmaster is in doubt about whether any matter is legally mailable, the postmaster may be held liable for any sender's sending nonmailable matter through the mail.

B. If the sender is ignorant of what it is that constitutes nonmailable matter, the sender is relieved of all responsibility for mailing nonmailable matter.

C. If a sender sends nonmailable matter, the sender is fully liable for law violation even though doubt may have existed about the mailability of the matter.

D. If the Postal Service has not expressly declared material mailable, it is nonmailable.

E. If the Postal Service has not expressly declared material nonmailable, it is mailable.

5. In evaluating education for a particular position, education in and of itself is of no value except to the degree in which it contributes to knowledge, skills, and abilities needed in the particular job. On its face, such a statement would seem to contend that general educational development need not be considered in evaluating education and training. Much to the contrary, such a proposition favors the consideration of any and

all training, but only as it pertains to the position for which the applicant applies.

The paragraph best supports the statement that

A. If general education is supplemented by specialized education, it is of no value.

B. If a high school education is desirable in any occupation, special training need not be evaluated.

C. In evaluating education, a contradiction arises in assigning equal weight to general and specialized education.

D. Unless it is supplemented by general education, specialized education is of no value.

E. Education is of value to the degree to which it is needed in the particular position.

6. Statistics tell us that heart disease kills more people than any other illness, and the death rate continues to rise. People over 30 have a fifty-fifty chance of escaping, for heart disease is chiefly an illness of people in late middle age and advanced years. Because there are more people in this age group living today than there were some years ago, heart disease is able to find more victims.

The paragraph best supports the statement that

A. If a person has heart disease, there is a 50% chance that he or she is over 30 years of age.

B. According to statistics, more middle-aged and elderly people die of heart disease than of all other causes.

C. Because heart disease is chiefly an illness of people in late middle age,

young people are less likely to be the victims of heart disease.

D. The rising birth rate has increased the possibility that the average person will die of heart disease.

E. If the stress of modern living were not increasing, there would be a slower increase in the risk of heart disease.

7. Racketeers are primarily concerned with business affairs, legitimate or otherwise, and prefer those that are close to the margin of legitimacy. They get their best opportunities from business organizations that meet the need of large sections of the public for goods or services that are defined as illegitimate by the same public, such as prostitution, illicit drugs, or liquor. In contrast to the thief, the racketeer and the establishments he or she controls deliver goods and services for money received.

The paragraph best supports the statement that

A. Because racketeers deliver goods and services for money received, their business affairs are not illegitimate.

B. Because racketeering involves objects of value, it is unlike theft.

C. Victims of racketeers are not guilty of violating the law, therefore racketeering is a victimless crime.

D. Because many people want services that are not obtainable through legitimate sources, they contribute to the difficulty of suppressing racketeers.

E. If large sections of the public are engaged in legitimate business with racketeers, the businesses are not illegitimate.

8. The housing authority not only faces every problem of the private developer, it must also assume responsibilities of which private building is free. The authority must account to the community; it must conform to federal regulations; it must provide durable buildings of good standard at low cost; and it must overcome the prejudices of contractors, bankers, and prospective tenants against public operations. These authorities are being watched by antihousing enthusiasts for the first error of judgment or the first evidence of high costs that can be torn to bits before a Congressional committee.

The paragraph best supports the statement that

A. Because private developers are not accountable to the community, they do not have the opposition of contractors, bankers, and prospective tenants.

B. If Congressional committees are watched by antihousing enthusiasts, they may discover errors of judgment and high costs on the part of a housing authority.

C. Although a housing authority must deal with all the difficulties encountered by a private builder, it must also deal with antihousing enthusiasts.

D. If housing authorities are not immune to errors in judgment, they must provide durable buildings of good standard and low cost, just like private developers.

E. If a housing authority is to conform to federal regulations, it must overcome the prejudices of contractors, builders, and prospective tenants.

9. Security of tenure in the public service must be viewed in the context of the universal quest for security. If we narrow our application of the term to employment, the problem of security in the public service is seen to differ from that in private industry only in the need to meet the peculiar threats to security in governmental organizations—principally the danger of making employment contingent on factors other than the performance of the workers.

The paragraph best supports the statement that

A. If workers seek security, they should enter public service.

B. If employment is contingent on factors other than work performance, workers feel more secure.

C. If employees believe that their security is threatened, they are employed in private industry.

D. The term of employment in public service differs from that in private industry.

E. The employment status of the public servant with respect to security of tenure differs from that of the private employee by encompassing factors beyond those affecting the private employee.

10. The wide use of antibiotics has presented a number of problems. Some patients become allergic to the drugs, so that the drugs cannot be used when they are needed. In other cases, after prolonged treatment with antibiotics, certain organisms no longer respond to them. This is one of the reasons for the constant search for more potent drugs.

The paragraph best supports the statement that

A. Because a number of problems have been presented by long-term treatment with antibiotics, antibiotics should never be used on a long-term basis.

B. Because some people have developed an allergy to specific drugs, potent antibiotics cannot always be used.

C. Because antibiotics have been used successfully for certain allergies, there must be a constant search for more potent drugs.

D. If antibiotics are used for a prolonged period of time, certain organisms become allergic to them.

E. Because so many diseases have been successfully treated with antibiotics, there must be a constant search for new drugs.

11. The noncompetitive class consists of positions for which there are minimum qualifications but for which no reliable exam has been developed. In the noncompetitive class, every applicant must meet minimum qualifications in terms of education, experience, and medical or physical qualifications. There may even be an examination on a pass/fail basis.

The paragraph best supports the statement that

A. If an exam is unreliable, the position is in the noncompetitive class.

B. If an applicant has met minimum qualifications in terms of education, experience, medical, or physical requirements, the applicant must pass a test.

C. If an applicant has met minimum qualifications in terms of education, experi-

rience, medical, or physical requirements, the applicant may fail a test.

D. If an applicant passes an exam for a noncompetitive position, the applicant must also meet minimum qualifications.

E. If there are minimum qualifications for a position, the position is in the noncompetitive class.

12. Two independent clauses cannot share one sentence without some form of connective. If they do, they form a run-on sentence. Two principal clauses may be joined by a coordinating conjunction, by a comma followed by a coordinating conjunction, or by a semicolon. They may also form two distinct sentences. Two main clauses may never be joined by a comma without a coordinating conjunction. This error is called a comma splice.

The paragraph best supports the statement that

A. If the violation is called a comma splice, two main clauses are joined by a comma without a coordinating conjunction.

B. If two distinct sentences share one sentence and are joined by a coordinating conjunction, the result is a run-on sentence.

C. When a coordinating conjunction is not followed by a semicolon, the writer has committed an error of punctuation.

D. Although a comma and a semicolon may not be used in the same principal clause, they may be used in the same sentence.

E. A bad remedy for a run-on sentence is not a comma splice.

13. The pay for some job titles is hourly; for others, it is annual. Official work weeks vary from 35 hours to 37.5 hours to 40 hours. In some positions, overtime is earned for all time worked beyond the set number of hours, and differentials are paid for night, weekend, and holiday work. Other positions offer compensatory time off for overtime or for work during unpopular times. Still other positions require the jobholder to devote as much extra time as needed to do the work without any extra compensation. And in some positions, employees who work overtime are given a meal allowance.

The paragraph best supports the statement that

A. If a meal allowance is given, there is compensation for overtime.

B. If the work week is 35 hours long, the job is unpopular.

C. If overtime is earned, pay in the job title is hourly.

D. If a jobholder has earned a weekend differential, the employee has worked beyond the set number of hours.

E. If compensatory time is offered, it is offered as a substitute for overtime pay.

14. All applicants must be of satisfactory character and reputation and must meet all requirements set forth in the Notice of Examination for the position for which they are applying. Applicants may be summoned for the written test before investigation of their qualifications and background. Admission to the test does not mean that the applicant has met the qualifications for the position.

The paragraph best supports the statement that

A. If an applicant has been admitted to the test, the applicant has met the qualifications for the position.

B. If an applicant has not been investigated, the applicant will not be admitted to the written test.

C. If an applicant has met all requirements for the position, the applicant will be admitted to the test.

D. If an applicant has satisfactory character and reputation, the applicant will not have his or her background investigated.

E. If an applicant has met all the requirements set forth in the Notice of Examination, the applicant will pass the test.

15. Although it has in the past been illegal for undocumented aliens to work in the United States, it has not, until now, been unlawful for employers to hire these aliens. With the passage of the new immigration law, employers will now be subject to civil penalties and ultimately imprisonment if they "knowingly" hire, recruit, or refer for a fee any unauthorized aliens. Similarly, it is also unlawful for employers to continue to employ an undocumented alien who was hired after November 6, 1986, knowing that he or she was or is unauthorized to work.

The paragraph best supports the statement that

A. Under the new immigration law, it is no longer illegal for undocumented aliens to be denied employment in the United States.

B. If an undocumented alien is not remaining on the job illegally, the worker was not hired after November 6, 1986.

C. If a person wants to avoid the penalties of the new immigration law, the person must not knowingly employ aliens.

D. If an employer inadvertently hires undocumented aliens, the employer may be subject to fine or imprisonment, but not both.

E. If an unauthorized alien was able to find an employer who would hire him or her after November 6, 1986, the alien was welcome to go to work.

16. The law requires that the government offer employees, retirees, and their families the opportunity to continue group health and/or welfare fund coverage at 102% of the group rate in certain instances where the coverage would otherwise terminate. All group benefits, including optional benefits riders, are available. Welfare fund benefits that can be continued under COBRA are dental, vision, prescription drugs, and other related medical benefits. The period of coverage varies from 18 to 36 months, depending on the reason for continuation.

The paragraph best supports the statement that

A. The period of coverage continuation varies depending on the reason for termination.

B. After retirement, welfare fund benefits continue at a 102% rate.

C. The law requires employees, retirees, and their families to continue health coverage.

D. COBRA is a program for acquiring welfare fund benefits.

E. If retirees or their families do not desire to terminate them, they can continue group benefits at 102% of the group rate.

17. Historical records as such rarely constitute an adequate or, more importantly, a reliable basis for estimating earthquake potential. In most regions of the world, recorded history is short relative to the time between the largest earthquakes. Thus the fact that there have been no historic earthquakes larger than a given size does not make us confident that they will also be absent in the future. It may alternatively be due to the short length of available historical records relative to the long repeat time for large earthquakes.

The paragraph best supports the statement that

A. If historic earthquakes are no larger than a given size, they are unlikely to recur.

B. Potential earthquakes do not inspire confidence in historical records as predictors of time between earthquakes.

C. If the time span between major earthquakes were not longer than the length of available records, history would have greater predictive value.

D. Because there have been no historic earthquakes larger than a given size, we are confident that there will be a long time span between major earthquakes.

E. In those regions of the world where recorded history is long, the time between the largest earthquakes is short.

18. A language can be thought of as a number of strings or sequences of symbols. The definition of a language defines which strings belong to the language, but because most languages of interest consist of an infinite number of strings, this definition is impossible to accomplish by listing the strings (or sentences). Although the number of *sentences* in a language can be infinite, the rules by which they are constructed are not. This may explain why we are able to speak sentences in a language we have never spoken before and to understand sentences we have never heard before.

The paragraph best supports the statement that

A. If there is an infinite number of sequences of symbols in a language, there is an infinite number of rules for their construction.

B. If we have never spoken a language, we can understand its sentences provided that we know the rules by which they were constructed.

C. A language is defined by its strings.

D. If the number of sentences in an unnatural language were not infinite, we would be able to define it.

E. If sequences of symbols are governed by rules of construction, then the number of sentences can be determined.

19. An assumption commonly made in regard to the reliability of testimony is that when a number of persons report the same matter, those details on which there is an agreement may generally be considered substantiated. Experiments have shown, however, that there is a tendency for the same errors to appear in the testimony of different individuals, and that, apart from any collusion, agreement of testimony is no proof of dependability.

The paragraph best supports the statement that

A. If details of the testimony are true, all witnesses will agree to it.

B. Unless there is collusion, it is impossible for a number of persons to give the same report.

C. If most witnesses do not independently attest to the same facts, the facts cannot be true.

D. If the testimony of a group of people is in substantial agreement, it cannot be ruled out that those witnesses have not all made the same mistake.

E. Under experimental conditions, witnesses tend to give reliable testimony.

20. In some instances, changes are made in a contract after it has been signed and accepted by both parties. This is done either by inserting a new clause in a contract or by annexing a rider to the contract. If a contract is changed by a rider, both parties must sign the rider for the rider to be legal. The basic contract should also note that a rider is attached by inserting new words to the contract, and both parties should also initial and date the new insertion. The same requirement applies if either party later changes any wording in the contract. What two people agree to do, they can mutually agree not to do, as long as they both agree.

The paragraph best supports the statement that

A. If two people mutually agree not to do something, they must sign a rider.

B. If both parties to a contract do not agree to attach a rider, they must initial the contract to render it legal.

C. If a rider to a contract is to be legal, that rider must be agreed to and signed by both parties, who must not neglect to initial and date that portion of the contract to which the rider refers.

D. If a party to a contract does not agree to a change, that party should initial the change and annex a rider detailing the disagreement.

E. If the wording of a contract is not to be changed, both parties must initial and date a rider.

21. Explosives are substances or devices capable of producing a volume of rapidly expanding gases that exert a sudden pressure on their surroundings. Chemical explosives are the most commonly used, although there are also mechanical and nuclear explosives. All mechanical explosives are devices in which a physical reaction is produced, such as that caused by overloading a container with compressed air. Although nuclear explosives are by far the most powerful, all nuclear explosives have been restricted to military weapons. The paragraph best supports the statement that

A. All explosives that have been restricted to military weapons are nuclear explosives.

B. No mechanical explosives are devices in which a physical reaction is produced, such as that caused by overloading a container with compressed air.

C. Some nuclear explosives have not been restricted to military weapons.

D. All mechanical explosives have been restricted to military weapons.

E. Some devices in which a physical reaction is produced, such as that caused by overloading a container with compressed air, are mechanical explosives.

22. A sanitizer is an agent, usually chemical in nature, that is used in hospitals to reduce the number of microorganisms to a level that has been officially approved as safe. Frequently, hospitals use stronger antimicrobial agents to ensure that stringent health standards are met. However, if no dangerous microorganisms that must be destroyed are known to be present in a given environment, sanitizers are used.

The paragraph best supports the statement that, in a given hospital environment

A. If dangerous microorganisms that must be destroyed are known to be present, then sanitizers are used.

B. If sanitizers are used, then some dangerous microorganisms that must be destroyed are known to be present.

C. If sanitizers are not used, then no dangerous microorganisms that must be destroyed are known to be present.

D. If only some dangerous microorganisms are known to be present, then sanitizers are used.

E. If sanitizers are not used, then dangerous microorganisms that must be destroyed are known to be present.

23. One use for wild land is the protection of certain species of wild animals or plants in wildlife refuges or in botanical reservations. Some general types of land use involve activities that conflict with this stated purpose. All activities that exhibit such conflict are, of course, excluded from refuges and reservations.

The paragraph best supports the statement that

A. All activities that conflict with the purpose of wildlife refuges or botanical reservations are general types of land use.

B. All activities excluded from wildlife refuges and botanical reservations are those that conflict with the purpose of the refuge or reservation.

C. Some activities excluded from wildlife refuges and botanical reservations are general types of land use.

D. No activities that conflict with the purpose of wildlife refuges and botanical reservations are general types of land use.

E. Some general types of land use are not excluded from wildlife refuges and botanical reservations.

24. Information centers can be categorized according to the primary activity or service they provide. For example, some information centers are document depots. These depots, generally government sponsored, serve as archives for the acquisition, storage, retrieval, and dissemination of a variety of documents. All document depots can provide a great range of user services, which may include preparing specialized bibliographies; publishing announcements, indexes, and abstracts; and providing copies.

The paragraph best supports the statement that

A. Some information centers are categorized by features other than the primary activity or service they provide.

B. Some document depots lack the capacity to provide a great range of user services.

C. No document depot lacks the capacity to provide a great range of user services.

D. All information centers are document depots.

E. Some places that provide a great range of user services are not document depots.

25. Authorities generally agree that the use of hyphens tends to defy most rules. The best advice that can be given is to consult the dictionary to determine whether a given prefix is joined solidly to a root word or is hyphenated. One reliable rule, however, is that if an expression is a familiar one, such as *overtime* or *hatchback*, it is a nonhyphenated compound.

The paragraph best supports the statement that

A. If an expression is a familiar one, then it is a hyphenated compound.

B. If an expression is a nonhyphenated compound, then it is a familiar expression.

C. If an expression is not a familiar one, then it is a hyphenated compound.

D. If an expression is a hyphenated compound, containing a suffix rather than a prefix, then it is not a familiar one.

E. If an expression is a hyphenated compound, then it is not a familiar one.

Answer Key

1.	A	11.	D	21.	E	
2.	B	12.	A	22.	E	
3.	B	13.	E	23.	C	
4.	C	14.	C	24.	C	
5.	E	15.	B	25.	E	
6.	C	16.	E			
7.	D	17.	C			
8.	C	18.	B			
9.	E	19.	D			
10.	B	20.	C			

23

Answer Explanations

1.   **(A)** The essential information from which the answer can be inferred is found in the second sentence. Because *a uniformed member while out of uniform* (in other words, an off-duty member) *may not indulge in intoxicants to an extent unfitting the member for duty,* it follows that the same member may drink liquor in moderation. Response B is incorrect because it directly contradicts the first sentence. Response C is incorrect because it introduces a concept not addressed in the paragraph—that of the uniformed member who reports unfit for duty. Response D is wrong because it reverses the meaning of the second sentence—the uniformed member in civilian clothes may drink to the extent that the member remains fit for duty. Response E is incorrect because it raises a topic never mentioned in the paragraph—that of the civilian member of the department in a uniform (what uniform?).

2.   **(B)** The paragraph makes the statement that the technician may sign documents that the tax specialist is not required to per-sonally sign. The paragraph also states the rules that apply to how the technician is to sign such documents: name and title of tax law specialist, followed by "by" and the name and title of the tax technician in ink. Responses C and D are incorrect because they address topics not mentioned in the paragraph—redelegation and requisitions. Response E is incorrect; the tax law specialist's name may be affixed by rubber stamp.

3.   **(B)** The first clause states that the retiree is entitled to an annuity; the second clause tells of the pension that is the equal of one service-fraction of final compensation multiplied by number of years of government service; and the last clause describes an additional pension that is the actuarial equivalent of any reserve-for-increased-take-home-pay to which the retiree might at that time be entitled. Response A is incorrect because it does not complete the explanation of the basis for the second pension. Responses C, D, and E are all hopelessly garbled misstatements.

4. **(C)** In effect, the paragraph is saying, "When in doubt, check it out." Ignorance of the nature of the material to be mailed or of how the law pertains to it does not excuse the mailer if the material was indeed subject to a prohibition. Response A misinterprets the role of the postmaster. The postmaster is the final authority as to mailability. Response B is incorrect in its direct contradiction of the paragraph that states, "Ignorance is no excuse." Responses D and E both interpret beyond the paragraph. The paragraph places all burden on the mailer.

5. **(E)** The last sentence makes the point that *any and all training* is valuable *but only as it pertains to the position for which the applicant applies.* Responses A and D miss the point. Any training or education is valuable *if it contributes to knowledge, skills, and abilities needed in the particular job.* Responses B and C make statements unsupported by the paragraph.

6. **(C)** The second sentence tells us that heart disease is an illness of late middle age and old age. Response A is totally wrong: Because heart disease is an illness of older people, the odds of a person with heart disease being over 30 are much more than 50%. The 50-50 statement refers to the likelihood of persons over 30 at some time developing heart disease. Response B confuses death from *all other illnesses.* Response D makes an unsupported assumption that only the rising birth rate contributes to the number of people above a certain age. (Actually, the longevity rate is much more crucial to this figure.) Response E makes a statement which, whether true or false, is in no way supported by the paragraph.

7. **(D)** If people want what they can't get through legitimate, entirely legal, channels, they will turn to those who supply those products or services. The consumers of less-than-legitimate products or services are unlikely to betray their suppliers. Response A is incorrect: Because racketeers deliver goods and services for money received, they are not engaged in theft, but not all "non-thieves" are engaged in legitimate business. Response B is incorrect because both racketeering and theft involve objects of value; the differences are along other dimensions. Response C makes no sense at all. Response E is unsupported by the paragraph.

8. **(C)** The first sentence tells us that the problems of the housing authority are legion, that it faces all the problems of private developers and problems peculiar to a public authority. Being *watched by antihousing enthusiasts* is one of these problems. Response A makes an unsupported statement: The paragraph does not enumerate the problems of private developers. Response B is incorrect: It is the antihousing authorities who watch for errors and cost overruns and then bring them to the attention of Congressional committees. Responses D and E make unsupported statements that do not make much sense as statements.

9. **(E)** *The peculiar threats to security in governmental organizations* to which the paragraph alludes are factors related to partisan, electoral politics. Other factors—job performance, needs of the marketplace, interpersonal relationships, and internal power plays—affect private and public employees in about equal propor-

tions. Response A is unsupported by the paragraph. Response B directly contradicts the paragraph. Responses C and D are entirely unsupported by the paragraph.

10. **(B)** Some people develop allergies to antibiotics so that when those specific antibiotics might be the drug of choice to counter illness, the antibiotics cannot be used for those people. Response A makes a categorical statement that is unsupported by the paragraph. Response C is incorrect because antibiotics do not *cure* allergies; they may *cause* allergies. Response D is incorrect because the organisms do not become allergic to antibiotics (people become allergic). Response E is incorrect because there would be no need to search for new drugs if the existing ones were unfailingly effective. We need new drugs precisely because some organisms have become resistant to current ones.

11. **(D)** The paragraph clearly states that *in the noncompetitive class, every applicant must meet minimum qualifications. . . .* There may or may not be a pass/fail examination, but there most definitely are minimum qualifications that must be fulfilled. Response A is a distortion of the first sentence. The sentence means that there are no reliable exams for noncompetitive positions, not that noncompetitive positions are filled by unreliable exams. Response B is incorrect because the paragraph states that there may be an exam, not that there will be an exam. Response C is incorrect because if there is a test, the applicant must pass it. Response E goes beyond the scope of the paragraph: The paragraph does not state that all positions

for which there are minimum qualifications are in the noncompetitive class.

12. **(A)** The paragraph defines a comma splice as the joining of two main clauses by a comma without a coordinating conjunction. Response B is incorrect because a run-on sentence is defined as two independent clauses sharing one sentence with no connective. Response C is incorrect because the paragraph suggests that a semicolon used as a connective can stand alone. Response D touches on a subject not addressed in the paragraph. Response E reverses the intent of the paragraph: A comma splice is a bad remedy for a run-on sentence.

13. **(E)** In some positions, overtime is earned for time worked beyond the set number of hours, other positions offer compensatory time for overtime. Compensatory time is an alternative to overtime pay. Responses A, B, and C make unsupported statements. Response D combines the additional payments for two different classes of services. Overtime pay is for hours in excess of the standard number; weekend differentials are for work on weekends, even if within the standard number of workweek hours.

14. **(C)** The paragraph makes clear that applicants may take the test before their backgrounds and qualifications have been investigated. If qualification is not even prerequisite to testing, certainly a qualified applicant will not be barred from the exam. Response A is incorrect in assuming that all persons admitted to the test are unqualified. The paragraph indicates only that their qualifications need not have yet been verified. Response B contradicts the

paragraph. Response D is incorrect: The investigation is made to verify satisfactory character and reputation. Response E is unsupported by the paragraph.

15. **(B)** Because it is illegal to continue employing an undocumented alien hired after November 6, 1986, it must not be illegal to retain an employee who was hired before that date. Response A is incorrect: It never was illegal to *deny* employment to undocumented aliens; it is now illegal to employ them. Response C misinterprets the paragraph: The paragraph applies only to undocumented or unauthorized aliens. Aliens who have authorizing documents or "green cards" may be employed legally. Response D is incorrect: Penalties are for "knowingly" hiring illegal aliens, not for inadvertent hiring. (You must limit your answers to the material presented in the paragraph, even though you may know of the burden on employers to verify documentation or face penalties.) Response E is in contradiction to the paragraph.

16. **(E)** COBRA provides for the continuation of health and welfare benefits after payment of 102% of the group premium. Response A misinterprets the variation in the length of continuing coverage to depend on the reason for termination of coverage rather than on the reason for continuation of coverage. Response B is incorrect because it is the cost to the subscriber that jumps to 102% of the group rate, not the extent of the coverage. Response C is incorrect because the law requires the employer to offer the opportunity to continue health coverage: it does not require employees, retirees, or their families to continue that coverage. Response D is wrong because, under COBRA, terminated employees and retirees can continue coverage but they cannot acquire new benefits.

17. **(C)** Recorded history is short relative to the time span between major earthquakes; therefore, history is inadequate as a predictive tool. Either a much longer period of recorded history or a much shorter span between major earthquakes would enhance the predictive value of historical data. Response A is not supported by the paragraph. Responses B and D are not only unsupported, they make no sense. Response E makes an assumption that goes beyond the paragraph.

18. **(B)** Basically, the last sentence of the paragraph is saying that if we know the rules of construction of a language, we can understand it. Response A contradicts the paragraph. The paragraph states that the number of rules is finite. Response C twists the second sentence, which states that definition of a language by listing its strings is impossible because the number of strings is finite. Response D introduces unnatural languages, which is not a subject of the paragraph. Response E makes an unsupported statement.

19. **(D)** Just as *agreement of testimony is no proof of dependability*, so agreement of testimony is no proof of undependability. Response A is incorrect because the thrust of the paragraph is that people's perceptions are sometimes in error. Response B contradicts the paragraph: It is reported that a number of witnesses may report the same erroneous observation even apart from collusion. Response C misses the point: Because witnesses can make mistakes, they

are just as likely to have not noticed the truth as to have "observed" that which did not happen. Response E is a misstatement.

20.   **(C)** If a contract is changed by a rider, both parties must sign the rider. The basic contract should note that a rider is being attached, and both parties should initial and date the notice in the basic contract. Response A is incorrect in that it creates a rider without necessarily having created a contract. A mutual agreement to refrain from an act may be a first point of agreement and not a change. Responses B and D are both incorrect because there can be no change unless both parties agree. Response E is incorrect because if there is to be no change, there is no call for a rider.

21.   **(E)** The answer can be validly inferred from the third sentence in the paragraph. This sentence states that *all mechanical explosives are devices in which a physical reaction is produced, such as that caused by overloading a container with compressed air*. From this, we can safely conclude that some devices in which a physical reaction is produced, such as that caused by overloading a container with compressed air, are mechanical explosives. Response A cannot be inferred because the paragraph does not provide sufficient information to enable the conclusion to be drawn that all explosives that have been restricted to military weapons are nuclear weapons. It may be that other explosives that are not nuclear weapons also have been restricted to military weapons. Responses B and C are incorrect because they contradict the paragraph. Response D is wrong because the paragraph

provides no information at all about whether or not mechanical explosives are restricted to military weapons.

22.   **(E)** The essential information from which the answer can be inferred is contained in the third sentence of the paragraph. An analysis of this sentence reveals that response E is validly inferable because if it were not true that *dangerous microorganisms that must be destroyed are known to be present*, then sanitizers would be used. In E, we are told that *sanitizers are not used*; therefore, we can conclude that *dangerous microorganisms that must be destroyed are known to be present*. Response A is wrong because the paragraph does not definitely state what is done if dangerous microorganisms that must be destroyed are known to be present. It may be that in such cases only stronger antimicrobial agents are used. Responses B and C are wrong because they run contrary to the information given in the paragraph to the effect that sanitizers are used if no dangerous microorganisms are known to be present. Response D is wrong because the information in the paragraph provides no evidence whatsoever about what measures would be adopted if only some (presumably specific) dangerous microorganisms are known not to be present.

23.   **(C)** The answer can be inferred from the second and third sentences in the paragraph. The second sentence tells us that *some general types of land use are activities that conflict with* the purpose of wildlife refuges and botanical reservations. The third sentence explains that *all activities that exhibit such conflict are . . . excluded from refuges and reservations.*

Therefore, we can conclude that *some activities excluded from refuges and reservations* (the ones that conflict with the purpose of refuges and reservations) *are general types of land use.* Response A is wrong because the paragraph does not give any information about whether all activities that conflict with the purpose of refuges and reservations are general types of land use. The paragraph only says that *all activities that exhibit such conflict are . . . excluded from refuges and reservations.* Response B cannot be inferred because the paragraph does not give enough information about all activities that are excluded from refuges and reservations. Thus, we must recognize that we only know about some excluded activities. Response D is incorrect because the paragraph states that *some general types of land use are activities that conflict with the purpose of refuges and reservations.* It follows that some activities that conflict with this purpose are general types of land use. Response E is incorrect because there is insufficient information to infer whether some general types of land use are not excluded from wildlife refuges.

24.   **(C)** This answer can be inferred from the information presented in the last sentence of the paragraph, which says in part that *all document depots have the capacity to provide a great range of user services.* In view of this statement, it is clearly the case that no document depot lacks such a capacity. Response A is incorrect because it goes beyond the information given in the paragraph. Although there may be other ways of categorizing information centers, the paragraph only provides information

about one method—by the primary activity or service provided. Statements about other methods would be speculation because they could not be inferred from the information in the paragraph. Response B is incorrect because it contradicts the information presented in the last sentence of the paragraph. Because all document depots have the capacity to provide a great range of user services, it cannot be true that some document depots lack this capacity. Response D is not supported by the paragraph because it draws an overly general conclusion from the information presented. The second sentence states that *some information centers are document depots.* It can be inferred from this that some document depots are information centers, but it cannot be inferred that all information centers are document depots. Response E goes beyond the information that is implicit in the last sentence of the paragraph. That sentence says that *all document depots have the capacity to provide a great range of user services.* From this statement, nothing can be inferred about whether or not there are places that provide a great range of user services but are not document depots.

25.   **(E)** The conclusion expressed in E can be derived from the information presented in the last sentence of the paragraph. That sentence says that *if an expression is a familiar one . . . then it is a non-hyphenated compound.* Therefore, if an expression is a hyphenated compound, it cannot be a familiar one. Response A is incorrect because it contradicts the information in the paragraph. By stating that a familiar expression is a hyphenated compound, re-

sponse A directly contradicts the last sentence of the paragraph. Response B is incorrect because the paragraph does not give us information about all non-hyphenated compounds, only those that are familiar expressions. It could be that there are words that are not hyphenated even though they are not familiar expressions. Response C is incorrect because the information in the paragraph is not complete enough to enable us to draw the conclusion that all expressions that are not familiar are hyphenated. The paragraph gives us complete information about familiar expressions (that is, they are not hyphenated) but it does not give us enough information about the entire class of expressions that are not familiar. Response D is incorrect because it represents an unwarranted inference from the information given in the paragraph. The paragraph provides no information whatsoever about compounds that have suffixes.

23

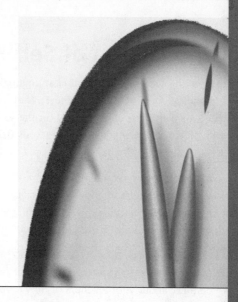

Hour 24

Sample Self-Rating Questions

What You'll Learn in This Hour

This hour presents sample self-rating questions. Although these questions are multiple choice and are timed like tests, they are not really tests at all. Rather, self-rating questions are designed to give examiners the best idea of where your true feelings and interests lie.

Here are your goals for this hour:

- Know the basis and design of self-rating questions
- Answer some sample self-rating questions

Basis and Design of Self-Rating Questions

The self-rating sections of federal examinations are set up to look like multiple-choice tests. Although they are timed like tests, they are not really tests at all. There are no right or wrong answers. You cannot study for the self-rating questions; your preparation consists only of gathering statistical records from your school years and thinking about what you achieved and when.

In a typical self-rating section of an exam, you will find questions about your best and worst grades in school and about your favorite and least favorite subjects; questions about your extracurricular activities in school and college (if you went to college) and about your participation in sports; questions about attendance, part-time jobs, and leadership positions.

Other questions refer to your working life or school relationships. These questions ask how you think about your teachers or how employers might rate you on specific traits. Similar questions ask you to suggest what your friends might say about you. Still other questions ask how you rate yourself against others.

Tip
Some of these questions offer hard choices, but during the actual exam, you won't have time to dwell on the answers. The self-rating sections are timed in the same manner as test questions. In this hour, you're given plenty of time to assess your responses and gather your thoughts—a process that can help you prepare for these questions on an actual exam. But on exam day, don't take the extra time we give you here. Just answer honestly and to the best of your ability.

Caution
Do not try to second-guess the questions and give the answers you think the examiners want. Some exams include two separate self-rating sections to check for honesty. Even where there is only one such section, it has built-in measures of general consistency.

There are no official self-rating sample questions. The following questions are representative. Because this hour presents 20 questions, use the following timed approach in answering the questions. By continually practicing taking sample tests under a specified time limit, you further enhance your abilities to concentrate under pressure, a benefit that can really pay off on test day.

1.   Allow yourself no more than three minutes for each question. Read each question carefully, thinking back to exactly how the question applies to your previous experiences.

2.   Before you "answer" the question, take a separate piece of paper and jot down three or four things that come to mind regarding the question. For example, are there certain aspects of your experiences related to the question that you particularly enjoyed? Are there memories of things you really didn't like? Write those down in your list.

3.   Next, answer the question, giving the most honest answer that applies to you.

4.   Finally, compare your "answer" to your short list of related issues. Does your answer "fit in" with your list? If so, then you probably have answered the question as honestly as possible. If your list doesn't seem to reflect your answer, try to reevaluate the answer you gave. Perhaps your "answer" is pointing you in a different direction (for example, an interest you were previously not aware of).

24

Answer Sheet

1. Ⓐ Ⓑ Ⓒ Ⓓ Ⓔ   6. Ⓐ Ⓑ Ⓒ Ⓓ Ⓔ   11. Ⓐ Ⓑ Ⓒ Ⓓ Ⓔ   16. Ⓐ Ⓑ Ⓒ Ⓓ Ⓔ

2. Ⓐ Ⓑ Ⓒ Ⓓ Ⓔ   7. Ⓐ Ⓑ Ⓒ Ⓓ Ⓔ   12. Ⓐ Ⓑ Ⓒ Ⓓ Ⓔ   17. Ⓐ Ⓑ Ⓒ Ⓓ Ⓔ

3. Ⓐ Ⓑ Ⓒ Ⓓ Ⓔ   8. Ⓐ Ⓑ Ⓒ Ⓓ Ⓔ   13. Ⓐ Ⓑ Ⓒ Ⓓ Ⓔ   18. Ⓐ Ⓑ Ⓒ Ⓓ Ⓔ

4. Ⓐ Ⓑ Ⓒ Ⓓ Ⓔ   9. Ⓐ Ⓑ Ⓒ Ⓓ Ⓔ   14. Ⓐ Ⓑ Ⓒ Ⓓ Ⓔ   19. Ⓐ Ⓑ Ⓒ Ⓓ Ⓔ

5. Ⓐ Ⓑ Ⓒ Ⓓ Ⓔ   10. Ⓐ Ⓑ Ⓒ Ⓓ Ⓔ   15. Ⓐ Ⓑ Ⓒ Ⓓ Ⓔ   20. Ⓐ Ⓑ Ⓒ Ⓓ Ⓔ

Sample Self-Rating Questions

> **Note**
> There are no right answers to these questions, so you will find no answer key or answer explanations at the end of this chapter.

1. My favorite subject in high school was
   A. Math
   B. English
   C. Physical education
   D. Social studies
   E. Science

2. My GPA at graduation from high school (on a 4.0 scale) was
   A. Lower than 2.51
   B. 2.51 to 2.80
   C. 2.81 to 3.25
   D. 3.26 to 3.60
   E. Higher than 3.60

3. In my second year of high school, I was absent
   A. Never
   B. Not more than 3 days
   C. 4 to 10 days
   D. More often than 10 days
   E. Do not recall

4. My best grades in high school were in
   A. Art
   B. Math
   C. English
   D. Social studies
   E. Music

5. While in high school, I participated in
   A. One sport
   B. Two sports and one other extracurricular activity
   C. Three nonathletic extracurricular activities
   D. No extracurricular activities
   E. Other than the above

6. During my senior year in high school, I held a paying job
   A. 0 hours a week
   B. 1 to 5 hours a week
   C. 6 to 10 hours a week
   D. 11 to 16 hours a week
   E. More than 16 hours a week

7. The number of semesters in which I failed a course in high school was
   A. None
   B. One
   C. Two or three
   D. Four or five
   E. More than five

8. In high school, I did volunteer work
   A. More than 10 hours a week
   B. 5 to 10 hours on a regular basis
   C. Sporadically
   D. Seldom
   E. Not at all

24

9. Of the skills I developed at college, the one I value most is
    A. Foreign language ability
    B. Oral expression
    C. Writing skills
    D. Facility with computers
    E. Analytical skills

10. I made my greatest mark in college through my
    A. Athletic prowess
    B. Success in performing arts
    C. Academic success
    D. Partying reputation
    E. Conciliatory skill with my peers

11. In the past six months, I have been late to work (or school)
    A. Never
    B. Only one time
    C. Very seldom
    D. More than five times
    E. I don't recall

12. My supervisors (or teachers) would be most likely to describe me as
    A. Competent
    B. Gifted
    C. Intelligent
    D. Fast working
    E. Detail oriented

13. My peers would probably describe me as
    A. Analytical
    B. Glib
    C. Organized
    D. Funny
    E. Helpful

14. According to my supervisors (or teachers), my greatest asset is
    A. My ability to communicate orally
    B. Written expression
    C. My ability to motivate others
    D. The way I organize my time
    E. My friendly personality

15. In the past two years, I have applied for
    A. No jobs other than this one
    B. One other job
    C. Two to four other jobs
    D. Five to eight other jobs
    E. More than eight jobs

16. In the past year, I have read strictly for pleasure
    A. No books
    B. One book
    C. Two books
    D. Three to six books
    E. More than six books

17. When I read for pleasure, I read mostly
    A. History
    B. Fiction
    C. Poetry
    D. Biography
    E. Current events

18. My peers would say of me that, when they ask me a question, I am
    A. Helpful
    B. Brusque
    C. Condescending
    D. Generous
    E. Patient

19. My supervisors (or teachers) would say that my area of least competence is

A. Analytical ability

B. Written communication

C. Attention to detail

D. Public speaking

E. Self-control

20. My peers would say that, when I feel challenged, my reaction is one of

A. Determination

B. Energy

C. Defiance

D. Caution

E. Compromise

24

Appendix A

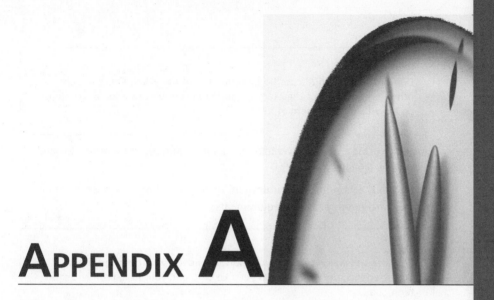

Choose the Position That's Best for You

Having read through this book, you're a lot more familiar with the many different law enforcement positions available than you were when you started. You may be excited about the prospect of a law enforcement career but don't know quite where to be begin.

A good place to start is to narrow your choices to those that fit your own qualifications, specific requirements, personal preferences, and of course, the availability of job openings.

You can begin the narrowing process by looking carefully at the Comparison Charts on pages 349 through 354.

1. With a pencil or pen, draw a line through those positions that do not appeal to you at all.

2. Cross out those positions for which you are disqualified because of age, education, physical condition, or experience.

3. If one of the exams seems particularly intimidating to you, you may want to discount positions that require it.

> **Caution**
> Don't rush to rule out a position just because of the exam! Check out all other requirements of the exam; if your interest in that position is still high, go ahead and take a shot at it!

4. Check out working hours, travel and relocation requirements, starting pay, and opportunities for advancement.

5. Rank positions according to their desirability to you. Eliminate those positions that do not meet your personal requirements.

> **Tip**
> Consider and weigh carefully your personal needs, your own personality characteristics, the surroundings you like best, and your long-term and short-term goals.

Some Questions to Consider as You Decide Which Position Is Right for You

Although it is in no way inclusive, the following questions can help you determine some positions that are—or are not—well suited for your law enforcement career:

-   Do you have parents or other family members who are going to need more and more of your time in the years ahead? If so, avoid a position that is likely to relocate you far from home.

-   Do you like to be home for dinner every night? Then choose a position with regularly scheduled hours (such as that of an Alcohol, Tobacco, and Firearms Inspector).

-   Are you physically handicapped? A number of great opportunities are available to you, including Import Specialist and Deportation Officer.

-   Do you hate crowds? Do you enjoy solitude in the wide-open spaces? Border Patrol Special Agent might just be the perfect job for you.

-   Did you drop out of scouting because you hated wearing a uniform? Avoid the uniformed services, of course!

-   Do you like to work closely with a few others? Criminal Investigators and Special Agents tend to work in teams.

-   Do you feel strongly that every citizen should serve some time in the Armed Forces? Consider the Customs Service. Employees of the Customs Service can take leave from their positions to enter the Armed Forces, be assured that their jobs await them when they return, and earn promotions and raises during their absence. Employees of the Customs Service can also serve in the military reserves and collect regular pay while attending summer training.

- Do you have young children and feel that you should be around the house a good deal right now, but that you yearn for a more exciting life (as if raising children isn't exciting enough)? A Postal Inspector must have postal experience: Consider joining the Postal Service in a regularly scheduled position now and plan to move into the position of Postal Inspector in the future.

- Do you thrive on long hours and look forward to lots of overtime pay? All law enforcement positions except Postal Inspector, which is paid at a higher-than-usual rate altogether, earn overtime pay for overtime work. The job descriptions tell you which positions demand greater overtime.

- Are you short of cash? Unless you borrow start-up money, you cannot be a Border Patrol Agent. Most of the uniformed services supply uniforms, but the Border Patrol Agent must buy his or her own uniforms, both rough duty and official, at a cost of over $1,200 (most agencies reimburse part of this cost to you) and must pay for travel to the first duty station (but not to and from the Federal Law Enforcement Training Facility in Georgia) as well.

A

Other Things to Consider When Choosing a Law Enforcement Career

You should supplement the information presented in this book with personal information, if possible. If you know anyone who holds a position in which you think you are interested, that person would make a natural—and potentially invaluable—resource for information. Consider the following when talking with such a person:

- Ask about working conditions, about special features of the job, about what the person likes most and least about the job.

- Evaluate the information in light of your own likes and dislikes and your own priorities.

- You might learn of low morale in a specific agency. This information might discourage you from applying, or you may choose to seize the opportunity for rapid advancement because of turnover at the top.

> **Tip**
> You must evaluate all information according to what is important to you. Remember, however, that polices do change, and that a condition described to you now may not exist by the time you are employed.

If you have no personal contacts in the agencies that interest you, check your phone book. If the agency has an office in your area, you may be able to arrange a meeting with an employee who would be willing to talk with you and answer your questions.

> **Caution**
> Any such person you contact through a phone call to an office would undoubtedly be quite enthusiastic about the agency, so be prepared to temper that enthusiasm with information you gain from other sources, as well as your own personal beliefs and interests.

The final and crucial element in choosing your law enforcement career is *availability*. Positions at the local, state, and county level open with some frequency. Contact your municipal, county, or state police and ask for an application. You may receive immediate satisfaction, or you may be referred to an employment division or a department of personnel or human resources.

> **Tip**
> Do not be discouraged if you are sent from one department to another. Follow through! Even divisions that really want and need you are bound by bureaucracy. Don't let the run-around get you down!

If you are interested in a federal position, you may find information at your State Employment Service. If the announcements you seek are not posted or filed at your State Employment Service, then call, write, or go to a Federal Job Information Center. The most convenient Federal Job Information Center should be listed in the blue pages of your telephone directory under the heading "U.S. Government."

> **Tip**
> One easy and efficient way to get information about federal law enforcement job openings throughout the country—and to get application materials—is to call the Career American Connection at (912) 757-3000. Although this is a toll call, it is a 24-hour automated service. Allow yourself at least one-half hour to search job categories and geographical areas.

A final, excellent source of information about the availability of federal law enforcement positions and application procedures is to call the agencies themselves. Call Washington, D.C., information and ask for the telephone number of the personnel office of the agency in which you are interested.

Comparison Charts

AGE AT ENTRY, RETIREMENT, EDUCATION

Position	Age at Entry	Retirement	Education
Police Officer	20 to 35	Varies	HS plus (varies)
Deputy Sheriff	21 to 29	Varies	HS and some college (varies)
State Police Officer	21 to 29	Varies	HS plus (varies)
BATF Inspector	Over 18	Unspecified	College or experience
BATF Special Agent	21 to 37	Eligible at 50 after 20 years	BA/BS and experience
DEA Special Agent	21 to 37	Eligible at 50 after 20 years	Advanced degree and experience
FBI Special Agent	23 to 37	Mandatory at 55	Advanced degree and experience
Federal Protection Officer	Over 21	Unspecified	2 years college or experience
Border Patrol Agent	21 to 37	Mandatory at 55	College or experience
Immigration Inspector	Over 18	Unspecified	College or experience
INS Criminal Investigator (Special Agent)	21 to 37	Mandatory at 55	College or experience
Deportation Officer	21 to 37	Mandatory at 55	College or experience
IRS Internal Security Inspector	21 to 37	Eligible at 50 after 20 years	College or experience
IRS Special Agent	23 to 37	Eligible at 50 after 20 years	BA/BS and advanced courses
Customs Aid	Over 18	Unspecified	2 years college or experience
Customs Inspector	Over 21	Unspecified	College or experience
Import Specialist	Over 20	Unspecified	College or experience
Customs Special Agent	Under 37	Unspecified	College and 2 years experience
Deputy U.S. Marshall	21 to 37	Eligible at 50 after 20 years	College or experience
Postal Police Officer	Over 20	Unspecified	No requirements
Postal Inspector	21 to 37	Eligible at 50 after 20 years	College or experience
Secret Service Uniformed Officer	Over 21	Eligible after 20 years	HS and police experience in a large city
Secret Service Special Agent	21 to 37	Mandatory at 55	College or experience

A

Exam, Physical Requirements, Training

Position	Exam	Physical Requirements	Training
Police Officer	Local	Varies	Varies
Deputy Sheriff	Local	Varies	Varies
State Police Officer	Local	Varies	State training school
BATF Inspector	ACWA	Not too strict	1 year on-the-job
BATF Special Agent	TEA	Very strict; near perfect vision	8 weeks FLETC and Special Agent School
DEA Special Agent	No written exam	Very strict; near perfect vision	12–15 weeks FLETC
FBI Special Agent	FBI's own	Very strict	15 weeks FBI Academy
Federal Protection Officer	An OPM-developed exam	Not too strict	8 weeks FLETC
Border Patrol Agent	Border Patrol Agent Exam	Very strict	17 weeks FLETC
Immigration Inspector	ACWA	Not too strict	14 weeks FLETC
INS Criminal Investigator (Special Agent)	ACWA	Very strict; perfect hearing	14 weeks FLETC
Deportation Officer	ACWA	Certain handicaps allowed	FLETC
IRS Internal Security Inspector	TEA	Not too strict	7 weeks FLETC and 2 weeks Internal Security
IRS Special Agent	TEA	Very strict	20 weeks FLETC
Customs Aid	Federal Clerical Exam	Not too strict	On-the-job
Customs Inspector	No written exam	Very strict	FLETC
Import Specialist	No written exam	Lenient, but no colorblindness	Classroom and on-the-job
Customs Special Agent	TEA	Strict, but glasses allowed	11 weeks FLETC
Deputy U.S. Marshall	TEA	Very strict	12 weeks FLETC
Postal Police Officer	Postal Police	Very strict	8 weeks FLETC
Postal Inspector	PO's own	Very strict	16 weeks Potomac Management Academy
Secret Service Uniformed Officer	SS's own	Very strict; near perfect vision	FLETC
Secret Service Special Agent	TEA and SS's own	Very strict; near perfect vision	FLETC

SPECIAL SKILLS, TRAVEL, RELOCATION, HOURS

Position	Special Skills	Travel	Relocation	Hours
Police Officer	None for entry	No	No	Rotating shifts and overtime
Deputy Sheriff	None for entry	Some	Unlikely	Rotating shifts; emergency overtime
State Police Office	None for entry	Some	Possible	Rotating shifts; emergency overtime
BATF Inspector	None for entry	Yes	Yes	Regular 40-hour week
BATF Special Agent	Courses in police science	Yes	Yes	Irregular 40-hour week plus overtime
DEA Special Agent	CPA, JD, or MS	Yes	Yes	Irregular hours plus overtime
FBI Special Agent	Advanced degree	Yes	Yes	40 hours plus overtime
Federal Protection Officer	None for entry	Little	Yes	Rotating shifts
Border Patrol Agent	Spanish	Yes	Yes	60-hour week in irregular shifts
Immigration Inspector	None for entry	No	Possible	Long and irregular
INS Criminal Investigator (Special Agent)	None for entry	Yes	Yes	Long and irregular
Deportation Officer	None for entry	Some	Possible	Regular 40-hour week; probable overtime
IRS Internal Security Inspector	None for entry	Yes	Yes	40 irregular hours plus overtime
IRS Special Agent	Accounting	Yes	Yes	40 irregular hours plus overtime
Customs Aid	None for entry	No	No	Rotating shifts; 40-hour week
Customs Inspector	None for entry	No	Once	Rotating shifts; 40-hour week
Import Specialist	None for entry	No	Once	Rotating shifts; 40 hours plus overtime
Customs Special Agent	Law or business	No	Yes	Rotating shifts; 40 hours plus overtime
Deputy U.S. Marshall	None for entry	Yes	Yes	Long and irregular
Postal Police Officer	None for entry 40-hour	No	No	Shifts; 40-hour week with overtime and night differential

SPECIAL SKILLS, TRAVEL, RELOCATION, HOURS (CONTINUED)

Position	Special Skills	Travel	Relocation	Hours
Postal Inspector	Postal experience	Yes	Often	Regular 48-hour week; emergency overtime
Secret Service Uniformed Officer	None for entry	No	Possible	Rotating shifts; 40 hours plus overtime
Secret Service Special Agent	None for entry	Yes	Yes	Rotating shifts; much overtime

APPENDIX B

Preparing for Training Programs

Understanding What the Police Academy Is All About

Surviving the hiring process is only the start of your exposure to the world of police service. The next phase of your development as an officer—your introduction to law enforcement—begins in the Police Academy. Every state and large municipal police department has its own training academy, and each offers its own specific training program and schedule. In the academy, you will spend the next four to six months of your life learning what it means to be a Police Officer. Different agencies require different things from their Police Officer trainees.

> **Note**
> Although the information presented here is structured around the Police Academy, most of it applies to any law enforcement training program.

Some departments (for example, the LAPD) stress extensive physical training sessions and spend a significant amount of time teaching recruits to speak Spanish. This emphasis on second-language skills reflects the culture of the area and is becoming more common in many municipalities in the United States.

Other agencies, such as the San Diego Police Department, have established a "phase training" program in which officer trainees rotate back and forth between academy classes and actual participation in street patrol with senior Field Training Officers. This hands-on experience helps prepare new officers for the stress of police work by introducing them to it in carefully controlled stages.

On the West Coast or East Coast, from a small Midwestern training center or from a large southern regional facility, you'll come away from your academy experience with the following traits and abilities:

- **Discipline.** You will know how to take orders and give them, especially during moments of extreme stress.
- **Teamwork.** You will recognize the need to work together as a unit, either with a partner or even with several dozen other officers.
- **Camaraderie.** You will establish personal friendships that last for your entire career and beyond.
- **Esprit-de-corps.** You will forge an intense commitment to your "brothers and sisters in arms" that permeates your working relationships and even your entire way of life.
- **Courtesy, tact, and control.** You will use these traits to handle any situation politely, safely, humanely, and above all, professionally.
- **Tactical survival skills.** You will receive the best officer safety material available and learn the latest patrol theories designed to save your life.
- **Professionalism.** You will become a total law enforcement professional, taught to protect and serve with skill and a strong sense of commitment that the career you have chosen is both right and necessary for our society today.

What's Involved in Pre-academy Preparations

In some instances, people who reach the academy stage find themselves quite disillusioned by the pressure, the workload, and the physical side of police work. This disillusionment often leads to their dismissal because of low test scores and poor physical performance. More frequently, they quit on their own.

To get through a tough Police Academy, you need more than just high test scores and physical strength—you need mental toughness as well. The biggest, "baddest," or smartest people don't always make it because the Police Academy calls for so many other characteristics from students. Humility, internal courage, and enthusiasm count for just as much as physical virtues.

> **Caution**
> A very common mistake regarding preparation for the Police Academy is underestimating the amount of classroom study required. Most academy programs are designed around a college curriculum, offering from 12 to 18 units to officer graduates. With today's programs, it just isn't possible to "wing it" and get by without extensive study. If you don't devote a substantial portion of your off-hours to study, you won't make it to graduation day.

Although you really can't prepare for the academic rigors of the academy, you can improve your physical fitness as you ready yourself for the academy. Most academy fitness programs stress the same three elements: upper body strength, cardiovascular endurance, and joint and muscle flexibility. The key to your success in these three demanding areas starts with your pre-academy fitness level, so work hard on getting into the best shape possible before your first day at the academy.

Dealing with the "Boot Camp" Environment

It's no secret that the Police Academy is much like military basic training. You'll be required to respond to orders quickly, march in a structured fashion to and from various locations, salute when necessary, answer your training officer with a stout "Yes, Sir!" or "Yes, Ma'am!" when called on, and generally assume the role of classic "cadet," "recruit," or "trainee." It may seem as if the academy training officers are always yelling and mostly at you. There are good reasons for this: discipline, obedience, and unity are the orders of the day.

> **Tip**
> Any attempt at horseplay, showing off, or other childish behavior that jeopardizes the safety and success of your classmates will be met with swift and decisive punishment.
>
> As one veteran instructor put it, "Unless you want to spend all your time doing push-ups or writing 500-word essays on the importance of discipline, you had better 'toe the mark' and do what we tell you!"

Some new recruits are quite comfortable with this enormous emphasis on the paramilitary. Other trainees find it terrifying and have a hard time concentrating on the tasks at hand. The people who seem to react the best are those who have previous military experience. Most officers who have gone through the academy training, however, say that after a time, it becomes easier to respond in this military fashion. What seems foreign and difficult at first gets easier, especially if you concentrate and work hard to conform. Still, you'll do better if you can develop a thick skin before you begin the academy programs. The trick is to follow orders, complete the tasks you're given, and show effort and enthusiasm at all times.

Tip
Don't take any verbal abuse from training instructors as a personal attack. Their job is to teach you to be the best officer you can be, and they will use various means—not all of which are pleasant!—to ensure that you are.

The rewards and punishments doled out by your training officers have a "one size fits all" flavor. You'll usually be rewarded as a group and punished as a group, too. Class unity is a constant goal, so if one trainee violates the rules, his or her associates may share the blame. This isn't to say that individual punishments don't exist, but rather that the instructors use their knowledge of group dynamics to teach discipline and order by involving everyone.

In short, the best way to deal with the rigors of the academy is to just accept them as part of your training process. Don't take anything too personally—it won't last forever. Monitor your stress level the best you can and realize that your training officers want you to succeed!

Understanding the Classroom Component of the Academy

The time you spend in the academy classroom represents about 60 percent of your total training time. Obviously, that's the majority of your time!

The course material itself is specifically written and created to stress the most important parts of each subject. There is very little "fat" in a standard Police Academy curriculum. The organizers know that they have only a limited amount of time to teach you and your classmates a wide variety of necessary information. As such, nearly everything your instructors discuss relates to material you must know to pass an exam.

> **Note**
> The instructors who teach the various academy subjects are responsible for explaining certain core material mandated by the state. Each state has its own learning requirements for its Police Officers, and the instructors are expected to teach to these criteria. This isn't to say that you won't hear an abundance of stories, bad jokes, or inside police gossip, just that you can expect the bulk of the classroom material to relate to specific, testable material you'll have to remember later in the academy and later in your career.

Most academy subjects are taught in blocks of instruction, ranging from 2-hour overviews to 80-hour, in-depth studies. Lectures for these blocks, however, usually last for 50 minutes at a time to allow for frequent breaks. At many academies, the break procedure is the same: You are dismissed by the instructor, "fall in" to ranks outside the classroom, wait to be marched to the break area, and are then dismissed for the break. Returning to the class is usually less structured, as long as you get back on time.

> **Note**
> The types of tests you can expect to take during your training are discussed at length in the various test sample hours in this book. Be sure that you look at the strategy hours that correspond to each sample test for strategies and other helpful hints, too!

The following list represents some of the topics you can be expected to cover in a typical academy curriculum:

- Alcoholic beverage control laws
- Chemical weapons training
- Citations
- Community relations
- Constitutional law
- Corrections
- The court system
- Courtroom testimony
- Criminal laws
- Deadly force issues
- Death cases

B

- Defensive tactics
- Disturbance calls
- Driver's licenses
- DWI arrests
- Evidence
- Firearms training
- First-aid training
- Interview and interrogations
- Officer safety and survival
- Patrol theory
- Penal code
- Physical training lectures
- Police history and ethical principles
- Report writing
- Traffic accident investigation
- Vehicle code
- Vehicle operations

Preparing for Academy Physical Training

The best way to succeed in PT is to be in shape before it begins. Some hard work on your part before the academy begins will save you much grief later. It's just not possible to get in shape when you get there. You don't have the luxury of time (or a stress-free training environment) to help you ease your way into it.

If you have any preconceived notions about Police Officers being the largest people around, get rid of them. The old days of the burly, door-filling cops on the beat are over. Today's officers are leaner, more health conscious, and more fit than ever. More officers are exercising and eating correctly; they do not smoke and are actually working to reduce their on-duty and off-duty stresses.

Your personal PT program should begin at least four months before the actual academy start date. This will give you plenty of time to get physically and mentally ready for the classroom courses and PT sessions. Consider these four steps as a part of your pre-academy training plan:

- **Quit smoking.** If you don't smoke, don't start! As stressful as police work can be, a cigarette won't help it be any less stressful. If you do smoke, you simply *must* quit. The Police Academy theory of PT is based on one simple idea: constant movement. Your lungs have to be in top shape to handle this tremendous burden on them, and smoking will decisively reduce their ability to perform for you. Moreover, many academies are now prohibiting smoking on academy grounds and do not allow "smoke breaks" of any kind.

- **Lose weight.** If you can lose any extra weight before the academy, you'll find it very easy to keep it off once the PT sessions start. The trick is to be strong and muscular, without any unnecessary muscle mass or fat to carry around. If you're too heavy, you're probably too slow as well. Lean and mean is the idea here. (Just remember that you'll have to carry any extra pounds with you on those long academy training runs!)

- **Walk, run, spring.** If you're more than a weekend athlete, you're probably already used to running or jogging at least three times per week. If so, continue your present training pace and add some long runs, some sprints and speed work, and plenty of pre-run and post-run stretching to your workouts. If you don't actively run now, do yourself a huge favor and start! Begin by walking briskly, then work your way into running. The secret is not to overdo it because injuries can be serious and set you back for months.

- **Use your body weight.** If you were to get a dime for every push-up you'll do at the academy, you could retire at an early age. As with running, if you haven't done this type of exercise before, you should practice before the academy begins. Also, do your back and stomach a favor and start a sit-up program along with your push-up regimen. Choose a target number and meet it every day, no exceptions! Finally, work hard to keep your knee joints strong and flexible. Think of your academy PT sessions as the gateway to a career of lifelong fitness and injury prevention.

The Federal Law Enforcement Training Center (FLETC)

The Federal Law Enforcement Training Center (FLETC) is an intra-agency training facility established in 1970 to serve the training needs of the federal enforcement community. This bureau within the Department of the Treasury provides training for personnel from almost 60 federal organizations.

The following programs are all part of the FLETC. Although the specifics of each vary according to what field of law enforcement you are interested in, these general requirements apply to all areas.

Basic Training at the FLETC

The majority of your weeks of training at the FLETC is devoted to basic programs for Criminal Investigators. These programs provide you with a combination of classroom instruction and "hands-on" practical exercises. These exercises often involve hired role-players who act as victims, witnesses, and suspects. As a student, you apply your classroom knowledge in exercises that include a scenario and simulate typical situations encountered on the job.

Various topics of study are available at the FLETC. The following list, although not comprehensive, provides a good overview of the variety of study available:

- Legal
- Enforcement techniques
- Behavioral sciences
- Enforcement operations
- Computer/economic crime
- Firearms
- Physical techniques
- Driver and marine techniques

Advanced Training at the FLETC

The FLETC provides the facilities, equipment, and support services to conduct advanced and specialized training for both uniformed Police Officers and Criminal Investigators. This training may be conducted entirely by center personnel, entirely by participating agency personnel, or by a combination of both. The courses vary in length depending on the subjects being taught.

Note
The training staff of the FLETC is made up of experienced instructors who have a minimum of five years of law enforcement experience. A portion of the instructors are federal officers and investigators on detailed assignment to the center from their parent agencies. This mix of permanent and detailed instructors creates a balance of experience and fresh insight from the field.

FLETC Facilities

Many facilities once used by the Navy have been adapted for use by the FLETC, including these:

- Classrooms
- Dormitories
- Recreation facilities
- Dining halls
- Administrative and logistical support facilities

Construction is on-going at the FLETC, with new facilities and renovations constantly under way.

For More Information

For more information on the FLETC, as well as excellent updates on federal law enforcement positions and opportunities in general, visit the FLETC Web site at www.ustreas.gov/fletc

B